When the first volume of this magnificent s... of Western philosophy began to appear, critics ... hailed it with superlative praises and realized the ... promise it predicted. Now that the series has prog...... to this present volume there is no doubt any longer that it will be the standard history of philosophy for many years to come. As each new volume comes from Father Copleston's pen, it is increasingly apparent that this series is a remarkable accomplishment due in no small measure to his continued thoroughness in presentation and dispassionate objectivity of exposition. A lucid, readable style coupled with great erudition and scholarship has produced an unequaled achievement of which the critics have said:

"This magnificent effort to probe man's quest for reality . . . states many of the problems which still face us."

The Commonweal

". . . meticulous scholarship, synthetic power, balance of emphasis, and breath of appreciation. The style is clear, flexible, and interesting. . . ."

Avery Dulles, S.J.

"Here is a continuation of the same objective, progressive, critical scholarship that marked the first volume producing a skillful, discerning analysis of the interplay of philosophical currents in Christian thought over eleven centuries."

America

"There can be no doubt that this is the best text of the history of philosophy now available in English."

The Historical Bulletin

W9-BRH-680

D0125233

Volumes of A HISTORY OF PHILOSOPHY now available
in Image Books:

A History of Philosophy

VOLUME 6

Modern Philosophy

PART II

Kant

by Frederick Copleston, S.J.

IMAGE BOOKS
A Division of Doubleday & Company, Inc.
Garden City, New York

Image Books Edition
by special arrangement with The Newman Press
Image Books Edition published September 1964

DE LICENTIA SUPERIORUM ORDINIS:
John Coventry, S.J., *Praep. Prov. Angliae*

NIHIL OBSTAT:
J. L. Russell, S.J., *Censor Deputatus*

IMPRIMATUR:
✠ Franciscus, *Archiepiscopus Birmingamiensis*
Birmingamiae, die 27 Februarii 1959

© Frederick Copleston, 1960
Printed in the United States of America

CONTENTS

Chapter   *Page*

The rational being as an end in itself – The autonomy of the will – The kingdom of ends – Freedom as the condition of the possibility of a categorical imperative – The postulates of practical reason: freedom, Kant's idea of the perfect good, immortality, God, the general theory of the postulates – Kant on religion – Concluding remarks.

Chapter Eleven

KANT (2):
THE PROBLEMS OF THE FIRST
CRITIQUE

*The general problem of metaphysics – The problem of
a priori knowledge – The divisions of this problem –
Kant's Copernican revolution – Sensibility, understanding, reason, and the structure of the first* Critique *– The
significance of the first* Critique *in the context of the
general problem of Kant's philosophy.*

1. If we look at the prefaces to the first and second editions
of the *Critique of Pure Reason* and at the foreword to and
first sections of the *Prolegomena to Any Future Metaphysics*,[1] we find the author placing an obvious emphasis on the
problem of metaphysics. Is metaphysics possible or not? Obviously, the question is not whether it is possible to write
metaphysical treatises or to indulge in metaphysical speculation. The question is whether metaphysics is capable of
extending our knowledge of reality. For Kant, the chief problems of metaphysics are God, freedom and immortality.
We can therefore express the question in this way. Is metaphysics capable of giving us sure knowledge of the existence
and nature of God, of human freedom, and of the existence
in man of a spiritual, immortal soul?

A question of this sort clearly presupposes a doubt. And
there is, in Kant's opinion, abundant reason for such initial
doubt, that is, for raising the problem of metaphysics. Time
was when metaphysics 'was called the queen of all the sciences; and if one takes the will for the deed, she certainly
deserved this title of honour on account of the outstanding
importance of her subject-matter'.[2] Kant never denied the
importance of the main themes of which metaphysics treats.
But now, he observes, metaphysics has fallen into disrepute.
And this is easily understandable. Mathematics and the natural sciences have advanced, and there is in these fields a
great area of generally accepted knowledge. Nobody seriously

questions this fact. But metaphysics appears to be an arena for endless disputes. 'One can point to no single book, as one can point to a Euclid, and say: This is metaphysics, here you will find the noblest object of this science, the knowledge of a supreme Being and of a future world, provided by the principles of pure reason.'[3] The fact of the matter is that metaphysics, unlike physics, has not found any sure scientific method the application of which will enable it to solve its problems. And this leads us to ask, 'why is it that here no sure path of science has yet been found? Is it perhaps impossible to find one?'[4]

The inconclusiveness of metaphysics, its inability hitherto to find a reliable method which will lead to certain conclusions, its constant tendency to retrace its steps and to start all over again; such characteristics have helped to produce a widespread indifference towards metaphysics and its claims. True, in one sense this indifference is unjustified; for it is 'vain to profess indifference in regard to such inquiries, the objects of which cannot be a matter of indifference to human nature'.[5] Moreover, those who profess to be indifferentists are prone to make metaphysical pronouncements of their own, even if they are unaware of the fact. At the same time this indifference is not, in Kant's view, the fruit of mere levity of mind: rather is it the expression of a contemporary maturity of judgment which refuses to be satisfied with illusory knowledge or pseudo-science. It should serve, therefore, as a stimulus to undertake a critical investigation of metaphysics, summoning the latter before the tribunal of reason.

What form must this critical investigation take? To be in a position to answer this question we must recall what metaphysics means for Kant. As we saw in the last chapter of PART I, he disagreed with Locke's theory that all our concepts are ultimately derived from experience. He did not, indeed, accept the opposite theory of innate ideas. But at the same time he believed that there are concepts and principles which the reason derives from within itself on the occasion of experience. A child is not born with, for example, an idea of causality. But on the occasion of experience its reason derives the concept from within itself. It is an *a priori* concept in the sense that it is not derived from experience but is applied to and in a sense governs experience. There are, therefore, *a priori* concepts and principles which are grounded in the mind's own structure. These concepts are 'pure', in the sense that they are, of themselves, empty of all empirical content or material. Now, the metaphysicians have assumed that reason can apply these concepts and principles so as to apprehend supersensible realities and things-in-themselves, that is, not merely as they appear to us. There have thus arisen the various systems of dogmatic metaphysics. But the assumption was over-hasty. We cannot take it for granted that the *a priori* concepts and principles of the reason can be used to transcend experience; that is, to know realities which are not given in experience. First of all we must undertake a critical investigation into the powers of the pure reason itself. This is the task which the dogmatic philosophers neglected, dogmatism being described as the assumption that it is possible to make progress in knowledge simply on the basis of pure philosophical concepts by employing principles which reason has long been in the habit of employing, 'without having inquired in what way and with what right reason has arrived at these principles. Dogmatism is thus the dogmatic procedure of the pure reason without previous criticism of its own powers.'[6] It is this criticism which Kant proposes to undertake.

The tribunal before which metaphysics is to be brought is, therefore, 'nothing else than the critical investigation (*Kritik*) of pure reason itself', which means 'a critical inquiry into the faculty of reason with reference to all the cognitions to which it may strive to attain independently of all experience'.[7] The question is, then, 'what and how much can understanding and reason[8] know, apart from all experience'.[9] Let us assume with Kant that speculative metaphysics is a non-empirical science (or alleged science) which claims to transcend experience, attaining to a knowledge of purely intelligible (non-sensible) realities by means of *a priori* concepts and principles. Given this view of metaphysics, the validity of its claim will obviously be determined by the answer to the question, what and how much can the mind know apart from experience.

To answer this question a critical inquiry into the faculty of reason, as Kant puts it, is required. What this means will, I hope, become clearer during the course of this chapter. But it may be as well to point out at once that Kant is not referring to a psychological inquiry into the nature of reason considered as a psychical entity; that is, with reason as an object among objects. He is concerned with reason in regard to the *a priori* cognition which it makes possible. That is to say, he is concerned with the pure conditions in the human subject as such for knowing objects. Such an inquiry is termed 'transcendental'.

One of the main tasks of the *Critique of Pure Reason* is to show in a systematic manner what these conditions are. And it is important to understand what sort of conditions Kant is talking about. There are obviously empirical conditions for perceiving things and for learning truths. For instance, I cannot see things in complete darkness; light is required for vision. And there are many scientific truths which cannot be discovered without the aid of instruments. Further, there are empirical conditions which are subjective, in the sense that they are conditions on the part of the knowing subject himself. I cannot see things if I am suffering from certain diseases of the eye in an advanced state. And there are obviously people who cannot, practically speaking, understand subjects which others understand with comparative ease. But Kant is not concerned with empirical conditions: he is concerned with the non-empirical or 'pure' conditions of human knowledge as such. In other words, he is concerned with the formal elements of pure consciousness. Tom, Dick and Harry, namely particular people with their particular limitations, do not enter into the matter at all. Or, rather, they enter into it only as exemplifying the human subject as such. That is to say, conditions of knowledge which hold for the human subject as such will obviously hold for Tom, Dick and Harry. But it is with the necessary conditions for knowing objects that Kant is concerned, not with variable empirical conditions. And if the conditions turn out to be such that realities transcending sense-experience cannot be objects of knowledge, the claims of speculative metaphysics will have been shown to be hollow and vain.

Now, Kant mentions Wolff with respect as 'the greatest of all dogmatic philosophers'.[10] And it is clear that when he speaks about dogmatic metaphysics, he has in mind principally, though not exclusively, the Leibniz-Wolffian system. We may be inclined to object, therefore, that his inquiry into the possibility or impossibility of metaphysics is really an inquiry into the capacity of a certain type of metaphysics to extend our knowledge of reality, and that it is thus too restricted in scope. For there are other ideas of metaphysics besides that of Wolff. But though it is quite true that Kant pays insufficient attention to other conceptions of metaphysics, it is possible to exaggerate the importance of this line of objection. For instance, concepts such as those of cause and substance are employed in other metaphysical systems besides that of Wolff. Yet if the status and function of these concepts were what Kant, in the course of the first *Critique*, declares them to be, they could not be used to attain knowledge of supersensible realities. The Kantian critique of the powers of reason would thus, if valid, affect many other metaphysical systems besides that of Wolff. In other words, Kant's field of inquiry may be too narrow in its starting-point, in the sense that metaphysics means for him a particular type of metaphysics; but the inquiry is developed in such a way that the conclusions arrived at have a very wide range of application.

It may be as well to note that Kant does not always use the term 'metaphysics' in precisely the same sense. The inquiry into the powers of reason in regard to pure *a priori* cognition is called critical philosophy, while the systematic presentation of the whole body of philsophical knowledge attained or attainable by the power of pure reason (that is, *a priori*) is called metaphysics. When the latter term is used in this sense, critical philosophy is a preparation for or propaedeutic to metaphysics, and thus falls outside metaphysics. But the term 'metaphysics' may also be given to the whole of pure (non-empirical) philosophy, including so-called critical philosophy; and in this case critical philosophy counts as the first part of metaphysics. Again, if we take the term 'metaphysics' as meaning the systematic presentation of the whole body of philosophical knowledge attained by the power of pure reason, we may mean by 'knowledge', knowledge in a strict sense, or we may include the pretended or illusory knowledge which many philosophers have thought to be attainable by pure reason. If we understand the word 'knowledge' in the first of these two senses, Kant obviously does not reject metaphysics. On the contrary, he thought that it could, at least in principle, be systematically and completely developed. And his own *Metaphysical First Elements of Natural Science* is a contribution. But if the term 'metaphysics' is used to mean pretended or illusory knowledge of supersensible realities, one of the tasks of the critical philosophy is to expose the hollowness of the claims made on behalf of this pseudo-science. Finally, we must distinguish between metaphysics as a natural disposition and metaphysics considered as a science. The mind has a natural tendency to raise such problems as those of God and immortality; and though we should try to understand why this is the case, Kant neither wishes to eradicate the tendency nor believes that it is possible to do so, even if it were desirable. Metaphysics as a natural disposition is actual, and therefore it is obviously possible. But metaphysics as a science, if we mean by this a scientific knowledge of supersensible beings, has never, according to Kant, been a reality. For all the alleged demonstrations hitherto produced can be shown to be invalid, that is, pseudo-demonstrations. Hence we can very properly ask whether metaphysics, considered as a science, is possible.

All this may sound very complicated and confusing. But it is not so confusing in practice as it sounds when briefly summarized. In the first place Kant himself refers to the different uses of the term 'metaphysics'.[11] In the second place the context makes it clear in what sense Kant is using the term in a particular passage. But the fact that the term bears more than one meaning in his writings is of some importance. For if one is ignorant of it, one may rashly conclude that he contradicts himself, admitting metaphysics in one place, rejecting it in another, when there is perhaps really no contradiction at all.

2. But though the possibility of metaphysics as a science (that is, as a science with objects of its own, transcending sense-experience) is for Kant an important problem, it is only part of the general problem considered in the *Critique of Pure Reason*. This general problem may be said to be that of the possibility of *a priori* knowledge.

Now, by *a priori* knowledge Kant does not mean knowledge which is relatively *a priori*; that is, in relation to this or that experience or to this or that kind of experience. If someone puts a garment too near the fire so that it is singed or burned, we may say that he might have known *a priori* that this would happen. That is to say, on the basis of past experience the man might have known antecedently to his action what its effect would be. He need not have waited to see what would happen. But this antecedent knowledge would be *a priori* only in relation to a particular experience. And it is not of such relatively *a priori* knowledge that Kant is thinking. He is thinking of knowledge which is *a priori* in relation to all experience.

But here we have to be careful not to draw the conclusion that Kant is thinking about innate ideas, supposed to be present in the human mind before experience in a temporal sense of the word 'before'. Pure *a priori* knowledge does not mean knowledge which is explicitly present in the mind before it has begun to experience anything at all: it means knowledge which is underived from experience, even if it makes its appearance as what we would ordinarily call 'knowledge' only on the occasion of experience. Consider the following famous and often-quoted statements. 'That all our knowledge begins with experience there can be no doubt. . . . But though all our knowledge begins *with* experience, it does not follow that it all arises *out of* experience.'[12] Kant agrees with the empiricists, such as Locke, to the extent of saying that 'all our knowledge begins with experience'. Our knowledge, he thinks, must begin with experience because the cognitive faculty, as he puts it, requires to be brought into exercise by our senses being affected by objects. Given sensations, the raw material of experience, the mind can set to work. At the same time, however, even if no knowledge is temporally antecedent to experience, it is possible that the cognitive faculty supplies *a priori* elements from within itself on the occasion of sense-impressions. In this sense the *a priori* elements would be underived from experience.

Now, why should Kant think that it is possible for there to be any *a priori* knowledge at all? The answer is that he was convinced that there evidently is such knowledge. He agreed with David Hume that we cannot derive necessity and strict universality[13] from experience. It follows, therefore, that 'necessity and strict universality are sure marks of *a priori* knowledge and are inseparably connected with one another'.[14] And it is easy to show that we possess knowledge which finds expression in necessary and universal judgments. 'If one desires an example from the sciences, one needs only to look at any proposition in mathematics. If one desires an example from the commonest operations of the understanding, the proposition that every change must have a cause can serve one's purposes.'[15] This last proposition is, in Kant's terminology, 'impure' in the sense that the concept of change is derived from experience. But the proposition is none the less *a priori*, even if it is not an example of pure *a priori* knowledge. For it is a necessary and strictly universal judgment.

There is, therefore, a considerable area of *a priori* knowledge. Kant acknowledged his debt to Hume. 'I freely confess that it was the thought of David Hume which many years ago first interrupted my dogmatic slumbers and gave an entirely new direction to my inquiries in the field of speculative philosophy.'[16] But though Kant had been convinced by Hume's discussion of the principle of causality that the element of necessity in the judgment cannot be justified on purely empiricist lines, he refused to accept Hume's psychological account of its origin in terms of the association of ideas. If I say that every event must have a cause, my judgment expresses *a priori* knowledge: it is not simply the expression of an habitual expectation mechanically produced by the association of ideas. The necessity, Kant insists, is not 'purely subjective';[17] the dependence of any event or happening or change on a cause is known, and it is known *a priori*. That is to say, my judgment is not simply a generalization from my experience of particular cases; nor does it stand in need of experiential confirmation before its truth can be known. Though, therefore, Hume was right in saying that a necessary relation between event and cause is not given in experience, his psychological explanation of the origin of the idea of necessity was inadequate. We have here an instance of *a priori* knowledge. But it is by no means the only instance. Hume may have devoted his attention principally to the causal relation; but Kant 'soon found that the concept of connection between cause and effect is by no means the only one through which the understanding thinks connections between things *a priori*'.[18] There is, therefore, a considerable area of *a priori* knowledge.

But if there certainly is *a priori* knowledge, why should Kant ask how it is possible? For if it is actual, it is obviously possible. The answer is, of course, that in the case of those fields (pure mathematics and pure physics) where, Kant is convinced, there evidently is *a priori* knowledge, the question is not how this knowledge is *possible* (better, *whether* it is possible) but *how* it is possible. Granted its possibility (for it is actual), how is it that it is possible? How is it that we can have the *a priori* knowledge which we have, for example, in mathematics?

In the case of speculative metaphysics, however, the claim to possess *a priori* knowledge is suspect. Here, therefore, we ask whether it is possible rather than how it is possible. If metaphysics provides us with knowledge of God or of immortality, for instance, such knowledge must, on Kant's view of metaphysics, be *a priori*. It must be independent of experience, in the sense that it does not logically depend on purely empirical judgments. But does speculative metaphysics provide us with such knowledge? Is it even capable in principle of doing so?

3. We must now try to make these problems more precise. And to do so we must refer to Kant's distinction between different types of judgment.

In the first place we must distinguish between analytic and synthetic judgments. Analytic judgments are those in which the predicate is contained, at least implicitly, in the concept of the subject. They are said to be 'explicative judgments' (*Erläuterungsurteile*)[19] because the predicate does not add to the concept of the subject anything which is not already contained in it, explicitly or implicitly. And their truth depends on the law of contradiction. We cannot deny the proposition without involving ourselves in logical contradiction. Kant cites as an example 'all bodies are extended'. For the idea of extension is contained in the idea of body. Synthetic judgments, however, affirm or deny of a subject a predicate which is not contained in the concept of the subject. They are called, therefore, 'ampliative' or 'augmentative judgments' (*Erweiterungsurteile*),[20] because they add something to the concept of the subject. According to Kant, 'all bodies are heavy' is an example of a synthetic judgment; for the idea of weight or heaviness is not contained in the concept of body as such.

We must now make a further distinction within the general class of synthetic judgments. In all synthetic judgments, as we have seen, something is added to the concept of the subject. A connection is affirmed (to restrict our attention to the affirmative judgment) between predicate and subject, but the predicate cannot be got out of the subject, so to speak, by mere analysis. Now, this connection may be purely factual and contingent: it is then given only in and through experience. And when this is the case, the judgment is synthetic *a posteriori*. Take the proposition, 'All members of tribe X are short', and let us suppose that this is a true proposition. It is synthetic: for we cannot elicit the idea of shortness by mere analysis from the concept of membership of tribe X.[21] But the connection between shortness and membership of the tribe is given only in and through experience; and the judgment is simply the result of a series of observations. Its universality is not strict but assumed and comparative. Even if there does not happen to be at the moment any member of the tribe who is not short, there may be one or more tall members in the future. We cannot know *a priori* that all members are short: it is simply a matter of contingent fact.

But, according to Kant, there is another class of synthetic propositions, in which the connection between predicate and subject, though not knowable by mere analysis of the concept of the subject, is none the less necessary and strictly universal. These are called synthetic *a priori* propositions. Kant gives us an example. 'Everything which happens has its cause.'[22] The proposition is synthetic because the predicate, having a cause, is not contained in the concept of what happens, that is, of an event. It is an ampliative, not an explicative judgment. But it is at the same time *a priori*. For it is characterized by necessity and strict universality, the marks of *a priori* judgments. The proposition, 'everything which happens has its cause', does not mean that, so far as our experience goes, all events have had causes and that it is reasonable to expect, until experience shows otherwise, that future events also will have causes. It means that every event, without any possible exception, will have a cause. The proposition is, of course, dependent on experience in one sense, namely that it is by experience that we become acquainted with things happening, with events. But the connection between predicate and subject is given *a priori*. It is not a mere generalization from experience, reached by induction; nor does it stand in need of experiential confirmation. We know *a priori* or in advance that every event must have a cause; and the observation of such a connection in the case of events falling within the field of an experience adds nothing to the certainty of the judgment.

It would be out of place, I think, to interrupt the course of Kant's problematic by discussing the highly controversial question of synthetic *a priori* propositions. But for the benefit of any reader who may not already be well aware of the fact, it is only fitting to note that the existence of synthetic *a priori* propositions is widely challenged by modern logicians, especially, of course, by empiricists and positivists. Their approach to the matter is rather different from that of Kant, but I do not wish to dwell upon this theme. The main point is that while the general distinction between analytic and synthetic propositions causes no difficulty, many philosophers refuse to admit that there are any synthetic propositions which are *a priori*. If a proposition is necessary, it is analytic. If a proposition is not analytic, it is synthetic *a posteriori*, to use Kant's language. In other words, the empiricist contention is that if a proposition does more than analyse the meanings of terms or illustrate the meanings of symbols, if, that is to say, it gives us information about non-linguistic reality, the connection between predicate and subject is not, and cannot be, necessary. In fine, all synthetic propositions are, in Kant's terminology, *a posteriori*. A proposition whose truth rests simply on the principle of contradiction is, as Kant said, analytic. A proposition whose truth does not rest on the principle of contradiction cannot be necessarily true. There is no room for a third class of propositions besides analytic propositions on the one hand and empirical propositions (corresponding to Kant's synthetic *a posteriori* judgments) on the other.

Kant, however, was convinced that there are synthetic *a priori* propositions; that is, propositions which are not merely 'explicative' but which extend our knowledge of reality and which are at the same time *a priori* (that is, necessary and strictly universal). The general problem, therefore, how is *a priori* cognition possible, can be expressed thus. How are synthetic *a priori* propositions possible? How is it that we can know anything at all about reality *a priori*? But this general question can be split up into several more particular questions by considering where synthetic *a priori* propositions are to be found.

They are to be found, in the first place, in mathematics. 'First of all it must be noted that mathematical propositions proper are always judgments *a priori* and not empirical, because they include the concept of necessity, which cannot be derived from experience.'[23] The proposition $7 + 5 = 12$ is not an empirical generalization admitting of possible exceptions. It is a necessary proposition. At the same time, however, this proposition, according to Kant, is not analytic in the sense described above: it is synthetic. The concept of twelve is not obtained, and cannot be obtained, by mere analysis of the idea of the union between seven and five. For this idea does not of itself imply the concept of twelve as the particular number resulting from the union. We cannot arrive at the notion of 12 except with the aid of intuition. 'The arithmetical proposition is therefore always synthetic.'[24] That is to say, it is synthetic *a priori*; for, as we have seen, it is a necessary proposition and so cannot be synthetic *a posteriori*.

Similarly, the propositions of pure geometry are also synthetic *a priori* propositions. For instance, 'that a straight line between two points is the shortest, is a synthetic proposition. For my concept of *straight* contains no notion of quantity, but only of quality. The concept of *the shortest* is thus wholly an addition, and it cannot be derived by any analysis from the concept of a straight line. Intuition must therefore lend its aid here, by means of which alone is this synthesis possible.'[25] But besides being synthetic the proposition is necessary, and so *a priori*. It is not an empirical generalization.

Geometers, Kant remarks, can make use of some analytical propositions; but he insists that all the propositions of pure mathematics proper are synthetic *a priori* propositions. Pure mathematics is not for him, as it was for Leibniz, a simply analytic science, depending on the principle of contradiction: it is constructional in character. Something more will be said in the next chapter about Kant's conception of mathematics, when we treat of his theory of space and time. Meanwhile it is sufficient to note the question which arises from his doctrine that mathematical propositions are synthetic *a priori* propositions; namely how is pure mathematical science possible? We certainly do know mathematical truths *a priori*. But how is it possible to do so?

In the second place, synthetic *a priori* propositions are also found in physics. Take, for instance, the proposition, 'in all changes of the corporeal (material) world the quantity of matter remains unchanged'. This proposition, according to Kant, is necessary and therefore *a priori*. But it is also synthetic. For in the concept of matter we do not think its permanence, but merely its presence in space, which it fills. Physics in general, of course, does not consist simply of synthetic *a priori* propositions. But 'natural science (physics) contains within itself synthetic *a priori* judgments as principles'.[26] And if we call the complex of these principles pure natural science or pure physics, the question arises, 'How is pure natural science or physics possible?' We possess *a priori* knowledge in this sphere. But how is it possible for us to possess it?

Kant believed that there are also *synthetic a priori* propositions in morals. But this subject can be left to the chapter on his ethical theory, as we are treating here of the problems raised and discussed in the *Critique of Pure Reason*. We come, therefore, to the subject of metaphysics. And if we consider metaphysics, we find that it does not aim simply at analysing concepts. It contains, indeed, analytic propositions; but they are not, properly speaking, metaphysical propositions. Metaphysics aims at extending our knowledge of reality. Its propositions must, therefore, be synthetic. At the same time, if it is not (and it is not) an empirical science, its propositions must be *a priori*. It follows, therefore, that if metaphysics is possible, it must consist of synthetic *a priori* propositions. 'And so metaphysics, according to its aim at least, consists simply of synthetic *a priori* propositions.'[27] As an example Kant cites the proposition, 'the world must have a first beginning'.[28]

But, as we have seen, the claim of metaphysics to be a science is in doubt. The question, therefore, is not so much *how* metaphysics as a science is possible as *whether* it is possible. At this point, however, we must refer to a distinction which we have already made, the distinction between metaphysics as a natural disposition and metaphysics as a science. As Kant believes that the human reason is naturally impelled to raise problems which cannot be answered empirically, he can quite properly ask how metaphysics, considered as a natural disposition, is possible. But inasmuch as he doubts whether the claim of metaphysics to constitute a science, capable of answering its own problems, is justified, the question here is really whether metaphysics considered as a science is possible.

We are faced, therefore, with four questions. First, how is pure mathematical science possible? Secondly, how is pure natural science or pure physics possible? Thirdly, how is metaphysics, considered as a natural disposition, possible? Fourthly, is metaphysics, considered as a science, possible? Kant treats of these questions in the *Critique of Pure Reason*.

4. If we consider the general question, how is *a priori* knowledge possible or how are synthetic *a priori* judgments possible, and if at the same time we bear in mind Kant's agreement with Hume concerning the impossibility of deriving necessity and strict universality from empirical data, we can see how difficult it would be for him to maintain that knowledge consists simply in the conformity of the mind to its objects. The reason for this is obvious. If, to know objects, the mind must conform itself to them, and if at the same time it cannot find in these objects, considered as empirically given, necessary connections, it becomes impossible to explain how we can make necessary and strictly universal judgments which are as a matter of fact verified and which, as we know in advance or *a priori*, must always be verified. It is not

merely that we find, for instance, that experienced events have causes: we also know in advance that every event must have a cause. But if we reduce experience to the merely given, we cannot discover there a necessary causal relation. It is thus impossible to explain our knowledge that every event must have a cause on the hypothesis that knowledge consists simply in the mind's conforming itself to objects.

Kant therefore suggested another hypothesis. 'Hitherto it has been assumed that all our knowledge must conform to objects. But all attempts to ascertain anything about them *a priori* by concepts, and thus to extend our knowledge, came to nothing on this assumption. Let us try, then, whether we may not make better progress in the tasks of metaphysics if we assume that objects must conform to our knowledge. This at all events accords better with the possibility which we are seeking, namely of a knowledge of objects *a priori*, which would determine something about them before they are given to us.'[29]

This hypothesis, Kant observes, is analogous to that proposed by Copernicus. The latter saw that though the sun appears to move across the earth from east to west, we cannot justifiably conclude from this that the earth is fixed and that the sun moves round a fixed earth, for the very good reason that the observed movement of the sun would be precisely the same (that is to say, the phenomena would be precisely what they are) if it were the earth which was moving round the sun, and the human observer with it. The immediate phenomena would be the same on either hypothesis. The question is whether there are not astronomical phenomena which can only be explained on the heliocentric hypothesis, or which at any rate are explained better and more economically on the heliocentric than on the geocentric hypothesis. And subsequent astronomical investigation showed that this is indeed the case. In an analogous manner, Kant suggests, empirical reality would remain what it is even on the hypothesis that for objects to be known (that is, for them to *be* objects, if we mean by 'object' an object of knowledge) they must conform to the mind rather than the other way about. And if *a priori* knowledge can be explained on the new but not on the old hypothesis, this is obviously an argument in favour of the former.

Kant's 'Copernican revolution' does not imply the view that reality can be reduced to the human mind and its ideas. He is not suggesting that the human mind creates things, as far as their existence is concerned, by thinking them. What he is suggesting is that we cannot know things, that they cannot be objects of knowledge for us, except in so far as they are subjected to certain *a priori* conditions of knowledge on the part of the subject. If we assume that the human mind is purely passive in knowledge, we cannot explain the *a priori* knowledge which we undoubtedly possess. Let us assume, therefore, that the mind is active. This activity does not mean creation of beings out of nothing. It means rather that the mind imposes, as it were, on the ultimate material of experience its own forms of cognition, determined by the structure of human sensibility and understanding, and that things cannot be known except through the medium of these forms. But if we speak of the mind imposing its own cognitive forms on the raw material, so to speak, of knowledge, this must not be taken to mean that the human subject does this deliberately, consciously and of set purpose. The object as given to conscious experience, the object *about* which we think (a tree, for instance), is already subjected to those cognitive forms which the human subject imposes by a natural necessity, because it is what it is; that is, because of its natural structure as a knowing subject. The cognitive forms thus determine the possibility of objects, if 'object' is taken to refer to object of knowledge precisely as such. If the word were taken to refer to things in themselves, that is, to things as they exist apart from any relation to the knowing subject, we could not, of course, say that they are determined by the human mind.

Perhaps the matter can be made a little clearer by reverting to the admittedly crude illustration of a man with red-tinted spectacles. On the one hand it is obvious that the man who sees the world as red because he is wearing red-tinted spectacles does not create the things which he sees in the sense in which God is Creator. Unless there existed things which affected him, that is, which stimulated his power of vision, he would not see anything at all. On the other hand nothing could be seen by him, that is, nothing could be for him an object of vision unless it were seen as red. At the same time, to make the analogy at all applicable, we must add the following important point. A man who puts on red-tinted spectacles does so deliberately: it is by his own choice that he sees things as red. We have to imagine, therefore, a man who is born with his power of vision so constituted that he sees all things as red. The world presented to him in experience is then a red world. This is really the point of departure for his reflection. Two hypotheses are then possible. It may be that everything *is* red. Or it may be that things have different colours,[30] but that they appear as red because of some subjective factor (as is, indeed, the case in the analogy). Spontaneously, the man would naturally embrace the first hypothesis. But it may be that in the course of time he finds a difficulty in explaining certain facts on this hypothesis. Thus he may be led to envisage and consider the alternative hypothesis. And if he finds that certain facts can be explained on this second hypothesis which cannot be explained on the hypothesis that all things are really red, he will embrace the second. He will never, indeed, be able to see the 'real' colours of things: appearances will be the same for him after his change of hypothesis as before, just as the apparent movement of the sun is precisely the same for the man who accepts the heliocentric hypothesis as it is for the man who accepts the geocentric hypothesis. But he will know why things appear as they do. The man who accepts the heliocentric hypothesis will know that the apparent movement of the sun round the earth is due to the earth's movement and to his own with it. The man who sees all things as red will have reason to suppose that this appearance of things is due to a condition in himself. Analogously, the man who accepts Kant's 'Copernican revolution' will have reason to believe, let it be assumed, that certain ways in which things appear to him (as spatially co-ordinated, for instance, and as connected with one another by necessary causal relations) are due to subjective *a priori* conditions of knowledge in himself. He will not, indeed, be able to know things apart from their subjection to these *a priori* conditions or forms; but he will know why the empirical world is what it is for his consciousness.

We have already noted Kant's reference in his foreword to the *Prolegomena* to Hume's influence on his thought. In the preface to the second edition of the *Critique of Pure Reason* he draws attention to the influence of mathematics and physics in suggesting to him the idea of his 'Copernican revolution'. In mathematics a revolution must have occurred at a very early stage. Whoever the Greek may have been who first demonstrated the properties of the isosceles triangle, a new light must have flashed upon his mind. For he saw that it was not sufficient to contemplate either the visible diagram of the triangle or the idea of it in his mind. He had to demonstrate the properties of the triangle by a process of active construction. And, in general, mathematics became a science only when it became constructional in accordance with *a priori* concepts. As for physics, the revolution in this sphere came at a much later date. With the experiments of Galileo, Torricelli and others a new light broke upon physicists. They understood at last that though the scientist must, indeed, approach Nature to learn from her, he must not do so simply in the spirit of a pupil. Rather must he approach Nature as a judge, compelling her to answer the questions which he proposes, as a judge insists on witnesses answering the questions proposed to them according to a plan. He must come to Nature with principles in one hand and experiment in the other and make her answer questions proposed according to his design or purpose. He must not allow himself simply to follow her about like a child in leading-strings. It was only when physicists saw that Nature must be made to conform, as it were, to their preconceived designs[31] that real progress in the science became possible. And these revolutions in mathematics and physics suggest that we may possibly get along better in metaphysics if we assume that objects must conform to the mind rather than the other way round. As Hume showed, *a priori* cognition cannot be explained on the second supposition. Let us see, therefore, if it can be explained on the first.

How can the 'Copernican revolution' help to explain *a priori* cognition? An example may help to give a preliminary idea. We know that every event must have a cause. But, as Hume showed, no amount of observation of particular events will serve to produce this knowledge. From this Hume concluded that we cannot be said to *know* that every event has a cause. All we can do is to try to find a psychological explanation of our belief or persuasion.[32] For Kant, however, we certainly do know that every event must have a cause. And this is an instance of *a priori* cognition. On what condition is it possible? It is possible only on condition that objects, to be objects (that is, to be known), must be subjected to the *a priori* concepts or categories of the human understanding, of which causality is one. For in this case nothing will ever enter the field of our experience except as exemplifying the causal relation, just as, to revert to our former illustration, nothing can ever enter the field of vision of the man whose power of vision is so constituted that he sees all things as red, except as red. If objects of experience are of necessity partially determined or constituted as such by the imposition of mental categories, and if causality is one of these, we can know in advance or *a priori* that nothing will ever happen, within the whole field of human experience, without a cause. And by extending this idea beyond the single example of causality we can explain the possibility of the whole range of *a priori* cognition.

Now, I have spoken of Kant's 'hypothesis'. And as regards its initial conception it was, of course, an hypothesis. 'Let us see whether we can get on better by assuming that . . .' represents the sort of way in which Kant introduces his idea. But he notes that, though the idea was suggested by the revolution in natural philosophy or physics, we cannot, in the critical philosophy, experiment with objects in a manner analogous to that in which the physicist can make experiments. We are concerned with the relation between objects and consciousness in general, and we cannot remove objects out of their relation to the knowing subject in order to see whether this does or does not make a difference to them. Such a procedure is impossible in principle. At the same time, however, if on the new hypothesis we can explain what cannot be explained in any other way, and if at the same time we succeed in demonstrating the laws which lie *a priori* at the basis of Nature (considered as the sum of possible objects of experience), we shall have succeeded in proving the validity of the point of view which was at first assumed as an hypothesis.

5. Now, 'there are two sources of human knowledge, which perhaps spring from a common but to us unknown root, namely sensibility and understanding. Through the former objects are *given* to us; through the latter they are *thought*.'[33] Kant here distinguishes between sense or sensibility (*Sinnlichkeit*) and understanding (*Verstand*), telling us that objects are *given* through sense and *thought* through the understanding. But this statement, if taken alone and without reference to the context, might easily give rise to a misconception of his meaning, and a few words of comment are necessary.

We have seen that Kant does not agree with the empiricists that all human knowledge is derived from experience. For there is *a priori* knowledge, which cannot be explained on purely empiricist principles. At the same time he agrees with the empiricists on this point, that objects are given to us in sense-experience. But the word 'given' can be misleading. To

the *a priori* forms of sensibility and shows how the synthetic *a priori* propositions of mathematics are possible. The *Transcendental Logic* is subdivided into *The Transcendental Analytic* (*Die transzendentale Analytik*) and *The Transcendental Dialectic* (*Die transzendentale Dialektik*). In the *Analytic* Kant treats of the pure concepts or categories of the understanding and shows how the synthetic *a priori* propositions of natural science are possible. In the *Dialectic* he considers two main themes, first the natural disposition to metaphysics, and secondly the question whether metaphysics (that is, speculative metaphysics of the traditional type) can be a science. As has already been remarked, he affirms the value of metaphysics considered as a natural disposition but denies its claim to constitute a true science which give us theoretical knowledge of purely intelligible reality.

The second of the two broad divisions of the *Critique of Pure Reason* is entitled *Transcendental Doctrine of Method* (*Transzendentale Methodenlehre*). In the place of speculative or 'transcendent' metaphysics, claiming to be a science of realities which transcend experience, Kant envisages a 'transcendental' metaphysics, which would comprise the complete system of *a priori* cognition, including the metaphysical foundations of natural science. He does not profess to provide this transcendental system in the *Critique of Pure Reason*. If we regard the complete system of *a priori* cognition as an edifice, we can say that the *Transcendental Doctrine of Elements*, the first broad division of the *Critique*, examines the materials and their functions, while the *Transcendental Doctrine of Method* considers the plan of the edifice and is 'the determination of the formal conditions for a complete system of pure Reason'.[36] Kant can say, therefore, that the *Critique of Pure Reason* sketches the plan of the edifice architectonically, and that it is 'the complete idea of transcendental philosophy, but not this science itself'.[37] Strictly speaking, the *Critique of Pure Reason* is only a propaedeutic to the system of transcendental philosophy or metaphysics. But if we use the latter term in a wider sense, we can, of course, say that the contents of the *Critique*, the doctrine of elements and the doctrine of method, constitute the first part of transcendental philosophy or metaphysics.

6. In the last chapter of PART I mention was made of the fact that in *Dreams of a Ghost-seer* Kant declared that metaphysics is the science of the boundaries or limits of human reason. In the *Critique of Pure Reason* he endeavours to ful-

fil this programme. But reason must be understood to mean the theoretical or speculative reason; better, reason in its theoretical function. We cannot have theoretical knowledge of realities which are not given in sense-experience or which are incapable of being so given. There is, of course, reason's critical reflection on itself; but the result of such reflection is primarily to reveal the conditions of scientific knowledge, the conditions of the possibility of objects. It does not open to us a world of supersensible reality as an object of theoretical knowledge.

At the same time this delimitation of the boundaries of theoretical or scientific knowledge does not show that God, for example, is unthinkable or that the term is meaningless. What it does is to put freedom, immortality and God beyond the range of either proof or disproof. The criticism of metaphysics, therefore, which is to be found in the *Transcendental Dialectic* opens the way for practical or moral faith, resting on the moral consciousness. Thus Kant can say[38] that he has to do away with knowledge to make room for faith, and that his destructive criticism of metaphysics' claim to be a science strikes a blow at the root of materialism, fatalism and atheism. For the truths that there is a spiritual soul, that man is free and that God exists no longer rest on fallacious arguments which afford a ground for those who deny these truths; they are moved to the sphere of the practical or moral reason and become objects of faith rather than of knowledge (this term being taken in a sense analogous to that in which it is used with reference to mathematics and natural science).

It is a great mistake to look on this theory as a mere sop to the orthodox and devout or as a mere act of prudence on Kant's part. For it is part of his solution to the great problem of reconciling the world of science on the one hand with, on the other, the world of the moral and religious consciousness. Science (that is, classical physics) involves a conception of causal laws which do not admit of freedom. And man, considered as a member of the cosmic system studied by the scientist, is no exception. But scientific knowledge has its limits, and its limits are determined by the *a priori* forms of human sensibility and understanding. There is thus no valid reason whatsoever for saying that the limits of our scientific or theoretical knowledge are identical with the limits of reality. And the moral consciousness, when its practical implications are developed, takes us beyond the sensible sphere. As a phenomenal being, man must be considered as subject to causal laws and as determined; but the moral consciousness, itself a reality, involves the idea of freedom. Though, therefore, we cannot demonstrate scientifically that man is free, belief in freedom is demanded by the moral consciousness.

This point of view is certainly beset with difficulties. Not only do we have the division between sensible, phenomenal reality and noumenal, purely intelligible reality, but we are also faced in particular with the difficult conception of man as phenomenally determined but noumenally free, as determined and free at the same time, though under different aspects. But it would be out of place to discuss the difficulties here. My point in mentioning Kant's point of view was twofold. First, I wished to draw attention once again to the general problem of the reconciliation of the world of Newtonian physics with the world of reality and religion. For if we bear this general problem in mind, we are less likely to lose sight of the wood for the trees. Secondly, I wished to indicate that the *Critique of Pure Reason* does not stand by itself in lonely isolation from Kant's other writings but that it forms a part of a total philosophy which is gradually revealed in successive works. True, the first *Critique* has its own problems, and to this extent it stands by itself. But, quite apart from the fact that inquiry into *a priori* cognition has yet to be pursued in the field of the practical reason, the conclusions of the first *Critique* form only a part of the solution to a general problem which underlies all Kant's thinking. And it is important to understand this fact from the start.

Chapter Twelve

KANT (3): SCIENTIFIC KNOWLEDGE

Space and time — Mathematics — The pure concepts or categories of the understanding — The justification of the application of the categories — The schematism of the categories — Synthetic a priori principles — The possibility of the pure science of Nature — Phenomena and noumena — The refutation of idealism — Concluding remarks.

1. The only way, says Kant at the beginning of the *Transcendental Aesthetic*, in which our knowledge can relate immediately to objects is by means of an intuition.[1] And an intuition can take place only in so far as an object is given to us. The divine intellect is said to be both intuitive and archetypal. That is to say, the divine intuition creates its objects. But this is not the case with human intuition, which presupposes an object. And this means that the human subject must be affected by the object in some way. Now, the capacity for receiving representations (*Vorstellungen*) of objects by being affected by them is named 'sensibility' (*Sinnlichkeit*). 'By means of sensibility, therefore, objects are given to us, and it alone provides us with intuitions.'[2]

If these remarks are taken purely by themselves, the term 'sensibility' has a wide meaning, being simply cognitive receptivity or the capacity for receiving representations of objects by being affected by them. But we must remember that Kant looks on the divine intuition, considered precisely in contrast with human intuition, as being not only archetypal but intellectual. It follows, therefore, that human intuition is sense intuition. And sensibility thus means the capacity for receiving representations of objects by being sensibly affected by them. 'The effect of an object upon the faculty of representation, so far as we are affected by the object, is sensation' (*Empfindung*).[3] Kant agrees, therefore, with the empiricists to the extent of saying that human cognition of objects requires sensation. The mind requires to be put in contact, as it were, with things through an affection of the senses. Kant takes it for granted that the senses are acted upon by external things; and the effect of this action upon the faculty of representation is called 'sensation'. The latter is thus a subjective representation; but this does not mean that it is caused by the subject.

Sense intuition cannot, however, be reduced simply to the *a posteriori* affections of our senses by things. The object of an empirical sensuous intuition is called by Kant 'appearance' (*Erscheinung*). And in the appearance we can distinguish two elements. First there is its matter. This is described as 'that which corresponds to sensation'.[4] Secondly, there is the form of appearance. And this is described as 'that which enables the manifold of appearance to be arranged in certain relations'.[5] Now, the form, as distinct from the matter, cannot be itself sensation, if the matter is described as that which corresponds to sensation. Hence, while the matter is given is *a posteriori*, the form must lie on the side of the subject: that is to say, it must be *a priori*, an *a priori* form of sensibility, pertaining to the very structure of sensibility and constituting a necessary condition of all sense intuition. According to Kant, there are two pure forms of sensibility, space and time. Space is not, indeed, a necessary condition of *all* empirical intuitions; but this point can be passed over for the moment. It is sufficient to note that Kant parts company with the pure empiricists by finding an *a priori* element in all sense-experience.

Perhaps at this point some remarks should be made about Kant's terminology, even at the cost of interrupting the exposition of his theory of space and time. First, the term 'representation' (*Vorstellung*) is used in a very wide sense to cover a variety of cognitive states. Hence the term 'faculty of representation' is pretty well equivalent to 'mind' (*Gemüt*), a term which is also used in an extremely wide sense. Secondly, the term object (*Gegenstand*) is not used consistently in one sense. Thus in the definition of sensation quoted above 'object' must refer to what Kant later calls thing-in-itself, and which is unknown. But 'object' generally means object of knowledge. Thirdly, in the first edition of the *Critique of Pure Reason* Kant distinguishes between 'appearance' and 'phenomenon'. 'Appearances, so far as they are thought as objects according to the unity of the categories, are called *phenomena*.'[6] Hence 'appearance' should mean the content of a sense intuition when this content is considered as 'undetermined' or uncategorized, while 'phenomenon' should mean categorized objects. In point of fact, however, Kant often uses the term 'appearance' (*Erscheinung*) in both senses.

A further remark. We have seen that the matter of appearances is described as that which 'corresponds to' sensation. Elsewhere, however, we are told that sensation itself can be called 'the matter of sense-knowledge'.[7] And perhaps these two ways of speaking can be regarded as expressions of two different tendencies in Kant's thought. The external thing which affects the subject is itself unknown; but by affecting the senses it produces a representation. Now, Kant sometimes tends to speak as though all appearances were subjective representations. And, when this point of view is dominant, it is natural for him to describe sensation itself as the matter of appearance. For sensation is described, as we have seen, as the effect of an object upon the faculty of representation. But Kant also speaks as though phenomena were objects which are not simply subjective representations; and this represents, indeed, his dominant outlook. If, then, we think away the contribution of the categories of the understanding to phenomena and come down to appearances (in the narrower sense of the word), it is natural to speak of the matter of an appearance as being that which 'corresponds to' sensation.

The last three paragraphs can be described, not as a digression, but as a series of footnotes in the text, if one may be permitted a contradiction in terms. However, a brief development of the idea suggested in the final sentence of the last paragraph may serve to clarify Kant's position and carry forward our account of it. The approach is proposed by Kant himself.[8]

The world of common experience obviously consists of things with various qualities, things which stand in various relations to one another. That is to say, we ordinarily talk about perceiving things, each of which can be described in terms of qualities, and each of which stands in various relations to other things. And perception in this sense is clearly the work of understanding and sense in co-operation. But from the total process we can try to abstract all that is contributed by the understanding, in order to arrive at empirical intuition, or perception in a narrow sense. We then come by logical analysis to appearances, to what we may call perhaps sense-contents or sense-data. But we can carry the analysis further. For within the content of sense-experience we can distinguish between the material element, that which corresponds to indeterminate sensation, and the formal element, the spatio-temporal relations of the manifold of appearance.[9] And the purpose of the *Transcendental Aesthetic* is to isolate and study the formal elements, considered as a necessary condition of experience.

The matter can be expressed in this way. The very lowest level conceivable of anything which could be called a knowledge of or acquaintance with objects involves at least an adverting to the representations produced by the action of things upon our senses. But we cannot advert to sensations without relating them in space and time. For instance, to advert to two sensations, that is, to be conscious of them, involves relating the one to the other within time, within an order of temporal succession. One sensation comes before or after or at the same time as another. Space and time constitute the framework, as it were, in which the manifold of sensation is ordered or arranged. They thus at the same time diversify and unify (in spatio-temporal relations) the indeterminate matter of appearance.

This does not mean, of course, that we are at first aware of unordered sensations, and that we then subject them to the *a priori* forms of space and time. For we are never faced, as it were, with unordered sensations. Nor could we be. Indeed, Kant's main point is that space and time are *a priori* necessary conditions of sense-experience. What is given, therefore, in empirical intuition, namely that of which we are aware, is, so to speak, already ordered. The ordering is a condition of awareness or consciousness, not a consequence of it. True, within the appearance we can distinguish, by a process of logical abstraction or analysis, between matter and form. But as soon as we abstract in thought the subjectively contributed form of appearance, the object of which we are aware disappears. In fine, the objects of sensuous or empirical intuition are, as given to consciousness, already subject to the *a priori* forms of sensibility. The ordering or relating takes place within sensuous intuition, not after it.

Attention can now be drawn to the distinction which Kant makes between outer or external sense, by means of which we perceive objects external to us (or, as he puts it, represent to ourselves objects as external to us), and inner or internal sense, by means of which we perceive our interior states.[10] Space is said to be 'the form of all appearances of the external senses, that is, the subjective condition of sensibility, under which alone external intuition is possible for us'.[11] All objects external to us are, and must be, represented as being in space. Time is said to be 'the form of the internal sense, that is, of the intuition of ourselves[12] and of our internal state'.[13] Our psychical states are perceived in time, as following one another or as simultaneous, but not as in space.[14]

Inasmuch as Kant immediately proceeds to say that time is the *a priori* formal condition of all appearances whatsoever, whereas space is the *a priori* formal condition of external appearances only, it may appear that he is contradicting himself. But his meaning is this. All representations (*Vorstellungen*), whether they have or have not external things as their objects, are determinations of the mind.[15] And, as such, they belong to our internal state. Hence they must all be subject to the formal condition of inner sense or intuition, namely time. But time is thus only the mediate condition of external appearances, whereas it is the immediate condition of all internal appearances.

Now, we have been speaking of space and time as pure forms of sensibility and as forms of intuition. But we have already drawn attention[16] to the different ways in which Kant uses the term 'intuition'. And in what he calls the 'metaphysical exposition' of the ideas of space and time he refers to them as being themselves *a priori* intuitions. They are not empirically derived concepts. I cannot derive the representation of space *a posteriori*, from the experienced relations between external appearances; for I cannot represent external appearances as having spatial relations except within space. Nor could I represent appearances as existing simultaneously or successively unless the representation of time were already present. For I represent them as existing simultaneously or successively within time. I can think away all external appearances, and the representation of space still remains, as a condition of their possibility. Similarly, I can think away all internal states, but the representation of time still remains. Space and time, therefore, cannot be empirically derived concepts. Further, they cannot be concepts at all, if we mean by concepts general ideas. Our ideas of spaces are formed by introducing limitations within a unitary space, which is presupposed as their necessary foundation; and our ideas of different times or stretches of time are formed in an analogous manner. But we cannot, according to Kant, split up general concepts in this way. Space and time are particulars rather than general concepts. And they are found on the perceptual

level; they are presupposed by the concepts of the understanding, not the other way round. We must conclude, therefore, that they are *a priori* intuitions on the level of sense,
though we must not, of course, take this as meaning that in
the representations of unitary space and time we intuit non-
mental existent realities. The representations of space and
time are necessary conditions for perception; but they are
conditions on the side of the subject.

Are space and time, therefore, unreal for Kant? The answer to this question depends on the meanings which we attach to the words 'real' and 'unreal'. Appearances, objects
given in empirical intuition, are, so to speak, already tem-
poralized and, in the case of appearances represented as external to ourselves, spatialized. Empirical reality is, therefore,
spatio-temporal, and it follows that space and time must be
said to possess empirical reality. If the question whether space
and time are real is equivalent to the question whether
empirical reality is characterized by spatio-temporal relations,
the answer must be affirmative. We experience only appearances, and appearances are what they are, possible objects of
experience, only through the union of form and matter; that
is, through the ordering of the indeterminate and formless
matter of sensation by the application of the pure forms of
sensibility. There can never be an object of outer sense which
is not in space; and there can never be any object, whether
of outer or inner sense, which is not in time.[17] Hence empirical reality must necessarily be characterized by spatial and
temporal relations. It is not proper to say that appearances
seem to be in space; they *are* in space and time. It may be
objected that, according to Kant, space and time are subjective forms of sensibility, and that they therefore should be
called ideal rather than real. But the point is that, for Kant,
there can be no empirical reality apart from the imposition
of these forms. They enter into the constitution as it were
of empirical reality; and they are thus themselves empirically
real.

At the same time, however, inasmuch as space and time
are *a priori* forms of human sensibility, the range of their
application is extended only to things as appearing to us.
There is no reason to suppose that they apply to things-in-
themselves, apart from their appearance to us. Indeed, they
cannot do so. For they are essentially conditions for the possibility of appearances. While, therefore, it is correct to say,
for instance, that all appearances are in time, it is quite in-

correct to say that all things or all realities are in time. If there are realities which cannot affect our senses and which cannot belong to empirical reality, they cannot be in space and time. That is to say, they cannot have spatio-temporal relations. By transcending empirical reality they transcend the whole spatio-temporal order. Moreover, those realities which do affect our senses, when taken as they are in themselves and apart from being objects of experience, are not in space and time. There may be some ground in things in virtue of which a thing possesses, as a phenomenon, certain spatial relations and not others; but this ground is unknown and it necessarily remains unknown. It is not itself a spatial relation. For space and time have no application to non-phenomenal reality.

Kant's formula is, therefore, this. Space and time are empirically real but transcendentally ideal. They are empirically real in the sense that what is given in experience is in space (if it is an object of the external senses) and in time. Space and time are not, Kant insists, illusions. We can distinguish between reality and illusion as well on his theory as on the opposite theory. But space and time are transcendentally ideal in the sense that the sphere of phenomena is the only sphere of their validity, and that they do not apply to things-in-themselves, considered apart from their appearance to us.[18] This transcendental ideality, however, leaves the empirical reality of the spatio-temporal order entirely unimpaired. Kant would not admit, therefore, that his view could properly be assimilated to the Berkeleian idealism, according to which to exist is to perceive or to be perceived. For he affirmed the existence of things-in-themselves, which are not perceived.[19] His Copernican revolution, he insists, no more impairs the empirical reality of the world of experience than the heliocentric hypothesis alters or denies the phenomena. It is a question of explaining phenomena, not of denying them. And his view of space and time is capable of explaining the *a priori* knowledge founded on these intuitions, which no other view is capable of explaining. To this *a priori* knowledge we must now turn.

2. Kant gives what he calls a 'transcendental exposition' of both space and time. 'By a transcendental exposition I understand the explanation of a conception as a principle from which the possibility of other synthetic *a priori* cognitions can be discerned. For this purpose it is required, first that such cognitions do really flow from the given conception, and secondly that these cognitions are possible only on the pre-

supposition of a given way of explaining this conception.'[20] In his transcendental exposition of time Kant does not tell us very much beyond the facts, first that the concept of change, and with it the concept of motion (considered as change of place), is possible only in and through the representation of time, and secondly that we cannot explain the synthetic *a priori* cognition exhibited in the general doctrine of motion except on the presupposition that time is an *a priori* intuition. When treating of space, however, he speaks at some length[21] of mathematics, in particular of geometry. And his general thesis is that the possibility of mathematical knowledge, which is synthetic *a priori* in character, can be explained only on the theory that space and time are pure *a priori* intuitions.

Let us take the proposition, 'It is possible to construct a figure with three straight lines'. We cannot deduce this proposition by mere analysis of the concepts of a straight line and of the number three. We have to construct the object (a triangle) or, as Kant puts it, to give ourselves an object in intuition. This cannot be an empirical intuition. For then it could not give rise to a necessary proposition. It must be, therefore, an *a priori* intuition. And from this it follows that the object (the triangle) cannot be either a thing-in-itself or a mental image, as it were, of a thing-in-itself. It cannot be a thing-in-itself, for things-in-themselves, by definition, do not appear to us. And even if we grant the possibility of intuiting a thing-in-itself, this intuition could not be *a priori*. The thing would have to be presented to me in an *a posteriori* intellectual intuition, if such were possible to us. Nor can we suppose that the object (the triangle) is a mental image or representation of a thing-in-itself. For the necessary propositions which we are enabled to make by constructing a triangle are made about the triangle itself. For instance, we can demonstrate the properties of *the* isosceles triangle, so to speak. And we have no warrant for supposing that what is necessarily true of a representation is true of a thing-in-itself. How, then, can we construct in intuition objects which enable us to enunciate synthetic *a priori* propositions? We can do so only on condition that there is in us a faculty (*Vermögen*) of *a priori* intuition, which is the universal, necessary condition for the possibility of objects of external intuition. Mathematics is not a purely analytic science which gives us information only about the contents of concepts or meanings of terms. It gives us information *a priori* about objects of external intuition. But this is not possible unless the intuitions required for the construction of mathematics are all grounded in *a priori* intuitions which are the necessary conditions for the very possibility of objects of external intuition. Thus 'geometry is a science which determines the properties of space synthetically, and yet *a priori*'.[22] But we could not determine the properties of space in this way unless space were a pure form of human sensibility, a pure *a priori* intuition which is the necessary condition for all objects of external intuition.

The matter can perhaps be made somewhat clearer by referring to Kant's discussion in the *Prolegomena* of the objectivity of mathematics, that is, of its applicability to objects. Geometry, to take one particular branch of mathematics, is constructed *a priori*. Nevertheless we know very well that its propositions are necessary, in the sense that empirical reality must always conform to them. The geometer determines *a priori* the properties of space, and his propositions will always be true of the empirical spatial order. But how can he make necessarily true *a priori* statements which have objective validity in reference to the external, empirical world? It is possible for him to do this only if the space, whose properties he determines, is a pure form of human sensibility, by which form alone objects are given to us and which applies only to phenomena, not to things-in-themselves. Once we accept this explanation, 'it is quite easy to understand and at the same time to prove indisputably that all external objects of our sensible world must necessarily accord in all strictness with the propositions of geometry'.[23]

Kant thus uses the *a priori* character of mathematics to prove his theory of space and time. And it is of interest to note the relation of his position to that of Plato. The latter also was convinced of the *a priori* character of mathematics. But he explained it by postulating an intuition of 'mathematical objects', intelligible particulars which are not phenomena and which subsist in some sense in their own right. This line of explanation is ruled out on Kant's principles; and he accuses Plato of abandoning the world of sense and taking flight into an empty ideal realm where the mind can find no sure support. However, he shares Plato's conviction of the *a priori* character of mathematical knowledge, though his explanation of it is different.

Some references to Leibniz may help to throw some further light on Kant's view of mathematics. For Leibniz all mathematical propositions, including axioms, can be demonstrated with the aid of definitions and the principle of contradiction. For Kant fundamental axioms cannot be demonstrated by recourse to the principle of contradiction. Geometry is thus axiomatic in character. But Kant maintains that the fundamental axioms of geometry express insights into the essential nature of space represented in a subjective *a priori* intuition. And it is obvious that it is possible to hold both that the axioms are indemonstrable and that they do not express insights into the essential nature of space. For they might be held to be free postulates, as, for instance, by the mathematician, D. Hilbert.

Again, in developing mathematical science the mind, according to Leibniz, proceeds analytically. We only require definitions and the principle of contradiction, and we can then proceed by analysis. For Kant, as we have seen, mathematics is not a purely analytic science: it is synthetic, requiring intuition and proceeding constructionally. And this is as true of arithmetic as it is of geometry. Now, if we accept the view, represented above all by Bertrand Russell, that mathematics is ultimately reducible to logic, in the sense that pure mathematics could in principle be deduced from certain primitive logical concepts and indemonstrable propositions, we shall naturally reject Kant's theory. We shall regard this theory as refuted by the *Principles of Mathematics* and *Principia Mathematica*. But Russell's view of mathematics as purely analytic is not, of course, by any means universally accepted. And if we think, with L. E. J. Brouwer for example, that mathematics does in fact involve intuition, we shall naturally attach more value to Kant's theory, even if we do not accept his account of space and time. However, as I am not myself a mathematician, I cannot profitably attempt to decide how much truth there is in the theory. I can only draw attention to the fact that modern philosophers of mathematics are by no means all agreed that mathematics is what Kant said it was not, namely a purely analytic science.

Attention must, however, also be drawn to a feature of Kant's theory of geometry which has led critics to maintain that the theory has been discredited by subsequent mathematical developments. By space Kant meant Euclidean space, and by geometry he meant Euclidean geometry.[24] It follows, therefore, that if the geometer reads off, so to speak, the properties of space, the geometry of Euclid is the only geometry. Euclidean geometry will necessarily apply to empirical reality, but no other geometrical system will apply. Since Kant's time, however, non-Euclidean geometries have been developed, and it has been shown that Euclidean space is but one of the conceivable spaces. Moreover, Euclidean geometry is not the only one which will fit reality, as it were; which geometry is to be used depends on the mathematician's purpose and the problems with which he has to deal. It would, indeed, be absurd to blame Kant for having a prejudice in favour of Euclidean geometry. At the same time the development of other geometries has rendered his position untenable.

To be accurate, it is rash to say without qualification that Kant excluded the possibility of any non-Euclidean geometry. For we find him saying, for instance, that 'there is no contradiction in the concept of a figure which is enclosed within two straight lines. For the concepts of two straight lines and of their intersection contain no negation of a figure. The impossibility is found, not in the concept in itself, but in the construction of the concept in space; that is, in the conditions and determinations of space. But these have their own objective reality; that is, they apply to possible things, because they contain in themselves *a priori* the form of experience in general.'[25] But even if we take this passage as saying by implication that a non-Euclidean geometry is a bare logical possibility, Kant clearly states that such a geometry cannot be constructed in intuition. And this is really, for Kant, the same thing as to say that there cannot be a non-Euclidean geometrical system. Non-Euclidean geometry may be thinkable in the sense that it is not ruled out simply by application of the principle of contradiction. But, as we have seen, mathematics for Kant does not rest simply on the principle of contradiction; it is not an analytic but a synthetic science. Hence constructibility is essential for a geometrical system. And to say that only Euclidean geometry can be constructed is really to say that there cannot be non-Euclidean systems.

If, therefore, we assume the constructional character of geometry, and if non-Euclidean geometries can be constructed, it follows at any rate that Kant's theory of geometry cannot be accepted as it stands. And if non-Euclidean systems can be applied, this tells against Kant's theory that the intuition of Euclidean space is a universal and necessary condition for the possibility of objects. But whether or not it would be possible to revise the Kantian theory of the subjectivity of space in such a way as to allow for subsequent mathematical developments is not a matter on which I feel disposed to offer any opinion. From the purely mathematical point of view it is not a question of any importance. From the philosophical point of view it has, indeed, importance; but then there may be other reasons for denying Kant's theory of the transcendental ideality of space and time.[26]

However, if we assume that Kant has proved the truth of his theory of space and time, he may be said to have answered his first question, namely how is mathematical science possible. How can we explain the possibility of the synthetic *a priori* cognition which we undoubtedly possess in mathematics? It is explicable if, and only if, space and time are empirically real but transcendentally ideal in the sense described above.

A final remark. It may have occurred to the reader that it is very odd of Kant to treat mathematics on the level of sensibility. But the latter did not imagine, of course, that arithmetic and geometry are developed by the senses without the use of the understanding. The question was what is the necessary foundation for the work of the mind in developing systems of mathematical propositions. And for Kant the *a priori* forms of sensibility, the pure intuitions of space and time, constitute this necessary foundation. In his view all human intuition is sensuous, and if intuition is required in mathematics, it must be sensuous in character. He may well have been wrong in thinking that all human intuition is necessarily sensuous. But at any rate he was not guilty of the absurdity of supposing that the senses construct mathematical systems without the co-operation of the understanding.

3. We can begin our treatment of the *Transcendental Analytic* by developing a little this important point of the co-operation of sense and understanding in human knowledge.

Human knowledge arises from two chief sources in the mind (*Gemüt*). The first is the faculty or power of receiving impressions; and through this an object is given to us. Sense intuition provides us with data, and we cannot obtain objects as data in any other way. The second main source of human knowledge is the power of thinking the data by means of concepts. The receptivity of the mind for impressions is called sensibility (*Sinnlichkeit*). The faculty of spontaneously producing representations is called understanding (*Verstand*). And the co-operation of both faculties is required for knowledge of objects. 'Without sensibility no object would be given to us, and without the understanding no object would be thought. Thoughts without content are empty; intuitions without concepts are blind. . . . These two powers or faculties cannot exchange their functions. The understanding is incapable of intuiting, and the senses are incapable of thinking. It is only from the united co-operation of the two that knowledge can arise.'[27]

But though the co-operation of both powers is required for knowledge, we ought not to overlook the differences between them. And we can distinguish between sensibility and its laws on the one hand and understanding and its laws on the other. The science of the laws of sensibility has already been considered. We must therefore now turn our attention to the science of the laws of the understanding, namely logic.

The logic with which we are here concerned is not, however, formal logic, which regards only the forms of thinking and abstracts from its content and from differences in the kinds of objects about which we can think.[28] We are concerned with what Kant calls 'transcendental logic'. It is not offered as a substitute for traditional formal logic, which Kant simply accepts. It is offered as an additional, and new, science. Like pure formal logic, it is concerned with the *a priori* principles of thought, but, unlike the former science, it does not abstract from all the content of knowledge, that is, from the relation of knowledge to its object. For it is concerned with the *a priori* concepts and principles of the understanding and with their application to objects; not, indeed, with their application to this or that particular kind of object, but with their application to objects in general. In other words, transcendental logic is concerned with the *a priori* knowledge of objects so far as this is the work of the understanding. Transcendental aesthetic, which we have already considered, studies the pure forms of sensibility as the *a priori* conditions necessary for objects being given to us in *sense intuition*. Transcendental logic studies the *a priori* concepts and principles of the understanding as necessary conditions for objects (that is, the data of sense intuition) being *thought*.

The matter can be put this way. It was Kant's conviction that there are in the understanding *a priori* concepts by which the manifold of phenomena is synthesized. Causality is one of them. There is room, therefore, for a systematic study of these concepts and of the principles grounded in them. In pursuing this study we shall discover the ways in which human understanding necessarily synthesizes phenomena and makes knowledge possible.

The second part of the *Transcendental Logic*, namely the *Transcendental Dialectic*, is concerned with the misuse of these *a priori* concepts and principles and with their illegitimate extension from the objects given in sense intuition to things in general, including those which cannot be given to us as objects in the proper sense. But consideration of this second part must be left for the next chapter. We are concerned at present with the first part, namely the *Transcendental Analytic*. And our first task is to ascertain the *a priori* concepts of the understanding (*Analytic of Concepts*).

But how are we to set about this task? Obviously, we are not called upon to make a complete inventory of all possible concepts and then to separate the *a priori* concepts from those which are *a posteriori* or empirical, abstracted from sense-experience. Even if this were practically possible, we should have to possess a criterion or method for distinguishing between *a priori* and empirical concepts. And if we were in possession of a method for ascertaining which concepts are purely *a priori*, it might be that the use of the method would enable us to achieve our purpose without making any such general inventory. The question is, therefore, whether there is in fact a way of ascertaining the *a priori* concepts of the understanding in a direct and systematic manner. We need a principle or, as Kant puts it, a 'transcendental clue' (*Leitfaden*) for discovering these concepts.

Kant finds this clue in the faculty of judgment, which for him is the same as the power of thought. 'We can reduce all operations of the understanding to judgments, so that the understanding can be represented as the power of judging. For it is, according to what has been said above, a power of thinking.'[29] Now, what is a judgment? To judge, which is the same as to think, is to unify different representations to form one cognition by means of concepts.[30] In judgment, therefore, representations are synthesized by means of concepts. Now, we can obviously set no limit to the number of possible judgments, if we are talking about particular judgments. But we can determine the number of possible ways of judging, that is, the number of logical types of judgment, considered according to their form. And, in Kant's opinion, logicians have already done so. But they have not carried the matter further and inquired into the reason why these, and only these, forms of judgment are possible. It is, however, precisely here that we can find our 'transcendental clue'. For each form of judgment is determined by an *a priori* concept. And in order, therefore, to discover the list of the pure *a priori* concepts of the understanding, we have only to examine the table of possible logical types of judgment.

We can put the matter in this way. The understanding does not intuit; it judges. And to judge is to synthesize. Now, there are certain fundamental ways of synthesizing (functions of unity in judgment, as Kant puts it), exhibited in the possible logical types or forms of judgment. And these exhibit the *a priori* structure of the understanding, considered as a unifying or synthesizing power. We can thus discover the fundamental synthesizing functions of the understanding. 'The functions of the understanding can thus all be found, if one can completely exhibit the functions of unity in judgments. And the following section will show that this can be done quite easily.'[31]

Hitherto we have generally spoken of the pure or *a priori* *concepts* of the understanding. But Kant also calls them *categories*. And this is probably a better word. The understanding, which is the unifying or synthesizing or judging power, possesses an *a priori* categorial structure. That is to say, because it is what it is, it necessarily synthesizes representations in certain fundamental ways, according to certain basic categories. Without this synthesizing knowledge of objects is not possible. Hence the categories of the understanding are *a priori* conditions for knowledge. That is, they are *a priori* conditions for the possibility of objects being thought. And without being thought the objects cannot really be said to be known. For, as we have seen, sensibility and understanding co-operate in the production of knowledge, though their functions differ and can be considered separately.

Kant's table of types of judgment or of logical functions of judgment can now be given. For the sake of convenience I give at the same time his table of categories. The total scheme shows which category corresponds, or is supposed to correspond, to which logical function. The tables are to be found in the first chapter of the *Analytic of Concepts*.[32]

Judgments	*Categories*
1. Quantity.	1. Quantity.
(i) Universal.	(i) Unity.
(ii) Particular.	(ii) Plurality.
(iii) Singular.	(iii) Totality.

Judgments	*Categories*
2. Quality.	2. Quality.
(iv) Affirmative.	(iv) Reality.
(v) Negative.	(v) Negation.
(vi) Infinite.	(vi) Limitation.
3. Relation.	3. Relation.
(vii) Categorical.	(vii) Inherence and subsistence (substance and accident).
(viii) Hypothetical.	(viii) Causality and dependence (cause and effect).
(ix) Disjunctive.	(ix) Community (reciprocity between agent and patient).
4. Modality.	4. Modality.
(x) Problematic.	(x) Possibility—impossibility.
(xi) Assertoric.	(xi) Existence—non-existence.
(xii) Apodictic.	(xii) Necessity—contingency.

Kant remarks about the list of categories that it has not been made in a haphazard fashion, like Aristotle's list of categories, but by the systematic application of a principle. It thus contains all the original pure concepts or categories of the understanding. There are, indeed, other pure concepts of the understanding but these are derived (*a priori*) and subsidiary. Kant proposes to call them *predicables*, to distinguish them from the categories (*praedicamenta*); but he does not undertake to give a list of them; that is, to work out the complete system of original and derived pure concepts of the understanding. It is enough for his purpose to have given the list of the original concepts or categories.

Kant was, however, over-optimistic in thinking that he had given a complete list of categories. For it is clear that his principle for determining what they were was dependent on the acceptance of certain views about judgment, which were taken from the logic of his time. And so it was open to his successors to revise his list, even when they accepted the general idea of *a priori* categories.

It is worth remarking, perhaps, that according to Kant the third category in each triad arises out of the combination of the second with the first. Thus totality is plurality regarded as unity; limitation is reality combined with negation; community is the causality of a substance reciprocally determining and determined by another substance; and necessity is existence given through the possibility of existence.[33] This interpretation of the triadic scheme may seem to be somewhat far-fetched; but in view of the central position occupied later in the Hegelian philosophy by the idea of triadic development through thesis, antithesis and synthesis it is worth while drawing attention here to Kant's remarks.

4. According to Kant, therefore, there are twelve *a priori* categories of the understanding. But what is the justification for their employment in synthesizing phenomena? What is the justification for their application to objects? Such a problem does not arise in connection with the employment of the *a priori* forms of sensibility. For, as we have seen, no objects can be given to us at all except through the subjection of the indeterminate matter of sensation to the forms of space and time. Hence it would be foolish to ask how we are justified in applying the forms of sensibility to objects. For these forms are a necessary condition of there being objects at all. But the situation in regard to the categories of the understanding is different. Objects are already there, so to speak, given in sense intuition. Might not these objects, namely appearances, be such that the application to them of the categories of the understanding distorts or misrepresents them? We need to show that the application is justified.

The giving of such a justification is called by Kant the transcendental deduction of the categories. The word 'deduction' can easily be misunderstood. For it suggests a systematic discovery of what the categories are. And this has already been done. In the present context, therefore, deduction means justification, as Kant indeed explains. As for the word 'transcendental', its meaning is best understood by contrasting it with the word 'empirical'. Kant is not concerned to justify the application of the categories by showing that their employment is empirically fruitful, in this or that science, for example. He is concerned to justify their application by showing that they are *a priori* conditions of all experience. He can say, therefore, that the whole aim of the transcendental deduction is to show that the *a priori* concepts or categories of the understanding are *a priori* conditions of the possibility of experience.

The problem can be defined more closely. Space and time are also *a priori* conditions of experience. But they are conditions which are necessarily required in order that objects should be given to us. The task of the transcendental deduction, therefore, is to show that the categories are conditions which are necessarily required for objects to be *thought*. In other words, a justification of the application of the categories to objects must take the form of showing that objects cannot be thought except through the synthesizing categories of the understanding. And as the thinking of objects is required for knowledge of them, to show that objects cannot be thought save through the categories is to show that they cannot be known except through the categories. And to show this is to show that the employment of the categories is justified; that is, that they have objective validity.

This line of thought is clearly involved in Kant's Copernican revolution. The use of the categories cannot be justified on the assumption that the mind must conform to objects. But if objects, to be known, must conform to the mind, and if this means that they must be subjected to the categories of the understanding in order to be objects in the full sense, no further justification of the use of the categories is required.

The argument of Kant's transcendental deduction is by no means easy to follow. But in the course of it he introduces an important idea; and some effort must be made to give a brief account of it, even at the risk of over-simplifying his line of thought. In making this attempt I shall confine my attention to the deduction as given in the second edition of the *Critique of Pure Reason*, which differs considerably from that given in the first edition.

An object of knowledge is defined by Kant as 'that in the concept of which the manifold of a given intuition is *united*'.[34] Without synthesis there can be no knowledge of objects. A mere stream, so to speak, of unconnected representations could not be called knowledge. Now, synthesis is the work of the understanding. 'The connection (*Verbindung* and *conjunctio* are the words used by Kant) of a manifold can never be given us by the sense . . . ; for it is an act of the spontaneity of the power of representation. And as one must call this faculty understanding, to distinguish it from sensibility, all connection, whether conscious or unconscious, whether of the manifold of intuition or of several concepts

. . . is an act of the understanding. And to this act we give the general name of synthesis.'[35]

Besides the concepts of the manifold and of its synthesis, the idea of connection or conjunction contains another element. This is the representation of the unity of the manifold. Hence connection can be described as 'the representation of the synthetical unity of the manifold'.[36]

Kant is not referring here to the *a priori* concept or category of unity which figures in the list of categories. He is not saying that all connection involves the application of this category. For the application of any category, whether it be unity or any other, presupposes the unity of which he is speaking. Of what, then, is Kant speaking? He is speaking of the unity which consists in relation to one perceiving and thinking subject. Objects are thought by means of the categories but without this unity they would not be thinkable. In other words, the understanding's work of synthesizing is not possible except within the unity of consciousness.

This means that the manifold of intuition or perception is incapable of being thought and so becoming an object of knowledge unless perceiving and thinking are so united in one subject that self-consciousness is capable of accompanying all representations. Kant expresses this by saying that the *I think* must be capable of accompanying all one's representations. It is not necessary that I should always think of my perceiving and thinking as *mine*. But without the *possibility* of such awareness no unity can be given to the manifold of intuition: no connection is possible. 'The *I think* must be capable of accompanying all my representations. For otherwise something could be represented in me which could not be thought at all. And this is equivalent to saying that the representation would be impossible or at least would be nothing to me. . . . Therefore every manifold of intuition has a necessary relation to the *I think* in the same subject in which this manifold is found.'[37] It would be absurd to speak of my having any idea unless self-awareness could accompany it. And it would be absurd to speak of the manifold of perception being thought, unless the same consciousness could accompany the perceiving and the thinking.

This relation between the subject and the manifold of intuition (namely the relation expressed by saying that the *I think* must be capable of accompanying them all) is called by Kant 'pure apperception', to distinguish it from empirical apperception, that is, the empirical and contingent awareness of a given psychical state as mine. The empirical consciousness which accompanies different representations is fragmentary. At one moment I exercise an empirical act of self-awareness, accompanying a given representation, at another I do not. The empirical consciousness, like the representations which it accompanies, is disunited. But the possibility of an identical *I think* accompanying all representations is a permanent condition of experience. And it presupposes a transcendental (not empirical) unity of self-consciousness which is not given to me as an object but which is the fundamental necessary condition for there being any objects at all for me. Unless the manifold of intuition could be brought, as it were, to the unity of apperception, there could be no experience, no knowledge. Or, to express it less subjectively, there could be no objects.

Kant does not mean, of course, that I have first to be aware of myself as a subject or ego before I can do any synthesizing. I have no prior consciousness of a permanent self-identical ego. It is only with acts directed towards the given that I become conscious of them as mine. Consciousness of self and consciousness of that which is cognitively related to the self are so bound up together in the self that consciousness of self is not a temporally prior experience. At the same time the unity of apperception (in the sense that the *I think* must be capable of accompanying all my representations) and the transcendental unity of consciousness are *a priori* conditions of experience. Without connection there is no experience. And connection entails the unity of apperception.

In speaking of the unity of consciousness, of the unity of perceiving and thinking in one subject, as a condition of experience, Kant may seem to be saying something obvious. But, if so, it is an obvious fact which seems to be passed over by those who forget, as it were, the subject as subject and so concentrate on the empirical ego as object that they feel justified in dissolving the self into a series of psychical events or in describing it as being simply a logical construction, that is, the class of such events. If we bear these phenomenalists in mind, Kant seems to be drawing attention to a point of great importance.

The question arises, however, what has all this to do with justifying the application of the categories? The answer is, in brief, as follows. No objective experience, no knowledge of objects, is possible unless the manifold of intuition is connected in one self-consciousness. But all synthesis is effected by the understanding, and it is thus by the understanding that the manifold of representations is brought into the unity of apperception. Now, the understanding synthesizes by means of its *a priori* categories. Hence no objective experience, no knowledge of objects, is possible except through the application of the categories. The world of experience is formed through the co-operation of perception and thinking in the application of the *a priori* forms of sensibility and of the categories of the understanding. Hence the categories refer to objects, that is, have objective reference, because all objects, to be objects, must conform to them.

Kant's own words are worth quoting. 'The manifold which is given in a sensuous intuition comes necessarily under the original synthetic unity of apperception. For thereby alone is the *unity* of intuition possible. But that operation of the understanding, through which the manifold of given representations (whether intuitions or concepts) is brought under one apperception, is the logical function of judgments. Thus all the manifold, so far as it is given in one empirical intuition, is *determined* in relation to one of the logical functions of judgment, through which, that is to say, it is brought under one consciousness. Now, the *categories* are nothing else but these functions of judgment, so far as the manifold in a given intuition is determined in relation to them. Consequently the manifold in a given intuition is necessarily subject to the categories.'[38] Again, 'a manifold which is contained in an intuition that I call mine is represented by means of the synthesis of the understanding as belonging to the *necessary* unity of self-consciousness. And this takes place by means of the category.'[39]

5. A further question, however, arises. We have on the one hand the manifold data of intuition and on the other a plurality of categories. What determines which category or categories are applied? We need some indication of a connecting link. There must be some proportion or homogeneity between the data of sense intuition and the categories if the former are to be subsumed under the latter. But 'the pure concepts of the understanding are quite heterogeneous when compared with empirical intuitions (or even with sensuous intuitions in general), and they can never be discovered in any intuition. How, then, is the *subsumption* of the latter under the former, and with it the application of the categories to appearances possible?'[40] This is the problem.

To solve this problem Kant has recourse to the imagination

(*Einbildungskraft*) conceived as a mediating power or faculty between understanding and sensibility. The imagination is said to produce and to be the bearer, as it were, of *schemata*. A schema is, in general, a rule or procedure for the production of images which schematize or delimit, so to speak, a category so as to permit its application to appearances. The schema is not itself an image but represents a general procedure for the constitution of images. 'This representation of a general procedure of the imagination for providing a concept with its image I call the schema for this concept.'[41] The schema, being general, has an affinity with the concept: the image, being particular, has an affinity with the manifold of intuition. Thus the imagination is able to mediate between the concepts of the understanding and the manifold of intuition.

Kant was not, of course, the first philosopher to emphasize the mediating function of the image. This function had been attributed to the image in, for example, mediaeval Aristotelianism. But the approach to this subject in the philosophy of Kant obviously is, and must be, different from that of the mediaeval Aristotelian. For the latter the image is the result of processes on the level of sense and serves in turn as a basis for intellectual abstraction. With Kant, however, the image is a spontaneous product of the power of imagination working according to a schema which it itself produces. We must never forget that for Kant the object must conform to the mind rather than the other way about.

To show the sort of thing he means Kant gives one or two examples from mathematics. I can produce, for instance, an image of the number five by placing five points one after the other in this way . . . . . But the schema of the number five is not itself this image or any other image: it is the representation of a method whereby a multiplicity can be represented in an image in accordance with a certain concept. The schema permits the bringing together, as it were, of the concept and the manifold of phenomena. That is to say, it permits the application of the concept to phenomena. Kant also cites the non-mathematical example of the concept of a dog. The schema of this concept is a rule for producing a representation which is required for applying the concept to a particular animal.

Such illustrations can be extremely misleading. For we are primarily concerned here, not with mathematical concepts, and still less with empirical *a posteriori* ideas such as that of

a dog, but with the pure categories of the understanding.
And we are concerned, not with schemata or rules for the
production of images which (schemata) we can choose or
alter, but with transcendental schemata which determine *a
priori* the conditions under which a category can be applied
to any manifold. However, Kant's examples, taken from the
application of mathematical concepts and of *a posteriori* ideas
to the data of perception, are intended to serve only as an
introduction to the general notion of a schema.

The transcendental schemata of the categories determine
the conditions under which the categories can be applied to
appearances. And for Kant this means determining the temporal conditions under which a category is applicable to appearances. For situation in time is the only feature which is
common to all appearances whatsoever, including the states
of the empirical self. Hence Kant can say that 'the schemata
are nothing but temporal determinations *a priori* in accordance with rules'.[42] Time is the formal condition of the connection or conjunction of all representations. And a transcendental determination of time, which is a product of the
imagination, has, as it were, a footing in both camps. It is
homogeneous with the category of which it is the schema in
that it is universal and rests on an *a priori* rule. It is homogeneous with appearances, in that time is contained in every
empirical representation of the manifold. 'Thus an application of the category to appearances becomes possible by means
of the transcendental determination of time which, as the
schema of the concepts of the understanding, permits the
subsumption of the latter (appearances) under the former.'[43]

Kant does not discuss at much length the particular schemata of particular categories. And what he does say is in some
instances extremely difficult to understand. As, therefore, I
do not wish to involve myself in lengthy problems of exegesis,
I shall mention only a few examples.

Turning to the categories of relation, we are told that the
schema of the category of substance is 'the permanence of
the real[44] in time, that is, the representation of it as a substratum of the empirical determination of time; as a substratum, therefore, which remains, while all else changes'.[45]
That is to say, in order that the concept of substance should
be applicable to the data of perception, it must be schematized or determined by the schema of the imagination;
and this involves representing substance as a permanent sub-

stratum of change in time. Only in this schematized form is the category applicable to appearances.

The schema of the category of cause is 'the real which, when posited, is always followed by something else. It consists, therefore, in the succession of the manifold, in so far as this succession is subject to a rule.'[46] Kant does not wish to say that the concept of causality is nothing but the concept of regular succession. What he means is that the category of cause is not applicable to appearances unless it is so schematized by the imagination that it involves the representation of regular succession in time.

The schema of the third category of relation, that of community or reciprocity between agent and patient, is 'the coexistence of the determinations (accidents) of the one with those of the other according to a general rule'.[47] Here again Kant does not mean that the coexistence of substances with their accidents is all that there is in the concept of interaction. But this concept cannot be applied to phenomena unless it is given a form which involves this representation of coexistence in time.

Finally, to take the last two categories of modality, the schema of the category of existence is being at a certain time, while the schema of the category of necessity is the being of an object in all time. Necessity, as a category, does not mean simply being in all time. It means, as we saw earlier, existence which is given through the very possibility of existence. But the category could not be applied, according to Kant, unless the imagination so determined it in respect of time as to involve the representation of being or existence in all time. This is a necessary condition of its applicability. We cannot represent to ourselves anything as necessary except by representing it as existing in all time. This idea belongs to the schematized category. And it is always the schematized category which is applied.

A problem arises which can be briefly indicated here. Kant, as we have seen, uses the terms category and pure or *a priori* concept to refer to the same thing. Now, the categories are described as logical functions. They are pure forms of the understanding which make synthesis possible but which, taken in themselves apart from their application to appearances, do not represent any objects. And in this case it can be asked whether the word 'concept' is not a misnomer. And in his commentary on the *Critique of Pure Reason*[48] we find Professor Kemp Smith maintaining that when Kant speaks about the categories he usually means the schemata. Hence the chapter on the schematism of the categories simply contains their delayed definitions. The categories proper, as pure forms of the understanding, are simply logical functions and have no determinate content or meaning. The concept of substance, for instance, would be what Kant calls the schema of the category of substance. There is no room, as it were, for a pure concept of substance other than the notion of substance defined in the schema.

There is certainly a good deal to be said for this point of view. And if we turn to mathematical concepts, it might be maintained that the representation of a general rule or procedure for the construction of triangles *is* the concept of triangle. At the same time, while Kant certainly says that the unschematized categories have no sufficient meaning to give us the concept of an object and that they are 'only functions of the understanding for the production of concepts',[49] he also attributes to them some content, even if this content is not sufficient to represent an object. 'Substance, for example, if we leave out the temporal determination of permanence, would mean nothing more than a something, which can be thought as subject, without being a predicate of anything else.'[50] It may be that I can 'make nothing' of this idea, as Kant puts it. But this means that I cannot apply it to represent an object, an object being a possible object of experience, and experience being sense-experience. The fact remains, however, that *some* meaning or content is attributed by Kant to the unschematized category. This meaning is not sufficiently determinate to give knowledge; but it is thinkable, as a logical possibility. According to Kant, metaphysicians have attempted to use the pure categories as a source of knowledge of things-in-themselves. And to use the pure categories in this way is to misuse them. But the very possibility of misuse presupposes that they have *some* meaning.

6. Now, the understanding produces *a priori* certain principles which state the conditions of the possibility of objective experience, that is to say, of experience of objects. Or, to put the same thing in another way, the understanding produces *a priori* certain principles which are rules for the objective use of the categories. To ascertain, therefore, what these principles are, we need only consider the table of schematized categories. 'The table of categories gives us the natural guide to the table of principles (*Grundsätze*), because

the latter are nothing else than rules for the objective use of the former.'[51]

The principles corresponding to the categories of quantity are called by Kant 'axioms of intuition'. He does not mention specific axioms; but he tells us that their general principle is, 'All intuitions are extensive magnitudes'.[52] This is a principle of the pure understanding, and so it cannot be (not that one would be tempted to think that it is) a mathematical principle. For mathematical principles are said to be derived from pure intuitions by the mediation of the understanding, not from the pure understanding itself. At the same time this principle of the axioms of intuition explains, according to Kant, why the synthetic *a priori* propositions of mathematics are applicable to experience. For instance, what geometry affirms of the pure intuition of space must be valid for empirical intuitions if all intuitions are extensive magnitudes. In fact, as the principle is itself a condition of objective experience, the applicability of mathematics is also a condition of objective experience. And we may add that if the principle of the axioms of intuition explains why the synthetic *a priori* propositions of mathematics are applicable to phenomenal reality, it also explains the possibility of mathematical physics.

The principles corresponding to the schematized categories of quality are called by Kant 'anticipations of experience'. The general principle of these anticipations is 'in all appearances the real which is an object of sensation has intensive magnitude, that is, a degree'.[53] In discussing the schema of the categories of quality Kant maintained that it involves the representation of degree of intensity, a notion which implies the possibility of increase in intensity and of decrease down to zero (negation). We are now told, in the general principle of the anticipations of experience, that all empirical perceptions, as involving sensation, must have degrees of intensity. This principle, therefore, affords an *a priori* basis for the mathematical measurement of sensation.

If we take these two principles together, namely the principle of the axioms of intuition and the principle of the anticipations of experience, we can see that they enable us to make predictions about future intuitions or perceptions. We cannot, indeed, predict *a priori* what our future perceptions will be; nor can we predict the quality of empirical perceptions (perceptions involving sensation). We cannot predict that the next object of perception will be red, for instance.

But we can predict that all intuitions or perceptions will be extensive magnitudes and that all empirical perceptions involving sensation will have intensive magnitude.

These two principles are grouped together by Kant as mathematical principles. Or, rather, they are principles of the mathematical use of the categories. By saying this Kant does not mean that the two principles are mathematical propositions. He means that they bear on intuition, and that they justify the applicability of mathematics.

The principles corresponding to the schematized categories of relation are named 'analogies of experience'. And their general underlying principle runs, 'Experience is possible only through the representation of a necessary connection of perceptions'.[54] Objective experience, that is, knowledge of objects of sense, is not possible without a synthesis of perceptions, implying the presence to consciousness of a synthetic unity of the manifold. But this synthetic unity, which comprehends connections, is contributed by the subject, that is, a priori. And a priori connections are necessary. Hence experience is not possible except through the representation of necessary connections between objects of perception.

The three analogies are regarded by Kant as rules or guides for the empirical use of the understanding in discovering concrete connections. And they correspond respectively to what Kant calls the three modi of time, namely permanence, succession and coexistence. What is meant by this can best be understood by considering the analogies themselves. They are stated as follows. First, 'In every change of appearances the substance remains, and its quantum in Nature neither increases nor diminishes'.[55] Secondly, 'All changes take place according to the law of connection of cause and effect'.[56] Thirdly, 'All substances, so far as they can be perceived as coexistent in space, are in thorough-going interaction'.[57]

These principles obviously correspond respectively to the schematized categories of relation, namely substance and accident, cause and effect, and community or interaction between agent and patient. They are a priori principles and thus antecedent to experience. But though they tell us about relations or proportions, they do not predict or enable us to predict the unknown term. They differ, therefore, as Kant notes, from mathematical analogies. The first analogy, for instance, does not tell us what the permanent substance in Nature is: it tells us rather that change involves substance, and that, whatever substance is, it conserves its total quantum. This will be true whether we decide on empirical grounds that the substance or substratum of change in Nature is to be called matter (as Kant thought) or energy or whatever it may be. To put the matter crudely, the analogy tells us that the total quantum of the basic stuff or substance in Nature is conserved unchanged; but it does not tell us what it is. We cannot discover this *a priori*. Again, the second analogy tells us that all changes are causal, and that any given effect must have a determining cause. But though we may know the effect, we cannot discover what the cause is by the mere use of the second analogy. We must have recourse to experience, to empirical investigation. The analogy or principle is regulative in character: it guides us in the use of the category of causality. As for the third analogy, it is quite obvious that it does not tell us either what things are coexistent in space or what are their interactions. But it tells us *a priori*, and in a general sense, what we should look for.

The principles corresponding to the categories of modality are called 'the postulates of empirical thought in general'. They are as follows.[58] First, 'That which agrees with the formal conditions of experience (intuition and concepts) is *possible*'. Secondly, 'That which is connected with the material conditions of experience (that is of sensation) is *real*'. Thirdly, 'That the connection of which with the real is determined according to general conditions of experience is (exists as) *necessary*'.

It is important to understand that, according to Kant, these postulates concern only the relation of the world, of the objects of experience, to our cognitive faculties. The first postulate, for instance, states that only that which can be subjected, as it were, to the formal conditions of experience is a possible existent, that is, an existent within empirical reality. It does not state that there can be no being or beings which transcend empirical reality by transcending the formal conditions of objective experience. God, for example, is not a possible existent in the physical world; but to say this is not to say that there is not, and cannot be, a God. An infinite spiritual being transcends the application of the formal conditions of experience, and it is, therefore, not possible as a physical or experienced object. But the divine being is logically possible, at least in the sense that no logical contradiction is discernible in the idea of it. And there may be grounds for belief in such a being.

The postulates are, as already stated, postulates of empirical thinking. The second postulate, therefore, gives us a definition or explanation of reality in the empirical use of the term. It amounts to saying that in the sciences nothing can be accepted as real which is not connected with an empirical perception, and so with sensation, according to the analysis of experience. As for the third postulate, it concerns inference from what is perceived to what is not perceived according to the analogies of experience and empirical laws. If we take, for instance, the second analogy of experience by itself, we can say only that, given a certain change or event, it must have a cause: we cannot determine *a priori* what the cause is. But, if we take into account the empirical laws of Nature, we can say that a certain definite causal relation is necessary, and that a certain cause must exist, not, of course, with absolute necessity, but with hypothetical necessity, on the hypothesis, that is to say, that a certain change or event occurs.

7. Not only, therefore, is mathematics applicable to Nature, but there are also a number of principles which are derived from the categories of the understanding and which are thus *a priori*. A pure science of Nature is therefore possible. Physics in the narrow sense is an empirical science. Kant never imagined that we could deduce the whole of physics *a priori*. But there is a universal science of Nature, a propaedeutic to physics, as Kant calls it in the *Prolegomena*[59] though he also speaks of it as a universal or general physics.[60] It is true that not all the concepts which are found in this philosophical part of physics, or propaedeutic to physics, are pure in the Kantian sense; for some are dependent on experience. Kant gives as examples the concepts of motion, impenetrability and inertia.[61] And not all the principles of this universal science of Nature are universal in a strict sense. For there are some which apply only to objects of the external sense, and not to objects of the internal sense (namely the psychical states of the empirical ego). But there are at the same time some principles which apply to all objects of experience, whether external or internal; for example, the principle that events are causally determined according to constant laws. In any case there is a pure science of Nature in the sense that it consists of propositions which are not empirical hypotheses but which enable us to predict the course of Nature, and which are synthetic *a priori* propositions.

It will be remembered that one of Kant's main problems in the *Critique of Pure Reason* was to explain the possibility of this pure science of Nature. And the question how it is possible has now been answered, namely in the preceding sections of this chapter. A pure science of Nature is possible because objects of experience, to be objects of experience, must of necessity conform to certain *a priori* conditions. Given this necessary conformity, we know that the complex of synthetic *a priori* propositions derived immediately or mediately from the *a priori* categories of the understanding will be always verified. In brief, 'the principles of possible experience are then at the same time universal laws of Nature, which can be known *a priori*. And thus the problem contained in our second question, *How is the pure science of Nature possible?* has been solved'.[62]

We can put the matter in another way. Objects, to be objects, must be related to the unity of apperception, to the unity of consciousness. And they are related by being subsumed under certain *a priori* forms and categories. The complex of possible objects of experience thus forms one Nature in relation to the unity of consciousness in general. And the necessary conditions for thus relating them are themselves the ground of the necessary laws of Nature. Without synthesis there is for us no Nature; and the *a priori* synthesis gives laws to Nature. These necessary laws are in a real sense imposed by the human subject; but they are at the same time objective laws, because they are valid, and necessarily valid, for the whole range of possible experience; that is, for Nature as the complex of possible objects of experience.

Kant has, therefore, settled to his own satisfaction the problems raised by Hume. Newtonian physics postulates the uniformity of Nature. But experience is incapable of proving the uniformity of Nature. It cannot show that the future will resemble the past, in the sense of showing that there are universal and necessary laws of Nature. But while Hume contented himself with observing that we have a natural belief in the uniformity of Nature and with attempting to give a psychological explanation of this belief, Kant attempted to prove this uniformity. As he agreed with Hume that it cannot be proved by empirical induction, he argued that it follows from the fact that Nature, as the complex of objects of possible experience, must conform to the *a priori* conditions of objective experience. It is this fact which enables us to know *a priori* certain truths which lie at the foundation of Newtonian physics.[63]

We can say, if we like, that Kant undertook to justify the

Newtonian physics. But the term 'justify' can, of course, be misleading. For in one sense the only justification needed by a scientific system is its fruitfulness. That is to say, it can be maintained that an *a posteriori* justification is the only kind which is really relevant. But Kant believed that the Newtonian physics involved presuppositions which cannot be theoretically justified *a posteriori*. The question arose, therefore, whether an *a priori* theoretical justification is possible. And Kant was convinced that it was possible on one condition, namely on the condition of accepting the standpoint of his Copernican revolution. Much that Kant says is doubtless either dated or highly disputable. But the questions whether natural science does or does not involve presuppositions and, if so, what is the logical status of these presuppositions are by no means dead questions. For instance, in *Human Knowledge, Its Scope and Limits* Bertrand Russell argues that there are a number of 'postulates' of scientific inference, which are not derived from experience and cannot be proved empirically. To be sure, he goes on to give an account, partly psychological and partly biological, of the genesis of these natural beliefs. And he thus treads in the footsteps of Hume rather than in those of Kant, who tried to show that the presuppositions of physics have objective reference and why they have objective reference and yield knowledge. At the same time Bertrand Russell agrees with both Hume and Kant that pure empiricism is inadequate as a theory of knowledge. In spite, therefore, of his hostility towards Kant he recognizes the reality of the *problem* with which Kant found himself faced. And this is the point which I wish to make.

8. The reader will have noticed that the categories of the understanding, taken by themselves, give us no knowledge of objects. And the schematized categories apply only to the data of sense intuition, that is to say, appearances. The categories can give us no knowledge of things 'except in so far as they can be applied to *empirical intuition*. That is to say, they serve only to make *empirical knowledge* possible. But this is called experience.'[64] Hence the only legitimate use of the categories, with respect to the knowledge of things, lies in their application to possible objects of experience. This, says Kant, is a conclusion of great importance, because it determines the limits of the use of the categories and shows that they are valid only for objects of sense. They cannot

give us theoretical or scientific knowledge of realities which transcend the sphere of sense.

The same must be said, of course, of the *a priori* principles of the understanding. They apply only to possible objects of experience, that is, to phenomena, to objects as given in empirical or sense intuition. 'The final conclusion of this whole section is, therefore, that all principles of the pure understanding are nothing more than *a priori* principles of the possibility of experience; and to this alone do all synthetic *a priori* propositions relate. Indeed, their possibility itself rests entirely on this relation.'[65] Hence the principles, for example, which have reference to substance and to determined causality hold good only for phenomena.

Our knowledge of objects is thus restricted to phenomenal reality. But though we cannot cross the bounds of phenomenal or empirical reality and know what lies beyond these bounds, we have no right to assert that there are only phenomena. And Kant introduces the idea of noumena, an idea which we must now examine.

Literally the word *noumenon* means object of thought. And Kant sometimes speaks of noumena as objects of the understanding (*Verstandeswesen*).[66] But to say that noumenon means object of thought does not carry us far towards a comprehension of Kant's doctrine. Indeed, it can be definitely misleading. For it may suggest that Kant divides up reality into *sensibilia* or objects of sense and *intelligibilia* or noumena considered as objects apprehended by pure thought. The word *noumenon* can, of course, be used in this way. 'Appearances, in so far as they are thought as objects according to the unity of the categories, are called *phenomena*. But if I assume (the existence of) things which are simply objects of the understanding and which at the same time can be given as objects to intuition, although not to sense but to intellectual intuition, things of this kind would be called *noumena* or *intelligibilia*.'[67] But though the word *noumenon* can be used in this way, the notion that human beings enjoy or can enjoy an intellectual intuition of noumena is precisely one of the positions which Kant is most concerned to exclude. For him at least all intuition is sense intuition. So it is best to drop all etymological considerations and to concentrate on Kant's actual use of the term, which he takes pains to elucidate.

In the first edition of the *Critique of Pure Reason* Kant distinguishes between 'transcendental object' and noumenon.

The idea of appearance involves the idea of something which appears. Correlative to the idea of a thing as appearing is the idea of a thing as not appearing; that is, of a thing as it is in itself, apart from its appearing. But if I try to abstract from all that in the object which has reference to the *a priori* conditions of knowledge, that is, of the possibility of objects of knowledge, I arrive at the idea of an unknown 'something', an unknown and, indeed, unknowable X. This unknowable X is completely indeterminate: it is merely something in general. For example, the idea of the X correlative to a cow is no different from the idea of the X correlative to a dog. Thus we have here the idea of the transcendental object; that is, 'the completely undetermined idea of something in general'.[68] But this is not yet the idea of a *noumenon*. To transform, as it were, the transcendental object into a noumenon, I must assume an intellectual intuition in which the object can be given. In other words, while the concept of the transcendental object is a mere limiting concept, the noumenon is conceived as an *intelligibile*, a positive reality which could be the object of an intellectual intuition.

Having made this distinction, Kant goes on to say that we possess no faculty of intellectual intuition, and that we cannot conceive even its possibility, not, that is, in a positive concept. Further, though the idea of a noumenon as a thing-in-itself (*ein Ding an sich*) does not contain a logical contradiction, we cannot see the positive possibility of noumena considered as possible objects of intuition. Hence the division of objects into phenomena and noumena is not to be admitted. At the same time the concept of the noumenon is indispensable as a limiting concept; and we can call things-in-themselves, that is, things considered in so far as they do not appear, *noumena*. But our concept is then problematical. We do not assert that there are noumena, which could be intuited if we possessed a faculty of intellectual intuition. At the same time we have no right to assert that appearances exhaust reality; and the idea of the limits of sensibility carries with it as a correlative concept the indeterminate, negative concept of the noumenon.

The trouble with this account is that Kant first says that the word *noumenon* means something more than what is meant by transcendental object and then he proceeds to exclude this something more and to give an interpretation of the noumenon which seems to differ not at all from his interpretation of the transcendental object. However, in the second edition he clears up this at least apparent confusion by carefully distinguishing two senses of the word *noumenon*, though his doctrine concerning the extent of our knowledge remains unaltered.

First there is the negative sense of the word *noumenon*. 'If by noumenon we understand a thing *in so far as it is not the object of our sensuous intuition*, thus abstracting from our mode of intuiting it, this is a noumenon in the negative sense of the term.'[69] The remark about abstracting from our mode of intuiting the noumenon must not be taken to imply that according to Kant we intuit, or can intuit, it in a non-sensuous manner. He means that if we understand by noumenon a thing in so far as it is not the object of sensuous intuition, and if at the same time we make no assumptions about the possibility of any other kind of intuition, we have the idea of a noumenon in the negative sense of the term.

This negative sense of the term is contrasted with a possible positive sense. 'If we understand by it (the noumenon) an object of a non-sensuous intuition, we then assume a particular kind of intuition, namely intellectual intuition, which, however, is not ours and of which we cannot see even the possibility; and this would be a noumenon in the *positive* sense of the term.'[70] Thus a noumenon in the positive sense of the term would be an *intelligibile*, the object of an intellectual intuition. But as, according to Kant, we do not enjoy any such intuition, we can disregard for the moment the positive sense of the term and return to the use of the term in its negative sense.

The concept of the noumenon, Kant insists, is indispensable; for it is bound up with his whole theory of experience. 'The doctrine of sensibility is also the doctrine of noumena in the negative sense.'[71] If we were prepared to say that the human subject is creative in the full sense of the word, we could drop the distinction between phenomena and noumena. But if the subject contributes, as it were, only the formal elements of experience, we cannot abandon the distinction. For the idea of things conforming to the *a priori* conditions of experience involves the idea of the thing-in-itself.

At the same time, given the restriction of the cognitive use of the categories to phenomenal reality, it follows not only that we cannot know noumena in the sense of knowing their characteristics, but also that we are not entitled to assert dogmatically that they exist. Unity, plurality and existence are categories of the understanding. And though we can think of noumena as existing, the application of the categories in this way beyond their proper range of application does not yield knowledge. The existence of noumena thus remains problematical; and the idea of the noumenon or thing-in-itself becomes a limiting concept (*Grenzbegriff*).[72] The understanding limits sensibility 'by giving the name *noumena* to things considered in themselves and not as phenomena. But it at the same time sets limits to itself, that is, of not knowing them by means of any categories and of thinking them simply as an unknown something.'[73]

Now, in the first section of this chapter we saw how Kant speaks about our being affected by objects. In other words, he started from the common-sense position that things produce an effect on the subject which give rise to sensation, sensation being defined as 'the effect of an object upon the faculty of representation, so far as we are affected by the object'.[74] But this common-sense point of view seems to involve the assertion that there are things-in-themselves. For it appears to involve inference from sensation as an effect to the thing-in-itself as cause. Thus in the *Prolegomena* we read that things-in-themselves are unknowable as they are in themselves but that 'we know them through the representations which their influence on our sensibility procures for us'.[75] But by talking in this way Kant obviously lays himself open to the charge of applying the principle of causality beyond the limits which he himself lays down. It has therefore been a common objection against the doctrine of noumena considered as things-in-themselves that their existence is asserted as a result of causal inference whereas, on Kant's principles, the category of cause is only applicable to phenomena. In asserting the existence of the noumenon as a cause of sensation, it has therefore been said, Kant contradicts himself; that is to say, he is inconsistent with his own principles. It is, indeed, understandable that Kant talks in this way. For he never believed that things can be reduced simply to our representations. And it was natural, for him, therefore, to postulate an external cause or external causes of our representations. But this does not alter the fact that he is guilty of a flagrant inconsistency. And if we wish to maintain the Kantian view of the function of the category of cause, we must abandon the notion of the noumenon as thing-in-itself.

However, though this line of objection is clearly relevant if we regard simply Kant's remarks about the cause of our representations, we have seen that when he discusses explicitly the distinction between phenomena and noumena he adopts a different approach. For the idea of the noumenon is represented as arising, not through inference to a cause of sensation, but as an inseparable correlate of the idea of the phenomenon. We are not presented with subjective representations on the one hand and their external causes on the other. Rather are we presented with the idea of an object which appears and corresponding to the idea we have, as a purely limiting concept, the idea of the object apart from its appearance. It is as though the noumenon were the other side of the picture, a side which we do not and cannot see but the indeterminate notion of which necessarily accompanies the idea of the side which we do see. Further, though Kant clearly believes that there are noumena, he abstains, in theory at least, from asserting their existence. And this line of approach does not seem to lay him open to the line of objection mentioned in the last paragraph. For, even if we use the category of cause to think the noumenon, the use is problematical, not assertorical. And no special difficulty is created by the application of this special category which is not also created by the use of any other category.

A final remark. In this section we have been considering the noumenon as the thing which appears, apart from its appearing. That is to say, we have been considering it as the so-called thing-in-itself (*Ding an sich*). But Kant also speaks about the free, non-empirical ego and about God as being noumena and as possessing noumenal reality. He also speaks occasionally of God as a thing-in-itself. This way of talking is, indeed, justified on his premises. For God is not a phenomenon and cannot possess phenomenal or empirical reality. He must be conceived, therefore, as a noumenon, as a thing-in-itself, and not as something appearing to us. Further, all that has been said about the non-applicability of the categories to noumena holds good in regard to God. At the same time, if God is thought of at all, He is not thought of as being simply a correlate of spatio-temporal appearances. The concept of God is not the concept of a thing which appears, considered as not appearing. For God cannot be said to appear. Hence the terms *noumenon* and *thing-in-itself*, as applied to God, do not bear precisely the same sense which they bear when applied in the manner described above. It is best, therefore, to reserve any further discussion of the idea of God until we come, in the next chapter, to a consideration of the *Transcendental Dialectic*. For it is in this part of the first *Critique* that Kant discusses the idea of God, when he is dealing with the transcendental Ideas of pure reason.

9. Kant's use of the word *idealism* differs at different stages of the development of his thought. There is no one invariable and consistent use of the term. However, his dislike of the label evidently diminished, and we find him calling his philosophy transcendental or critical or problematical idealism. But when he speaks in this way, he is thinking of the doctrine of the unknowability of things-in-themselves. He does not intend to assert that in his view there are only the human ego and its ideas. Indeed, this is a doctrine which he attacks, as will be seen shortly. And if we can speak of Kant's philosophy as critical idealism, we could also speak of it as critical realism. For he resolutely refused to abandon the idea of things-in-themselves. However, I have no wish to embark on a profitless discussion of the proper nomenclature for Kant's philosophy. And I turn instead to his refutation of idealism; that is, of what he called empirical or material idealism in contrast with transcendental or formal idealism. In his view the acceptance of the latter involves the denial of the former.

Both editions of the *Critique of Pure Reason* contain a refutation of idealism; but I shall confine my remarks to the version given in the second edition. In it Kant distinguishes two kinds of idealism, problematic and dogmatic. According to the first kind, attributed to Descartes, the existence of external things in space is doubtful and indemonstrable, there being only one certain empirical proposition, *I am*. According to dogmatic idealism, attributed to Berkeley, space, together with all the objects of which it is the inseparable condition, is impossible, so that objects in space are mere products of the imagination.

These summaries, if considered as summaries of the actual positions of Descartes and Berkeley, are inadequate, to put it mildly. Berkeley did not hold that all external objects are mere products of the imagination in the sense which would naturally be given to this description. As for Descartes, he certainly maintains that we can apply 'hyperbolical' doubt to the existence of external finite things; but he also maintained that reason can overcome this doubt. Kant may have held that Descartes' demonstration of the existence of finite things other than the self was invalid. But this conviction would not justify his saying that according to problematic idealism the existence of external things in space is indemonstrable, and then ascribing this view to Descartes. However, the accuracy of Kant's historical remarks is of minor importance in comparison with his treatment of the two positions.

Of dogmatic idealism Kant says very little. He just remarks that it is unavoidable if we hold that space is a property of things-in-themselves; for in this case space, together with all the objects of which it is an inseparable condition, is a nonentity (*ein Unding*). But this position has been excluded in the *Transcendental Aesthetic*. In other words, if space is alleged to be a property of things-in-themselves, the concept of space can be shown to be a concept of something unreal and impossible. And it involves in its ruin the things of which it is supposed to be a property, and which must therefore be accounted mere products of the imagination. But it has been shown in the *Critique* that space is an *a priori* form of sensibility which applies only to phenomena and not to things-in-themselves. The latter are left intact, so to speak, while space is shown to possess empirical reality.

The treatment of problematic idealism, ascribed to Descartes, is rather more careful. The main point is that Descartes' approach is all wrong. For he assumes that we possess consciousness of ourselves independently of and prior to experience of external things, and then asks how the ego, certain of its own existence, can know that there are external things. Against this position Kant argues that internal experience is possible only through external experience.

Kant's argument is, indeed, somewhat involved. I am conscious of my own existence as determined in time.[76] But all determination in time, in respect, that is, of succession, presupposes the existence of something permanent in perception. But this something permanent cannot be something within myself. For it is the condition of my existence in time. It follows, therefore, that the perception of my own existence in time is possible only through the existence of something real outside me. Consciousness in time is thus necessarily connected with the *existence* of external things; that is, not merely with the *representation* of things external to me.

The point made by Kant is thus that I cannot be conscious of myself except mediately, that is to say, through the immediate consciousness of external things. 'The consciousness of my own existence is at the same time an immediate consciousness of the existence of other things outside me.'[77]

In other words, self-consciousness is not a prior datum: I become conscious of myself in perceiving external things. The question of inferring the existence of external things does not, therefore, arise.

Kant obviously makes a good point here, namely that I become aware of myself concomitantly with acts of attention directed to what is other than myself. But to use this point against Descartes he has to show that this becoming aware of myself is impossible unless external things *exist* and are not merely my representations or ideas. And to show this is, indeed, the burden of his argument. But he then finds himself compelled to admit that 'it does not follow that every intuitive representation of external things involves at the same time the existence of these things; for it may be the mere effect of the power of imagination in dreams as well as in madness.'[78] He argues, however, that these imaginative products are reproductions of previous external perceptions, which would be impossible unless external objects existed. 'Our task here has been to prove only that internal experience in general is possible only through external experience in general.'[79] Whether a particular perception is purely imaginative or not must be decided on the merits of the case.

This treatment of idealism may leave a good deal to be desired; but it at least throws into relief Kant's insistence on the empirical reality of the world of experience as a whole. Within the sphere of empirical reality we cannot justifiably accord a privileged status to the empirical self, reducing external objects, either dogmatically or problematically, to ideas or representations of the empirical self. For the empirical reality of the subject is inseparable from the empirical reality of the external world. That is to say, awareness of the two factors, subject and object, cannot be so divided that the alleged problem of inferring the existence of objects other than the self becomes a real problem.

10. There are many detailed criticisms of Kant's theory of experience which can be made from within the general framework of the Kantian philosophy, that is, by those who accept the philosopher's general point of view and who would call themselves Kantians or Neo-Kantians. For instance, dissatisfaction may be felt with Kant's idea that he had provided a complete table of categories, based on the table of judgments which he took over, with some changes, from the formal logic with which he was familiar. But such dissatisfaction would not by itself necessitate an abandonment of the general

standpoint represented by the theory of categories. Again, it is possible to criticize the ambiguity involved in Kant's habit of referring sometimes to 'categories' and sometimes to *a priori* concepts. But it might be possible to clear up the ambiguity without being compelled at the same time to throw overboard the whole theory. However, the detailed criticisms which can be brought from within the general framework of the system need not concern us here. Something will be said about the Neo-Kantians in a later volume.

If we look on Kant's theory of experience as an attempt to explain the possibility of synthetic *a priori* knowledge, our judgment about it will obviously depend very largely on whether we admit or reject the existence of synthetic *a priori* propositions. If we think that there are no such propositions, we must obviously draw the conclusions that the problem of explaining synthetic *a priori* knowledge does not arise. We shall say, for example, that Kant was mistaken in thinking that the geometrician reads off the properties of space from an *a priori* intuition. In Kantian terminology all propositions are either analytic or synthetic *a posteriori*. If, however, we think that there are synthetic *a priori* propositions, we shall recognize at least that the Kantian problem was a real problem. For *mere* sense-experience does not present us with necessary connections and with true universality.

It does not follow, however, that if we accept the existence of synthetic *a priori* knowledge, we are bound to accept also the hypothesis of Kant's Copernican revolution. For it is possible to allow that there are synthetic *a priori* propositions and at the same time to hold that there is an intellectual intuition which grounds such propositions. I certainly do not wish to commit myself to the view that the geometrician enjoys an intuition of space and that he reads off, as it were, its properties. I am prescinding altogether from the problem of mathematics. That is to say, when I speak about synthetic *a priori* propositions I am thinking, not of the propositions of pure mathematics, but of metaphysical principles, such as the principle that everything which comes into being has a cause. And by intuition I do not mean a direct apprehension of spiritual realities, such as God, but an intuitive apprehension of being, implied by the existential judgment concerning the concrete object of sense-perception. In other words, if the mind can discern, in dependence on sense-perception, the objective, intelligible structure of being, it can enunciate synthetic *a priori* propositions which have objective validity for things in themselves. I do not wish to develop this point of view any further. My intention in mentioning it is simply to indicate that we are not confined to choosing between empiricism on the one hand and the critical philosophy of Kant on the other.

Chapter Thirteen

KANT (4): METAPHYSICS UNDER FIRE

Introductory remarks – The transcendental Ideas of pure reason – The paralogisms of rational psychology – The antinomies of speculative cosmology – The impossibility of proving the existence of God – The regulative use of the transcendental Ideas of pure reason – Metaphysics and meaning.

1. If we presuppose the analysis of objective experience[1] described in the last chapter, it may appear that there is really nothing further to be said about metaphysics. For certain general conclusions about the subject follow directly from the *Transcendental Aesthetic* and *Transcendental Analytic* taken together. First, to the extent that transcendental criticism can itself be called metaphysics, the metaphysics, that is to say, of objective experience, metaphysics is possible, and possible as a science. Secondly, if the entire system of synthetic *a priori* propositions relating to pure natural science were worked out, we should have a developed metaphysics of Nature or of natural science. Thirdly, in so far as the unschematized categories can be used by the mind to think things-in-themselves and to form ideas which contain no logical contradiction, metaphysics of the traditional type is a psychological possibility. It is psychologically possible, for example, to think of things-in-themselves as substances. But fourthly, inasmuch as this procedure involves applying the categories beyond their legitimate field of application, it cannot yield knowledge. The cognitive function of the categories lies in their application to objects as given in sense intuition, that is, to phenomena. Things-in-themselves are not, and cannot be, phenomena. And we possess no faculty of intellectual intuition which could supply objects for a meta-phenomenal application of the categories. Hence metaphysics of the classical type is excluded, when it is considered as a possible source of objective knowledge. To take the same example, application of the category of substance to things-in-themselves yields no knowledge whatsoever about the latter. Fifthly, we cannot

use the principles of the understanding to infer the existence of supersensible beings such as God. For the principles of the understanding, like the categories on which they are founded, are of limited application. That is to say, their objective reference is to phenomena alone. Hence they cannot be used to transcend experience (in the Kantian sense).

But Kant's attitude towards metaphysics, as manifested in the *Critique of Pure Reason,* is more complex than this series of conclusions might lead one to expect. As we have already seen, he believed that the impulse to metaphysics is an ineradicable impulse in the human mind. Metaphysics considered as a natural disposition is possible. Moreover, it possesses value. In the *Transcendental Dialectic* Kant tends at least to make of the pure reason (*Vernunft*) a faculty distinct, or distinguishable, from understanding (*Verstand*). It produces transcendental Ideas which cannot, indeed, be used to increase our scientific knowledge of objects, but which at the same time have a positive 'regulative' function to perform. It remains for him, therefore, to investigate the origin and system of these Ideas and to determine their precise function.

Further, Kant is not content with saying simply that the knowledge which traditional speculative metaphysics claims to provide is illusory. He wishes to illustrate and confirm the truth of his contention by a detailed criticism of speculative psychology, speculative cosmology and natural or philosophical theology. This is done in the second book of the *Transcendental Dialectic.*

What did Kant mean by 'transcendental dialectic'? He thought that the Greeks understood by dialectic the art of sophistical disputation. This idea of the historical use of the word is extremely inadequate. But this does not matter for our purposes. The point is that Kant thought of dialectic as a 'logic of semblance' (*eine Logik des Scheins*)[2] or illusion. But he obviously did not wish to produce sophistical illusions. So dialectic came to mean for him a critical treatment of false or sophistical reasoning. And transcendental dialectic meant a critique or criticism of understanding and reason in regard to their claims to provide us with knowledge of things-in-themselves and supersensible realities. 'The second part of the transcendental logic must be, therefore, a critique of this dialectical semblance (or illusion). And it is called transcendental dialectic, not as an art of producing dogmatically such illusion (an art which is unfortunately too current among the practitioners of manifold metaphysical jugglery), but as a critique of the understanding and reason in regard to their metaphysical use. Its purpose is to expose the false illusion involved in the groundless pretensions of these faculties, and to substitute for their claims to discover new truths and enlarge our knowledge, which they imagine they can do simply by the use of transcendental principles, their proper function of protecting the pure understanding from sophistical delusion.'[3]

Here we have a purely negative conception of the function of transcendental dialectic. But inasmuch as the abuse of transcendental ideas and principles presupposes their rise and presence, and inasmuch as they possess a certain value, transcendental dialectic has also the positive function of determining in a systematic manner what are the transcendental Ideas of pure reason and what is their legitimate and proper function. 'The Ideas of the pure reason can never be, in themselves, dialectical; it is their misuse only which brings it about that we are involved in a deceptive illusion by means of them. For they arise in us through the very nature of our reason; and this supreme tribunal for judging the rights and claims of our speculation cannot possibly contain in itself original deceptions and illusions. We can presume, therefore, that these Ideas will have their sound and proper function, determined by the constitution of our reason.'[4]

2. One characteristic which Kant had in common with Wolff was a respect, not to say passion, for systematic arrangement and deduction. We have seen how he deduced the categories of the understanding from the forms of judgment. In the *Transcendental Dialectic* we find him deducing[5] the Ideas of pure reason from the forms of mediate inference, mediate inference meaning for him syllogistic inference.[6] The deduction seems to me highly artificial and not very convincing. But the general idea can be conveyed by means of the following steps.

The understanding (*Verstand*) is concerned directly with phenomena, unifying them in its judgments. The reason (*Vernunft*) is not directly concerned with phenomena in this way, but only indirectly or mediately. That is to say, it accepts the concepts and judgments of the understanding and seeks to unify them in the light of a higher principle. As an example let us take a syllogism suggested by Kant himself: 'All men are mortal; All scholars are men; Therefore all scholars are mortal.' The conclusion is seen as following from the major premiss by means of, or on the condition of, the minor premiss. But we can obviously go on to seek the condition for the truth of the major premiss. That is to say, we can try to exhibit the major premiss, namely 'All men are mortal', as being itself the conclusion of a prosyllogism. This is achieved, for instance, in the following syllogism: 'All animals are mortal; All men are animals: Therefore all men are mortal.' Our new major premiss can then be seen as unifying a whole series of judgments, such as 'All men are mortal', 'All cats are mortal', 'All elephants are mortal'. And we can then go on to subject the major premiss 'All animals are mortal' to a similar process, exhibiting it as the conclusion of a prosyllogism and thus unifying a wider range of different judgments.

Now, in the examples given it is obvious that reason did not produce the concepts and judgments from itself. It was concerned with the deductive relationship between judgments contributed by the understanding in its empirical use. But it is a peculiar feature of reason that it is not content with stopping this process of unification at any particular premiss which is itself conditioned; that is, which can itself be exhibited as the conclusion of a prosyllogism. It seeks the unconditioned. And the unconditioned is not given in experience.

At this point we must mention a distinction made by Kant, which is important for the line of thought expressed in the *Transcendental Dialectic*. To proceed ever upwards, so to speak, in the chain of prosyllogisms is a logical maxim of pure reason. That is to say, the logical maxim of reason bids us seek an ever greater unification of knowledge, tending more and more towards the unconditioned, towards an ultimate condition which is not itself conditioned. But the logical maxim, taken by itself, does not assert that the chain of reasoning ever does reach an unconditioned. It does not assert that there is an unconditioned: it merely tells us to act as though there were, by telling us to endeavour constantly to complete, as Kant puts it, our conditioned knowledge. When, however, it is assumed that the sequence of conditions reaches the unconditioned, and that there is an unconditioned, the logical maxim becomes a principle of pure reason. And it is one of the main tasks of the *Transcendental Dialectic* to show whether this principle is objectively valid or not. The purely logical maxim is not called in question. But are we justified in assuming that the sequence of conditioned judgments actually is unified in the unconditioned? Or is this assumption the source of deception and fallacy in metaphysics?

Now, there are, according to Kant, three possible types of syllogistic inference, namely categorical, hypothetical and disjunctive. These three types of mediate inference correspond to the three categories of relation, namely substance, cause and community or reciprocity. And corresponding to the three types of inference there are three kinds of unconditioned unity, postulated or assumed by the principles of pure reason. In the ascending series of categorical syllogisms reason tends towards a concept which stands for something which is always subject and never predicate. If we ascend by a chain of hypothetical syllogisms, reason demands an unconditioned unity in the form of a presupposition which itself presupposes nothing else; which is, that is to say, an ultimate presupposition. Finally, if we ascend by a chain of disjunctive syllogisms, reason demands an unconditioned unity in the form of an aggregate of the members of the disjunctive division of such a kind that it makes the division complete.

The reason why Kant endeavours to derive the three kinds of unconditioned unity from the three types of syllogistic inference is, I think, evident. When deducing the categories of the understanding he wished to avoid the haphazard kind of deduction of which he accuses Aristotle of being guilty, and to substitute a systematic and complete deduction. In other words, he wished to show at the same time what the categories are and why there are just these categories and no others. Hence he tried to deduce them from the logical types of judgment, presupposing that his classification of these types was complete. Similarly, in deducing the Ideas of the pure reason he wishes to show at the same time what these Ideas are and why there must be just these Ideas (or, as he puts it, classes of Ideas) and no others. Hence he tries to derive them from the three types of mediate inference which, in accordance with the formal logic which he accepts, are the only possible types. In the whole process we see Kant's passion for systematic arrangement and architectonic at work.

In the course of deducing the Ideas of pure reason, however, Kant introduces a supplementary line of thought which makes the whole matter considerably easier to understand. He introduces, that is to say, the idea of the most general relations in which our representations can stand. These are three. First, there is the relation to the subject. Secondly, there is the relation of our representations to objects as phenomena. Thirdly, there is the relation of our representations to objects as objects of thought in general, whether phenomena or not. We can consider these relations separately.

In the first place it is required for the possibility of experience, as we saw in the last chapter, that all representations should be related to the unity of apperception, in the sense that the *I think* must be capable of accompanying them all. Now, reason tends to complete this synthesis by assuming an unconditioned, namely a permanent ego or thinking subject, conceived as a substance. That is to say, reason tends to complete the synthesis of the inner life by passing beyond the empirical, conditioned ego to the unconditioned thinking self, the substantial subject which is never predicate.

In the second place, turning to the relation of our representations to objects as phenomena, we recall that the understanding synthesizes the manifold of sense intuition according to the second category of relation; namely the causal relation. Now, reason seeks to complete the synthesis by reaching an unconditioned unity conceived as the totality of causal sequences. Understanding provides us, as it were, with causal relations, each of which presupposes other causal relations. Reason postulates an ultimate presupposition which does not presuppose anything else (in the same order), namely the totality of the causal sequences of phenomena. There thus arises the idea of the world, conceived as the totality of causal sequences.

In the third place, that is, in regard to the relation of our representations to objects of thought in general, reason seeks an unconditioned unity in the form of the supreme condition of the possibility of all that is thinkable. Thus arises the conception of God as the union in one Being of all perfections.[7]

We have, therefore, three principal Ideas of pure reason, namely the soul as permanent substantial subject, the world as the totality of causally related phenomena, and God as absolute perfection, as the unity of the conditions of objects of thought in general. These three Ideas are not innate. At the same time they are not derived empirically. They arise as a result of the pure reason's natural drive towards completing the synthesis achieved by the understanding. This does not mean, as has already been mentioned, that the pure reason carries further the synthesizing activity of the understanding considered as constituting objects by imposing the *a priori* conditions of experience known as the categories. The Ideas of pure reason are not 'constitutive'. But the reason has a natural drive towards unifying the conditions of experience, and this it does by proceeding to the unconditioned, in the three forms already mentioned. In doing this it obviously passes beyond experience. Hence the Ideas of the pure reason are called by Kant 'transcendental Ideas', though he later goes on to speak of the third Idea, that of God, as the 'transcendental Ideal'. For God is conceived as supreme and absolute perfection.

These three Ideas form the principal unifying themes of the three branches of speculative metaphysics according to the Wolffian classification. 'The thinking subject is the object-matter of *psychology*, the totality of all phenomena (the world), the object-matter of *cosmology*, and the entity which contains the supreme condition of the possibility of all that can be thought (the Being of all beings) is the object-matter of *theology*. Thus the pure reason provides its Idea for a transcendental doctrine of the soul (*psychologia rationalis*), for a transcendental science of the world (*cosmologia rationalis*), and finally for a transcendental doctrine of God (*theologia transcendentalis*).'[8]

Now, inasmuch as we do not possess, according to Kant, any faculty of intellectual intuition, objects corresponding to these Ideas cannot be given to us in this way. Nor can they be given through experience in the sense described in the last chapter. The substantial soul, the world as the totality of all appearances, the supreme Being, God: none of these can be given in experience. They are not, and cannot be, phenomena. And the Ideas of them arise, not through the subjection of the material of experience to the *a priori* conditions of experience, but through unifying the conditions of experience as far as the unconditioned. It is only to be expected, therefore, that if reason makes what Kant calls a 'transcendent' use of them, claiming to prove the existence and nature of corresponding objects and so to enlarge our theoretical knowledge of objects, it will be involved in sophistical arguments and in antinomies. To show that this is in fact the case, and must be the case, is the aim of Kant's critical examination of rational psychology, speculative cosmology and philosophical theology. And we must now consider each of these in turn.

3. Kant conceives rational psychology as proceeding on Cartesian lines and as arguing from the *I think* to the soul as a simple substance which is permanent in the sense that it remains self-identical in time; that is, throughout all accidental changes. In his view rational psychology must proceed

a priori; for it is not an empirical science. Hence it starts from the *a priori* condition of experience, the unity of apperception. 'I *think* is thus the only text of rational psychology, from which it must develop its whole system.'[9]

If we bear in mind the contents of the last chapter, it is easy to see what line Kant's criticism will take. It is a necessary condition for the possibility of experience that I *think* should be capable of accompanying all one's representations. But the ego as a necessary condition for experience is not given in experience: it is a transcendental ego, not the empirical ego. Hence while it is psychologically possible to think of it as a unitary substance, the application of categories such as substance and unity cannot yield knowledge in this context. For this cognitive function lies in their application to phenomena, not to noumena. We can argue to the conclusion that the transcendental ego, as a logical subject, is a necessary condition of experience, in the sense that experience is unintelligible unless objects, to be objects, must be related to the unity of apperception; but we cannot argue to the existence of the transcendental ego as a substance. For this involves a misuse of categories such as existence, substance and unity. Scientific knowledge is bounded by the world of phenomena; but the transcendental ego does not belong to the world; it is a limiting concept. Thus Kant might say with Ludwig Wittgenstein that 'the subject does not belong to the world but it is a limit of the world'.[10]

According to Kant, rational psychology contains a fundamental paralogism; that is, a logically fallacious syllogism. This syllogism can be expressed as follows:

'That which cannot be thought otherwise than as subject, does not exist otherwise than as subject and is therefore substance:

Now, a thinking being, considered simply as such, cannot be thought otherwise than as subject:

Therefore it exists only as such, that is, as substance.'[11]

That this syllogism is a paralogism follows from the fact that it contains four terms. That is to say, the middle term, 'that which cannot be thought otherwise than as subject', is understood in one sense in the major and in another sense in the minor premiss. In the major premiss the reference is to objects of thought in general, including objects of intuition. And it is true that the category of substance applies to an object which is given, or can be given, in intuition, and which can be thought only as subject, in the sense of that which cannot be thought as a predicate. But in the minor premiss that which cannot be thought otherwise than as subject is understood in relation to self-consciousness as the form of thought, not in relation to an object of intuition. And it by no means follows that the category of substance can be applied to a subject in this sense. For the ego of pure self-consciousness is not given in intuition, and so it is not a candidate, so to speak, for the application of the category.

It is to be noted that Kant does not question the truth of either premiss when taken by itself. In fact each premiss is, according to him, an analytical proposition. For instance, if the thinking being, considered purely as such, of the minor premiss is understood as the ego of pure apperception, it is analytically true that it cannot be thought otherwise than as subject. But then the word 'subject' is not being used in the same sense in which it is used in the major premiss. And we are not entitled to draw the *synthetic* conclusion that the ego of pure apperception exists as substance.

It is not necessary to enter further into Kant's discussion of rational psychology in order to see the important place in his criticism which is occupied by the concept of intuition. The permanent ego is not given in intuition; on this point Kant agrees with Hume. Hence we cannot apply to it the category of substance. But obviously someone might wish to call in question the view that the permanent ego is not given in intuition. And even if it is not given in intuition as interpreted by Kant, we might well consider that his idea of intuiton is too narrow. In any case it might be argued that the presupposition and necessary condition of all experience is precisely a permanent ego; and that if experience is real, its necessary condition must be real. If to say this involves using the categories beyond their allotted sphere, this restriction of their use becomes questionable. If, however, we once admit all Kant's premisses, we can hardly avoid drawing his conclusions. The validity of the *Transcendental Dialectic* obviously depends to a great extent on the validity of the *Transcendental Aesthetic,* and *Analytic.*

It is worth noting that inasmuch as Kant believes that all phenomenal events are causally determined, it is in a sense in his interest to keep the permanent ego in the sphere of noumenal reality beyond experience. For this will enable him later to postulate freedom. At the same time, by placing the permanent self in the noumenal sphere and beyond the range

of intuition, he makes it impossible to argue to the existence
of the self in this sense. We can assert, of course, the existence of the empirical ego; for this is given in internal intuition. But the empirical ego is the self as studied in psychology. It is an object in time and is reducible to successive
states. The ego which is not reducible to successive states
and which cannot be thought except as subject is not given
in intuition, is not an object and cannot therefore be dogmatically asserted to exist as a simple substance.

4. We have seen that speculative cosmology, according to
Kant, centres round the idea of the world as the totality of
the causal sequence of phenomena. The speculative cosmolo-
gist seeks to extend our knowledge of the world, as a totality
of phenomena, through synthetic *a priori* propositions. But
this procedure, Kant maintains, leads to antinomies. An antinomy arises when each of two contradictory propositions can
be proved. And if speculative cosmology inevitably leads to
antinomies in this sense, the conclusion must be drawn that
its whole aim is mistaken, namely the aim of building up a
science of the world considered as the totality of phenomena.
This branch of speculative metaphysics is not, and cannot be,
a science. In other words, the fact that speculative cosmology
is productive of antinomies shows that we cannot make scientific use of the transcendental Idea of the world as the
totality of phenomena.

Kant discusses four antinomies. Each of them is supposed
to correspond to one of the four classes of categories. But
there is no necessity to dwell upon this typical piece of systematic correlation. I propose to pass it over and to come at
once to a brief discussion of each of the four antinomies.

(i) The conflicting propositions of the first antinomy are
as follows. 'Thesis: The world has a beginning in time and is
also limited in regard to space. Antithesis: The world has no
beginning and no limits in space, but is infinite in respect
both of time and space.'[12]

The thesis is proved as follows. If the world has no beginning in time, an infinite series of events must have occurred.
That is to say, before the present moment an infinite series
must have been completed. But an infinite series can never
be completed. Therefore the world must have had a beginning in time. As for the second part of the thesis, if the world
is not limited in regard to space, it must be an infinite given
total of coexistent things. But we cannot think an infinite
given total of coexistent things filling all possible spaces ex-

cept by successively adding part to part or unit to unit until the addition is complete. But we cannot regard this addition or synthesis as completed except by regarding it as completed in infinite time. And this involves looking on an infinite time as having elapsed, which is impossible. Hence we cannot regard the world as an infinite given total of coexistent things filling all possible spaces. We must look on it as spatially limited or finite.

The *antithesis* is proved as follows. If the world began in time, there must have been empty time before the world began. But in empty time no becoming or beginning is possible. It makes no sense to speak of something coming into being in empty time. Hence the world has no beginning. As for the world being spatially infinite, let us suppose, for the sake of argument, that it is finite and limited in space. It must then exist in a void or empty space. And in this case it must have a relation to empty space. But empty space is nothing; and a relation to nothing is itself nothing. Hence the world cannot be finite and spatially limited: it must be spatially infinite.

At first sight Kant seems to adopt a position diametrically opposed to that of St. Thomas Aquinas.[13] For while the latter maintained[14] that it had never been philosophically demonstrated either that the world had a beginning in time or that it had no beginning in time, Kant appears to be saying that both theses can be demonstrated. And we may note in passing that his proof of the thesis that the world had a beginning in time is the same as that advanced by St. Bonaventure[15] in support of this thesis, a proof the validity of which was denied by Aquinas. But both proofs rest, for Kant, on false assumptions. The proof of the thesis rests on the assumption that we can apply to phenomena the principle of pure reason that if the conditioned is given, the totality of conditions, and consequently the unconditioned, is also given. The proof of the antithesis rests on the assumption that the world of phenomena is the world of things-in-themselves. It is assumed, for instance, that space is an objective reality. Given the required assumptions, the proofs are valid.[16] But the fact that each of two contradictory propositions can be proved shows that the assumptions are unwarranted. We can avoid the antinomy only by adopting the standpoint of the critical philosophy and by abandoning the standpoints both of dogmatic rationalism and of uncritical common sense. This is the point which Kant really intends to bring out, though it can hardly be claimed that he does so very clearly. And it would, therefore, be misleading, even if true in a sense, to say that in the long run Kant comes to the position of St. Thomas Aquinas. For, according to Kant's point of view, the inherent futility of trying to prove philosophically either that the world had a beginning in time or that it had no beginning in time can be seen only by adopting a philosophy which was certainly not that of Aquinas.

(ii) The second antinomy is as follows. '*Thesis:* Every composite substance in the world consists of simple parts, and there does not exist anything which is not either itself simple or composed of simple parts. *Antithesis:* No composite thing in the world consists of simple parts, and there does not anywhere exist any simple thing.'[17]

The proof of the *thesis* takes this form. If composite substances did not consist of simple parts, then, if we thought away all composition, nothing at all would remain. But this can be excluded. For composition is merely a contingent relation. The composite must, therefore, consist of simple parts. And it follows from this that everything which exists must be either itself simple or composed of simple parts.

As for the *antithesis*, it can be proved in this way. A composite substance occupies space. And this space must consist of as many parts as there are parts in the composite substance. Therefore every part of the latter occupies a space. But everything which occupies a space must consist of a manifold of parts. And each of these will occupy a space, and will thus itself contain parts. And so on indefinitely. There cannot, therefore, be any composite thing which consists of simple parts. Nor can there be any simple thing.

As in the first antinomy, the thesis represents the position of dogmatic rationalism. All composite substances consist of simple substances, such as the Leibnizian monads. And, again as in the first antinomy, the antithesis represents an empiricist attack on dogmatic rationalism. But the thesis treats noumena as though they were phenomena, objects given in experience; and the antithesis treats phenomena, extended bodies, as though they were noumena. Again, the only way out of the antinomy is to adopt the position of the critical philosophy, and to recognize that what is true of phenomena as phenomena cannot be asserted of noumena, while of the latter we possess no objective knowledge.[18]

(iii) The third antinomy relates to free causation. '*Thesis:* Causality according to the laws of Nature is not the only causality from which the phenomena of the world can be derived. To explain them, it is necessary to assume another causality, causality through freedom. *Antithesis:* There is no freedom, but everything in the world happens solely according to the laws of Nature.'[19]

The *thesis* is proved thus. Let us suppose that there is only one kind of causality, namely causality according to the laws of Nature. In this case a given event is determined by a previous event, and so on indefinitely. There can then be no first beginning; and consequently the series of causes cannot be completed. But the law of Nature is that nothing happens without a cause sufficiently determined *a priori*. And this law is not fulfilled if the causality of every cause is itself an effect of an antecedent cause. There must therefore be an absolutely spontaneous causality which originates a series of phenomena proceeding according to natural causes.

The proof of the *antithesis* is, in brief, this. Spontaneous, free causation presupposes a state of the cause which stands in no causal relation (that is, as effect) to the preceding state. But this presupposition is contrary to the natural causal law, and it would render impossible the unity of experience. Consequently freedom is not to be found in experience and is a mere fiction of thought.

In this antinomy it is not at all clear in the first place what Kant is talking about. The proof of the thesis naturally suggests that he is thinking about the origination of the natural causal series by a first cause, the causal activity of which is entirely spontaneous in the sense that it does not itself depend on a previous cause. And in his observations on the thesis he explicitly states that he had in mind the origin of the world. But he then goes on to say that if there is a free cause of the total series of phenomenal causal sequences, we are justified in admitting, within the world, free causes of different series of phenomena.

As for the antithesis, it is natural to understand it as referring to human freedom. *Prima facie* at least it makes sense to speak of one state of the human subject being causally determined by another state; but it makes no sense at all to raise the question of the causal relation between states in regard to God. In his observations on the antithesis, however, Kant introduces the idea of a free cause existing outside the world. Even if we admit the existence of such a cause, we cannot, he remarks, admit free causes within the world.

In view of this ambiguity, that is, of the indefinite range of application of thesis and antithesis, it is difficult to maintain that the antinomy is resolved by observing that the thesis and antithesis refer to different things. However, there can be no antinomy at all, in the proper sense, unless thesis and antithesis refer to the same things. If the thesis asserts that a free cause of the total series of phenomenal causal sequences can be proved, while the antithesis states that it can be proved that there is no such cause, we have an antinomy. And if the thesis states that it can be proved that there is free causality within the world, while the antithesis states that it can be proved that there is no free causality within the world, we have again an antinomy. But if the thesis states that it can be proved that there is a free cause of the total series of phenomenal causal sequences, this free cause being outside the series, while the antithesis states that there is no free causality within the phenomenal series, there is, properly speaking, no antinomy at all.

It is not my intention to deny that the third antinomy falls to a great extent into the general pattern of Kant's antinomies. The proof of the thesis, if the latter is understood as referring to a first cause of the total series of phenomenal causal sequences, is valid only on the assumption that we can, as it were, complete the series, using the transcendental Idea of the world as a totality to extend our theoretical knowledge. The thesis, therefore, represents the standpoint of dogmatic rationalism. And the antithesis, whether it is taken as stating that no proof of the existence of a first cause of the total series is possible or as stating that there can be no free causes within the series, represents the empiricist standpoint. But if the antinomy can be resolved only by adopting the standpoint of the critical philosophy, the latter point of view should not be introduced into the proof of either thesis or antithesis. Yet it is at least arguable that this is precisely what Kant does in proving the antithesis. For he states that the admission of free causality destroys the possibility of the unity of experience. And though it may not be necessary to understand this statement in terms of his own peculiar point of view, it is difficult to avoid the impression that this is in fact how it should be understood.

What happens, however, to the antinomy when we explicitly adopt the critical point of view? The proof of the thesis, if the latter is taken as referring to a spontaneous cause of the total series of phenomena, is seen to rest on a misuse of the transcendental Idea of the world. As for the antithesis, the denial of freedom, this is seen to be valid only for the sphere of phenomena. The way is therefore left open for Kant to say later that man is noumenally free and phenomenally determined. If we adopt this point of view we can say that for Kant both thesis and antithesis, when rightly understood, are true. The thesis, that causality 'according to the laws of Nature' is not the only kind of causality, is true, though it is not true that we can prove that this is the case. The antithesis, that there is no freedom, is true if it is taken as referring solely to the phenomenal world, though it is not true if it is taken as referring to all reality whatsoever. For Kant it is only when we adopt the standpoint of the critical philosophy that we can sift out what is true from what is false in thesis and antithesis and rise above the flat contradictions in which reason, in its dogmatic use, has involved itself.

(iv) The fourth antinomy concerns the existence of a necessary being. '*Thesis:* There belongs to the world, either as part of it or as its cause, something which exists as an absolutely necessary being. *Antithesis:* There nowhere exists any necessary being as the cause of the world, either in the world or out of it.'[20]

The *thesis* is proved, as far as the existence of a necessary being is concerned, by the supposed fact that the series of conditions presupposes a complete series of conditions up to the unconditioned, which exists necessarily. Kant then argues that this necessary being cannot be thought of as transcending the world of sense, and that it must therefore be either identical with the whole cosmic series or a part of it.

The *antithesis* is proved by showing that there can be no absolutely necessary being either in or outside the world. There cannot be a first member of the series of changes, which is itself necessary and uncaused. For all phenomena are determined in time. Nor can the whole cosmic series be necessary if no single member is necessary. Therefore there can be no necessary being in the world, either as identical with the latter or as a part of it. But there cannot be a necessary being existing outside the world, as cause of the latter. For if it causes the series of cosmic changes, it must begin to act. And if it begins to act, it is in time. And if it is in time, it is within the world, not outside it.

There is obviously considerable overlapping between the third and fourth antinomies. For though in the fourth antinomy Kant introduces a new term, 'absolutely necessary being', he uses the same line of argument to prove the thesis which he has already used in the third antinomy to prove that there must be a purely spontaneous cause of the series of phenomena. There is thus something to be said in favour of the view that Kant supplies the fourth antinomy precisely in order to make up the number four, each antinomy being supposed to correspond with one of the four classes of categories. It is true, indeed, that the categories of necessity and contingency belong to the fourth class of categories, those of modality, whereas causality belongs to the third class, the categories of relation. But Kant, in proving the thesis of the fourth antinomy, makes use precisely of a causal argument.

It is a remarkable fact, according to Kant in his observations on the antithesis of the fourth antinomy, that the same grounds which serve to prove the thesis serve also to prove the antithesis. But he then goes on to say that reason often falls into discord with itself by considering the same object from different points of view. And if thesis and antithesis represent different points of view, it seems to follow that both may be true. That is to say, the antithesis may be correct in so far as it represents the contentions that there is no necessary being in the world, whether as identical with the latter or as part of it, and that no proof can be forthcoming of the existence of such a being outside the world. But the thesis may be true in stating that there is such a being, existing outside the world, though we can never be said to *know* that this is the case.

In regard to the antinomies as a whole, the theses are supposed to represent the point of view of dogmatic rationalist metaphysics, while the antitheses are supposed to represent the empiricist point of view. And Kant sides, of course, with the latter to the extent that he regards as thoroughly sound the empiricist criticism of the pretensions of metaphysics to increase our knowledge. At the same time it is important to understand that he does not commit himself to the empiricist philosophy as such. In his view empiricism, though sound in its negative criticism of speculative metaphysics, is itself a dogmatic system which dogmatically limits reality to phenomena and thus treats them as though they were things-in-themselves. It is not the pretensions of speculative metaphysics alone which have to be exposed. While accepting the empiricist criticism of metaphysical arguments, we have to rise above the narrow limits of dogmatic empiricism (equated pretty well with materialism) and leave room, as it were, for noumenal reality. Further, metaphysics is itself sustained by moral and religious interests. And though this fact easily leads metaphysicians into advancing arguments which are unsound, we must acknowledge that metaphysics represents levels of human life which are not catered for, so to speak, by sheer empiricism. In the critical philosophy, however, Kant maintains, we can avoid both the fallacies of metaphysics and the dogmatic materialism and mechanism of sheer empiricism. We rise above the antinomies by limiting knowledge to its proper sphere while at the same time we leave room for practical faith based on moral experience. Human freedom, for example, cannot be admitted within the phenomenal sphere; but it may be a reality, and later on it turns out to be a necessary postulate of the moral consciousness.

5. The third transcendental Idea of pure reason is called by Kant the transcendental Ideal. Originally, so to speak, it is the idea of the sum total of all possible predicates, containing *a priori* the data for all particular possibilities. That is to say, the mind, ascending the series of disjunctive syllogisms, finds the unconditioned condition of all particular predicates, each of which excludes contradictory or incompatible predicates, in the idea of an aggregate of all predicates. This is the idea of the aggregate or sum total of all possible perfections. But inasmuch as this sum total is thought of as the unconditioned condition of all particular perfections, it is thought of as the prototype of the latter, as that from which the latter are derived and to which they approximate, and not as a mere abstract concept of the conflation, so to speak, of all particular, empirical perfections. It is thought of, therefore, as a real being, indeed as the supreme reality. The idea of the most perfect Being, the *Ens perfectissimum*, is also the idea of the most real Being the *Ens realissimum*. This Being cannot be thought of as a conflation or juxtaposition, so to speak, of empirical, limited and often mutually exclusive perfections. It must be thought of as the union of unlimited, pure perfections in one simple Being. Further, the unconditioned condition of all possible limited perfection and reality is thought of as existing necessarily. We thus reach the idea of God as an individual, necessarily existing, eternal, simple and all-perfect supreme Being, which is not the aggregate of finite realities but their unconditioned condition and ultimate cause. And this idea forms the subject-matter of natural or philosophical theology.[21]

Kant's conception of the procedure of pure reason is clear. The reason seeks the unconditioned unity of all possible predicates. It cannot find this in the aggregate, in a literal sense, of empirical perfections, but has to pass beyond the conditioned. It thus objectifies the indeterminate goal of its search as the *Ens perfectissimum*. This is then 'hypostatized' as the *Ens realissimum*, an individual being. And finally it is personified as the God of theism. But by this procedure of objectification the reason passes beyond all possible experience. We have no right to assert that there *is* a Being which is *Ens perfectissimum* and *Ens realissimum*; that is, that there is an object corresponding to the representation of a sum total of all possible perfections. And even though reason goes on to say that we can possess only an analogical (or symbolic) knowledge of the supreme Being, the very fact of objectifying the idea of a totality of perfection means that we extend the categories beyond their proper field of application.

It is obvious that on Kant's premises no proof of God's existence is possible. But he wishes to make this impossibility clear by showing that every line of proof is fallacious. The task is not so great as one might suppose. For according to Kant there are only three ways of proving God's existence in speculative metaphysics. The reason can start with what we might call the *how* of the sensible world; that is, with its character as apparently manifesting finality, and proceed to God as cause of this finality. We then have the 'physico-theological' argument. Or reason can start from empirical existence and proceed to God as ultimate cause of this existence. And we then have the 'cosmological' argument. Or reason may proceed from the idea of God to the divine existence. And we then have the 'ontological' argument.

In treating these three lines of proof Kant starts with the third. For the movement of the mind towards God in metaphysics is always guided by the transcendental Ideal of pure reason, which is the goal of its striving. And it is thus only proper to start with the *a priori* argument from the idea of God to the divine existence. Further, it is Kant's conviction that in order to reach God by the other lines of argument reason is forced in the end to make use of the ontological argument. The latter is thus the fundamental argument and the one which must be considered first.

(i) The general form of the ontological argument which Kant has in mind can be stated as follows.[22] In the concept of a most perfect being existence is included. For if it were not, the concept would not be the concept of a most perfect being. Therefore if such a being is possible, it necessarily exists. For existence is included in the full complement of its possibility. But the concept of a most perfect being is the concept of a possible being. Therefore such a being necessarily exists.

Or the argument can be expressed thus. The idea of the *Ens realissimum* is the idea of an absolutely necessary being. And if such a being is possible, it exists. For the idea of a merely possible (and not actually existent) necessary being is a contradictory idea. But the idea of an absolutely necessary being is the idea of a possible being. Therefore an *Ens realissimum*, namely God, exists.

Kant objects that it is nonsense to talk about the idea of a merely possible necessary being being a contradictory idea. To think of such a being as merely possible I have to think away its existence. But then there is nothing left which could give rise to a contradiction. 'If you think away its existence, you think away the thing with all its predicates. How, then, can there be room for any contradiction?'[23] If someone says that God does not exist, he is not suppressing existence and leaving predicates such as omnipotence: he is suppressing all predicates, and the subject with them. The judgment that God does not exist is not, therefore, self-contradictory, even if it is false.

It may be said that the case of the *Ens realissimum* is unique. I can deny the existence of any other being without involving myself in self-contradiction: for existence does not belong to the concept or idea of any other being. But it does belong to the concept of the *Ens realissimum*. Hence I cannot without self-contradiction admit the possibility of the *Ens realissimum* and at the same time deny its existence.

Kant's answer is on these lines. In the first place, our inability to see any logical contradiction in the idea of God does not constitute a proof that the *Ens realissimum* is positively possible. In the second place, any argument from the idea of the *Ens realissimum* to its existence is worthless; for it is reducible to a mere tautology. If I introduce existence into the idea of a being, then, of course, I can conclude that it exists. But all I am saying is that an existent being exists. And this is true but tautological. I can draw the conclusion that the being exists from its concept or idea only because I have already put existence into the idea, thus begging the whole question. To say that I am arguing from possibility to

actuality is self-deception if possibility is made to includ
actuality.

It is Kant's contention, therefore, that every existenti;
proposition is synthetic and that none is analytic. Hence an
existential proposition can be denied without contradictio.
The defenders of the ontological argument would reply, ir
deed, that Kant is missing the whole point of the argumen'
In all other cases existential propositions are synthetic; bu
the case of the most perfect being is unique. For in this case
and in this case alone, existence is contained in the idea of th
subject. Hence it can be got out of it, so to speak, by analysi;
Kant may say that this is possible only because we have a
ready put it there, thus begging the question; but the point i
that existence is a predicate which belongs necessarily to th
subject.

For Kant, however, existence is not really a predicate a
all. If it were, then it would follow that when I affirm exis'
ence of anything, I am adding to the idea of this thing. An
in this case I do not affirm exactly the same thing which i
represented in my idea. The truth of the matter is that whe'
I say that something exists I simply affirm or posit the subjec
with all its predicates. Hence if I deny God's existence I ar
not denying a predicate of a subject: I am simply annihila'
ing in thought the total subject, together with all its pred
cates. And no logical contradiction arises.

We can conclude, therefore, that 'all the trouble and l;
bour bestowed on the famous ontological or Cartesian proc
of the existence of a supreme Being from concepts alone i
trouble and labour wasted. A man might as well expect t
become richer in knowledge by the aid of mere ideas as
merchant to increase his wealth by adding some noughts t
his cash-account.'[24]

(ii) Kant's formulation of the cosmological argument fc
God's existence is based on Leibniz. 'If anything exists, a
absolutely necessary being must also exist. Now, I at leas
exist. Therefore there also exists an absolutely necessary b
ing. The minor premiss contains an experience; the majc
premiss reasons from an experience in general to the existenc
of a necessary being.'[25]

It is obvious enough what Kant's line of criticism of th
argument as thus presented will be. In his view the majc
premiss rests on a 'transcendent' use, and therefore on
misuse, of the principle of causality. Everything contingen
has a cause. This principle is valid within the realm of sens

experience and it is only there that it possesses significance. We cannot use it to transcend the world as given in sense-experience. Further, the cosmological argument, according to Kant, involves completing the series of phenomena in the unconditioned unity of a necessary being. And though reason has a natural impulse to do this, surrender to the impulse cannot increase our knowledge.

To enter further into this line of criticism is unnecessary. For it follows immediately from Kant's view of the limits of human knowledge. But there is one point in his treatment of the cosmological argument to which attention must be drawn here. It is Kant's contention that in order to pass from the idea of a necessary being to the affirmation of God's existence recourse must be had, at least covertly, to the ontological argument.

The concept of a necessary being is indeterminate. Even if we grant that reflection on experience leads us to a necessary being, we cannot discover its properties by experience. We are forced, therefore, to seek for the concept which is adequate to the idea of a necessary being. And reason believes that it has found what is required in the concept of an *Ens realissimum*. It asserts, therefore, that the necessary being is the *Ens realissimum*, the most real or perfect being. But to do this is to work with concepts alone, which is the characteristic of the ontological argument. Further, if a necessary being is an *Ens realissimum*, an *Ens realissimum* is a necessary being. And here we are saying that the concept of a supremely real or perfect being comprises absolute necessity of existence; which is precisely the ontological argument.

A good many philosophers and historians of philosophy seem to have assumed without more ado that Kant's attempt to show that the cosmological argument necessarily relapses into the ontological argument was successful. But to me it seems singularly unconvincing. Or, rather, it is convincing only on one assumption, namely that the argument based on experience brings us, not to an affirmation of the existence of a necessary being, but only to the vague *idea* of a necessary being. For in this case we should have to look about, as Kant puts it, for a determining concept which would include existence in its content, so that existence could be deduced from the determined idea of a necessary being. And then we should be involved in the ontological argument. If, however, the argument based on experience brings us to the affirmation of the *existence* of a necessary being, the attempt to determine *a priori* the necessary attributes of this being has nothing to do with the ontological argument, which is primarily concerned with deducing existence from the idea of a being as possible, and not with deducing attributes from the idea of a being the existence of which has already been affirmed on other grounds than possibility. It may be said that it was precisely Kant's assumption that the argument based on experience brings us only to the vague idea of a necessary being. But this is no adequate reason for saying that the cosmological argument necessarily relapses into the ontological argument. The question whether the argument based on experience is valid or invalid is not really relevant to the precise point at issue. For if someone is convinced, even unjustifiably, that he has already proved the existence of a necessary being on grounds other than the *a priori* possibility of such a being, his subsequent attempt to determine the attributes of this being is not the same procedure as that adopted in the ontological argument.

(iii) Kant opens his discussion of the physico-theological proof by once more repeating general points of view which exclude from the start any *a posteriori* demonstration of God's existence. For example, 'all laws regarding the transition from effects to causes, yes, all synthetic extension of our knowledge, relate solely to possible experience, and thus to the objects of the sensible world; and it is only in relation to the latter that they have significance.'[26] This being the case, no argument from design in Nature to a transcendent cause can possibly be a valid proof.

The chief steps in the physico-theological argument are these. First, we observe in the world manifest signs of purposeful arrangement; that is, of adaptation of means to ends. Secondly, this adaptation of means to ends is contingent, in the sense that it does not belong to the nature of things. Thirdly, there must exist, therefore, at least one cause of this adaptation, and this cause or these causes must be intelligent and free. Fourthly, the reciprocal relations existing between the different parts of the world, relations which produce an harmonious system analogous to a work of art, justify our inferring that there is one, and only one, such cause.

Kant thus interprets the proof of God's existence from finality as based on an analogy from human constructive adaptation of means to ends. And the proof had indeed been presented in this way in the eighteenth century.[27] But, quite apart from any objections which can be raised on this score,

Kant remarks that 'the proof could at most establish the existence of an *architect of the world*, whose activity would be limited by the capacity of the material on which he works, and not of a *creator of the world*. . . .'[28] This contention is obviously true. The idea of design brings us, by itself, to the idea of a designer, and not immediately to the conclusion that this designer is also creator of finite sensible things according to their substance. Kant argues, therefore, that to prove the existence of God in the proper sense the physico-theological proof must summon the aid of the cosmological proof. And this, on Kant's view, relapses into the ontological argument. Thus even the physico-theological proof is dependent, even though indirectly, on the *a priori* or ontological argument. In other words, apart from any other considerations God's existence cannot be proved without the use of the ontological argument, and this is fallacious. All three proofs, therefore, have some fallacies in common; and each has also its own fallacies.

Natural theology or, as Kant often calls it, 'transcendental theology' is, therefore, worthless when it is regarded from one particular point of view, namely as an attempt to demonstrate God's existence by means of transcendental ideas or of theoretical principles which have no application outside the field of experience. But to say simply that Kant rejected natural theology would be apt to give a misleading impression of his position. It is, indeed, a true statement. For he describes natural theology as inferring 'the attributes and existence of an author of the world from the constitution of the world and from the order and unity observable in it'.[29] And the attempt to do this is 'completely fruitless'.[30] At the same time the purely negative statement that Kant rejected natural theology may give the misleading impression that he rejected all philosophical theology altogether. In point of fact, however, he admitted what he sometimes called 'moral theology'.[31] 'We shall show later that the laws of morality do not merely presuppose the existence of a supreme Being, but postulate it with right (though only, of course, from the practical point of view), as these laws are themselves absolutely necessary in another relation.'[32] And when we have arrived at practical (moral) faith in God, we can use the concepts of the reason to think the object of our faith in a consistent manner. True, we remain always in the sphere of practical faith; but, if we remember this fact, we are entitled to use the concepts of reason to construct a rational theology.

These last remarks put the statement that Kant rejected natural theology in a rather different light. That is to say, they help to delimit its meaning. The criticism of natural theology has a twofold function. It exposes the fallacies in the theoretical proofs of God's existence, and shows that God's existence cannot be demonstrated. At the same time the very nature of the criticism shows also that the non-existence of God can never be demonstrated. By reason we cannot either prove or disprove God's existence. The criticism of natural theology thus leaves the way open for practical or moral faith. And, when faith is presupposed, the reason can correct and purify our conception of God. Although reason in its speculative use cannot prove God's existence, 'it is, however, of the greatest use in correcting our knowledge of the supreme Being, supposing that this knowledge can be derived from some other source, in making it consistent with itself and with all other concepts of intelligible objects, and in purifying it from all that is incompatible with the concept of a supreme Being and from all admixture of empirical limitations.'[33]

Further, the alleged proofs of God's existence, even though they are fallacious arguments, can be of positive use. Thus the physico-theological argument, for which Kant always retained a real respect, can prepare the mind for theological (practical) knowledge and give it 'a right and natural direction',[34] even though it cannot provide a sure foundation for a natural theology.

6. We have already seen that the transcendental Ideas of pure reason have no 'constitutive' use. That is to say, they do not give us knowledge of corresponding objects. The schematized categories of the understanding, applied to the data of sense intuition, 'constitute' objects and thus enable us to know them. But the transcendental Ideas of pure reason are not applicable to the data of sense intuition. Nor are any corresponding objects supplied by a purely intellectual intuition. For we enjoy no such power of intellectual intuition. Hence the transcendental Ideas have no constitutive use and do not increase our knowledge. If we make use of them to transcend the sphere of experience and to assert the existence of realities not given in experience, we inevitably involve ourselves in those fallacies which it is the aim of the *Transcendental Dialectic* to expose.

At the same time, so Kant tells us, the human reason has a natural inclination to overstep the limits of experience, and he even speaks of the transcendental Ideas as being the parents of 'irresistible illusion'.[35] He does not mean, of course, that it is impossible to correct these illusions. But the impulse which produces them is a natural impulse, and the correction follows, as it were, a natural surrender to them. Historically speaking, speculative metaphysics preceded the *Dialectic*. And the latter, though enabling us in principle to avoid metaphysical illusions, cannot destroy the impulse to produce them and surrender to them. The reason for this is that 'transcendental Ideas are just as natural (to reason) as are the categories to the understanding'.[36]

Now, if the transcendental Ideas are natural to the reason, this suggests that they have a proper use. 'Thus the transcendental Ideas will, in all probability, have their proper and consequently *immanent* use.'[37] That is to say, they will have a use in relation to experience, though this use will not consist in enabling us to know objects corresponding to the Ideas. For there are no such objects *immanent* in experience. And if we give the Ideas a transcendent use, we are, as we have seen, inevitably involved in illusion and fallacy. What, then, is the proper employment of the Ideas? It is what Kant calls their 'regulative' use.

The special task of reason is to give systematic arrangement to our cognitions. We can say, therefore, that 'the understanding is an object for reason, as sensibility is for the understanding. To produce a systematic unity in all possible empirical operations of the understanding is the business of reason, just as the understanding unites the manifold of phenomena by means of concepts and brings them under empirical laws.'[38] In this process of systematization the Idea acts as a regulative principle of unity.

In psychology, for example, the Idea of the ego as a simple, permanent subject stimulates and leads us on to an ever greater unification of psychical phenomena, such as desires, emotions, acts of imagination, and so on; and empirical psychology endeavours to bring them together under laws and to form a unified scheme. In this task it is greatly assisted by the transcendental Idea of the ego as a simple, permanent subject. True, this transcendental ego is not given in experience. And if we are misled by the presence of the Idea into asserting dogmatically the existence of a corresponding object, we go beyond what is legitimate. But this does not alter the fact that the Idea is of great value as a kind of heuristic principle.

As for the cosmological Idea of the world, this would be a hindrance to science if it were taken to involve the assertion that the world is a closed totality, so to speak, a completed series. But, when taken without this assertion, the Idea of the world as an indefinite series of events stimulates the mind to proceed ever further along the causal chain. Kant explains that he does not mean to say that in following up a given natural series we are forbidden to find any relatively first term. For instance, we are not forbidden to find the primal members of a given organic species if the empirical evidence so warrants. The cosmological Idea does not tell us what to find or what not to find by scientific investigation. It is a stimulus, a heuristic principle, making us discontented, as it were, with present perceptions and urging us indefinitely to further scientific unification of natural phenomena according to causal laws.

Finally, the transcendental Idea of God as a supreme intelligence and the cause of the universe leads us to think of Nature as a systematic teleological unity. And this presupposition aids the mind in its investigation of Nature. Kant does not mean, of course, that investigation of the eye, for instance, should stop short with saying that God gave eyes to certain creatures for a certain purpose. To assert this would in any case involve asserting something which we do not and cannot know. But if we think of Nature *as if* it were the work of an intelligent work of an intelligent author, we shall be prompted, in Kant's opinion, to carry on the work of scientific investigation by subsumption under causal laws. Perhaps one can interpret Kant's meaning in this way. The idea of Nature as the work of an intelligent creator involves the idea of Nature as an intelligible system. And this presupposition is a spur to scientific investigation. In this way the transcendental Idea of a supreme Being can have a regulative and immanent use.

The transcendental Ideas thus form the basis for a philosophy of *As-if*, to borrow the title of Vaihinger's famous work. It is of practical use in psychology to act *as if* psychical phenomena were related to a permanent subject. It is of use in scientific investigation in general to act *as if* the world were a totality stretching back indefinitely in causal series, and *as if* Nature were the work of an intelligent creator. This utility does not show that the Ideas are true, in the sense of having corresponding objects. Nor is Kant saying that the truth of the statement that there is a God consists in the 'immanent' usefulness of the Idea of God. He is not offering a pragmatist interpretation of truth. At the same time it is easy to see how pragmatists have been able to look on Kant as a forerunner of their philosophy.

7. It will be remembered that Kant's two questions about metaphysics were these. How is metaphysics possible as a natural disposition? Is metaphysics possible as a science? The answers to these questions have, indeed, already been given. But it may be worth while to connect the answers with the foregoing section on the regulative use of the transcendental Ideas of pure reason.

Metaphysics as a natural disposition (that is, the natural disposition to metaphysics) is possible because of the very nature of the human reason. The latter, as we have seen, seeks by its very nature to unify the empirical cognitions of the understanding. And this natural impulse to systematic unification gives rise to the Ideas of an unconditioned unity in different forms. The only proper cognitive use of these Ideas is regulative, in the sense explained above, and therefore 'immanent'. At the same time there is a natural tendency to objectify the Ideas. And then reason seeks to justify this objectification in the various branches of metaphysics. In doing so it oversteps the limits of human knowledge. But this transgression does not alter the fact that the Ideas are natural to reason. They are not abstracted from experience; nor are they innate, in the proper sense of innate. But they arise out of reason's very nature. Hence there is nothing to take exception to in the Ideas considered simply as such. Further, they make possible the development of the necessary postulates of moral experience. The transcendental Ideal (the idea of God), for example, makes possible 'moral theology'; that is, a rational theology based on consideration of the moral consciousness. There is no question, therefore, of dismissing the natural impulse to metaphysics as something perverse in itself.

Metaphysics as a science is, however, impossible. That is to say, speculative metaphysics is supposed to be a science concerning objects corresponding to the transcendental Ideas of pure reason; but there are no such objects. Hence there can be no science of them. The function of the Ideas is not 'constitutive'. Of course, if we mean by 'objects' simply realities, including unknown and, indeed, unknowable realities, we are not entitled to say that there are no 'objects' corresponding to the Ideas of the permanent, simple ego and of

God.[39] But the word 'object' should be used as a term correlative to our knowledge. Those things are possible objects which can be given to us in experience. But realities, if there are any, corresponding to the transcendental Ideas cannot be given in experience in the absence of any faculty of intellectual intuition. Hence it is perfectly correct to say that there are no objects corresponding to the Ideas. And in this case there obviously cannot be any science of them.

Now, though there are, strictly speaking, no objects corresponding to the transcendental Ideas, we can *think* realities to which the Ideas of the soul and of God refer. And even if we do not project the Ideas, so to speak, into corresponding realities, the Ideas have content. Hence metaphysics is not meaningless. We cannot know by means of the speculative reason that there is a permanent, simple soul or that God exists; but the Ideas of the soul and of God are free from logical contradiction. They are not mere meaningless terms. Alleged metaphysical knowledge is pseudo-knowledge, illusion, not knowledge at all; and all attempts to show that it is knowledge are fallacious. But metaphysical propositions are not meaningless simply because they are metaphysical.

This seems to me to be Kant's representative position, so to speak, and it differentiates him from the modern positivists who have declared metaphysics to be so much meaningless nonsense. At the same time it must be admitted that the interpretation of Kant's position is by no means such plain sailing as this account would suggest. For sometimes he appears to say, or at least to imply, that speculative metaphysics is meaningless. For instance, he tells us that 'the concepts of reality, substance, causality, and even of necessity in existence lose all meaning and become empty signs of concepts, without any content, if I venture to employ them outside the field of the senses'.[40] And this is not a unique example of this line of thought.

It may well be, as some commentators have suggested, that the apparent diversity in Kant's ways of speaking about the meaning of terms employed in traditional metaphysics is connected with a diversity implicit in his account of the categories. The latter are called *a priori* concepts of the understanding. And in so far as they are concepts, even the unschematized categories must have some content. Hence even in their application outside the field of experience they possess at least some meaning. But the pure categories are also said to be logical functions of judgments. In this case it seems to follow that they become concepts, as it were, or give rise to concepts only when they are schematized. The unschematized categories would have no content in themselves. They would therefore be meaningless if applied outside the field of experience. Terms such as *Ens realissimum* and *necessary being* would be void of content.

It might be argued, therefore, that Kant's thought points in the direction of the conclusion that the propositions of speculative metaphysics are meaningless. But even if this conclusion appears to follow from one strand in his thought, it certainly does not represent his general position. It seems to me perfectly obvious that a man who insisted on the abiding importance of the fundamental problems of metaphysics, and who tried to show the rational legitimacy of practical faith in freedom, immortality and God did not really believe that metaphysics is simply meaningless nonsense. What he did hold, however, was that if the categories are applied to God, they are not only unable to give knowledge of God but are also of such indeterminate and vague content that they are simply symbols of the unknown. We can, indeed, think God; but we think Him simply by means of symbols. We produce a symbolical conception of the unknown. To think of God in terms of the schematized categories would be equivalent to bringing Him into the sensible world. We therefore try to think away the schematization, as it were, and to apply the term substance, for instance, in an analogical sense. But the attempt to eliminate the concept's reference to the world of sense leaves us with a mere symbol, void of determinate content. Our idea of God is thus symbolical only.

As far as the regulative and so-called immanent use of the transcendental Ideal is concerned, the vagueness of our idea does not matter to Kant. For in making a regulative use of the idea of God we are not asserting that there exists a Being corresponding to this idea. What God may be in Himself, if He exists, can be left indeterminate. We use the idea as 'a point of view' which enables reason to perform its function of unification. 'In a word, this transcendental thing is simply the schema of that regulative principle by means of which reason extends, so far as it can, systematic unity to all experience.'[41]

We may add in conclusion that the Kantian philosophy of religion is grounded in reflection on the practical reason; on reason in its moral use. And it is primarily to Kant's moral theory that we have to look for light on the way in which he thought about God. In the *Critique of Pure Reason* he is concerned with delimiting the range of our theoretical knowledge; and his remarks about the regulative use of the idea of God must not be taken as an account of the meaning of the idea for the religious consciousness.

Chapter Fourteen

KANT (5): MORALITY AND RELIGION[1]

Kant's aim – The good will – Duty and inclination – Duty and law – The categorical imperative – The rational being as an end in itself – The autonomy of the will – The kingdom of ends – Freedom as the condition of the possibility of a categorical imperative – The postulates of practical reason: freedom, Kant's idea of the perfect good, immortality, God, the general theory of the postulates – Kant on religion – Concluding remarks.

1. We have seen that Kant took for granted our ordinary knowledge of objects and our scientific knowledge. Physical science meant for him the Newtonian physics. And it is obvious that he did not consider it the philosopher's business to substitute for the classical physics some other system or to tell us that all our ordinary knowledge of things is no knowledge at all. But, given our ordinary experience and our scientific knowledge, the philosopher can distinguish by a process of analysis between the formal and material, the *a priori* and *a posteriori* elements in our theoretical knowledge of objects. It is the business of the critical philosopher to isolate and exhibit these *a priori* elements in a systematic way.

Now, besides our knowledge of objects which are originally given in sense intuition there is also moral knowledge. We can be said to know, for example, that we ought to tell the truth. But such knowledge is not knowledge of what is, that is to say, of how men actually behave, but of what ought to be, that is to say, of how men ought to behave. And this knowledge is *a priori*, in the sense that it does not depend on men's actual behaviour. Even if they all told lies, it would still be true that they ought not to do so. We cannot verify the statement that men ought to tell the truth by examining whether they in fact do so or not. The statement is true independently of their conduct, and in this sense is true *a priori*. For necessity and universality are marks of apriority. Of course, if we say 'men ought to tell the truth', our knowledge that there are men depends on experience. But there must be at least an *a priori* element in the judgment. And for Kant the primary task of the moral philosopher should be that of isolating the *a priori* elements in our moral knowledge and showing their origin. In this sense we can depict the moral philosopher as asking how the synthetic *a priori* propositions of morals are possible.

The performance of this task obviously does not involve dismissing all our ordinary moral judgments and producing a brand new system of morality. It means discovering the *a priori* principles according to which we judge when we make moral judgments. In the last chapter we saw that there are, according to Kant, certain *a priori* categories and principles of judgment. But Kant did not imagine that he was supplying for the first time a brand new set of categories. What he wished to do was to show how the categories which ground the synthetic *a priori* principles of our theoretical knowledge have their origin in the structure of the understanding. He wanted to connect them with the pure reason (the word 'reason' being here used in its wider sense). So now he wishes to discover the origin in the practical reason of the fundamental principles according to which we all judge when we judge morally.

Kant does not mean to imply, of course, that we are all explicitly aware of the *a priori* principles of morality. If we were, the task of isolating them would be superfluous. As it is, our moral knowledge taken as a whole contains a variety of elements; and it is the primary task, though not the only possible task, of the moral philosopher to lay bare the *a priori* element, freeing it from all empirically derived elements, and to show its origin in the practical reason.

What is the practical reason? It is reason[2] in its practical (moral) use or function. In other words, 'ultimately (there is) only one and the same reason which has to be distinguished simply in its application'.[3] Though ultimately one, reason can be concerned, we are told, with its objects in two ways. It can determine the object, the latter being originally given from some other source than reason itself. Or it can make the object real. 'The first is *theoretical*, the second *practical* rational knowledge.'[4] In its theoretical function reason determines or constitutes the object given in intuition, in the sense explained in the last chapter. It applies itself, as it were, to a datum given from another source than reason itself. In its practical function, however, reason is the source of its objects; it is concerned with moral choice, not with applying categories to the data of sense intuition. We can say that it is concerned with the production of moral choices or decisions in accordance with the law which proceeds from itself. We are told, therefore, that whereas reason in its theoretical function is concerned with objects of the cognitive power, in its practical use it is concerned 'with the grounds of the determination of the will; which is a power either of producing objects corresponding to ideas or of determining itself to produce them (whether the physical power to do so is sufficient or not), that is, of determining its causality'.[5] In plain language, theoretical reason is directed towards knowledge, while practical reason is directed towards choice in accordance with moral law and, when physically possible, to the implementation of choice in action. It should be added that while Kant sometimes speaks of practical reason as though it were distinct from will and influenced the latter, he also sometimes identifies it with will. The former way of speaking suggests the picture of practical reason moving the will by means of the moral imperative. The latter way of speaking shows that for Kant the will is a rational power, not a blind drive. Both ways of speaking seem to be required; for practical reason takes the form of willing in accordance with a principle or a maxim,[6] and we can distinguish the cognitive and voluntary aspects involved. But we must not so emphasize the cognitive aspect, knowledge of a moral principle, as to identify it with practical reason to the exclusion of will. For practical reason is said to produce its objects or to make them real. And it is will which produces choice and action in accordance with moral concepts and principles.

Now, we have said that for Kant the moral philosopher must find in the practical reason the source of the *a priori* element in the moral judgment. We cannot say, therefore, that Kant expects the philosopher to derive the whole moral law, form and content, from the concept of the practical reason. This follows, indeed, from the statement that the philosopher is concerned with finding the source in practical reason of the *a priori* element in the moral judgment. For the statement implies that there is an *a posteriori* element, which is given empirically. This is perfectly obvious, of course, in the case of a singular moral judgment such as the judgment that I am morally obliged here and now to reply to a certain letter from a particular person. We can distinguish between the concept of moral obligation as such and the empirically given conditions of this particular duty. Further, when Kant

speaks of the practical reason or rational will as the fount of
the moral law, he is thinking of practical reason *as such*, not
of the practical reason as found in a specific class of finite
beings, that is, in human beings. True, he does not intend to
state that there *are* finite rational beings other than men. But
he is concerned with the moral imperative as bearing on all
beings which are capable of being subject to obligation,
whether they are men or not. Hence he is concerned with
the moral imperative regarded as antecedent to consideration
of human nature and its empirical conditions. And if practical
reason is looked on in this extremely abstract way, it follows
that moral laws, in so far as they make sense only on the supposition that there are human beings, cannot be deduced from
the concept of practical reason. For instance, it would be
absurd to think of the commandment 'Thou shalt not commit adultery' applying to pure spirits, for it presupposes
bodies and the institution of marriage. We have to distinguish between pure ethics or the metaphysics of morals, which
deals with the supreme principle or principles of morality
and with the nature of moral obligation as such, and applied
ethics, which applies the supreme principle or principles to
the conditions of human nature, calling in the aid of what
Kant calls 'anthropology', knowledge of human nature.

The general notion of the division between the metaphysics
of morals and applied ethics is reasonably clear. Physics, as
we saw, can be divided into pure physics or the metaphysics
of Nature and empirical physics. Analogously, ethics or moral
philosophy can be divided into the metaphysics of morals
and applied ethics or practical anthropology. But when we
come down to the details of the division, certain difficulties
arise. We would expect the metaphysics of morals to prescind
altogether from human nature and to be concerned exclusively with certain fundamental principles which are afterwards applied to human nature in so-called practical anthropology. But in the introduction to the *Metaphysics of Morals*
(1797) Kant admits that even in the metaphysics of morals
we often have to take account of human nature as such in
order to exhibit the consequences of universal moral principles. True, this does not mean that the metaphysics of morals
can be founded on anthropology. 'A metaphysics of morals
cannot be founded on anthropology, but may be applied to
it.'[7] But if the application of moral principles to human nature is admissible in the metaphysical part of ethics, the second part of ethics, namely moral or practical anthropology,

tends to become a study of the subjective conditions, favoura-
ble and unfavourable, for carrying out moral precepts. It will
be concerned, for example, with moral education. And it is,
indeed, with such themes that practical anthropology is said
to be concerned when Kant describes its function in the introduction to the *Metaphysics of Morals*.

The difficulty, therefore, is this. According to Kant, there is
need for a metaphysic of morals which will prescind from all
empirical factors. And he blames Wolff for having mixed up
a priori and empirical factors in his ethical writing. At the
same time there seems to be a tendency on Kant's part to
push into the metaphysical part of ethics moral laws which
seem to include empirical elements. Thus we are told that
'the commandment, *Thou shalt not lie*, is not valid only for
human beings as though other rational beings had no need
to bother with it; and so with all other moral laws in the
proper sense'.[8] But though this precept is *a priori* in the
sense that it holds good independently of the way in which
human beings actually behave, it is questionable whether it
is *a priori* in the sense that it does not depend in any way on
'anthropology'.[9]

However, the main point which Kant wishes to make is
that 'the basis of obligation must not be sought in human
nature or in the circumstances of the world in which he
(man) is placed, but *a priori* simply in the concepts of pure
reason'.[10] We must work out a pure ethics which, 'when applied to man, does not borrow the least thing from the knowledge of man himself, but gives laws *a priori* to him as a rational being'.[11] We are really concerned with finding in
reason itself the basis of the *a priori* element in the moral
judgment, the element which makes possible the synthetic
a priori propositions of morals. We are certainly not concerned with deducing all moral laws and precepts by mere
analysis from the concept of the pure practical reason. Kant
did not think that this can be done.

But though we cannot deduce all moral laws and precepts
from the concept of pure practical reason alone, the moral
law must ultimately be grounded in this reason. And as this
means finding the ultimate source of the principles of the
moral law in reason considered in itself, without reference to
specifically human conditions, Kant obviously parts company
with all moral philosophers who try to find the ultimate basis
of the moral law in human nature as such or in any feature
of human nature or in any factor in human life or society. In

the *Critique of Practical Reason* he refers to Montaigne as founding morality on education, to Epicurus as founding it on man's physical feeling, to Mandeville as founding it on political constitution, and to Hutcheson as founding it on man's moral feelings. He then remarks that all these alleged foundations are 'evidently incapable of furnishing the general principle of morality'.[12] We can also note that Kant's moral theory, by grounding the moral law on reason, is incompatible with modern emotive theories of ethics. In a word, he rejects empiricism and must be classed as a rationalist in ethics, provided that this word is not taken to mean someone who thinks that the whole moral law is deducible by mere analysis from some fundamental concept.

In the following outline of Kant's moral theory we shall be concerned primarily with the metaphysical part of morals. That is to say, we shall be concerned primarily with what Kant calls the metaphysics of morals, not with speculative metaphysics. For Kant did not believe that morality should be founded on natural theology. For him belief in God is grounded in the moral consciousness rather than the moral law on belief in God. And our treatment will be based on the *Groundwork* and the second *Critique*. The work entitled *Metaphysics of Morals* does not seem to add much, if anything, which is required for a brief outline of the Kantian moral theory.

In the *Groundwork of the Metaphysics of Morals* (called by Abbott *Fundamental Principles of the Metaphysics of Morals*) we are told that the metaphysics of morals is concerned to investigate 'the source of the practical principles which are to be found *a priori* in our reason'.[13] The *Groundwork* itself is said to be 'nothing more than the investigation and establishment of *the supreme principle of morality*',[14] and thus to constitute a complete treatise in itself. At the same time it does not profess to be a complete critique of the practical reason. Hence it leads on to the second *Critique*. This fact is indicated, indeed, by the titles of the main divisions of the *Groundwork*. For the first part deals with the transition from common or ordinary moral knowledge to philosophical moral knowledge; the second part with the transition from popular moral philosophy to the metaphysics of morals; and the third with the final step from the metaphysics of morals to the critique of the pure practical reason.

The structure of the *Critique of Practical Reason* recalls the structure of the first *Critique*. There is, of course, nothing corresponding to the *Transcendental Aesthetic*. But the work is divided into an *Analytic* (proceeding from principles to concepts rather than, as in the first *Critique*, from concepts to principles) and a *Dialectic*, dealing with the illusions of reason in its practical use, but also putting forward a positive standpoint. And Kant adds a *Methodology of Pure Practical Reason*, treating of the method of making the objectively practical reason also subjectively practical. That is to say, it considers the way in which the laws of the pure practical reason can be given access to and influence on the human mind. But this section is brief, and it is perhaps inserted more to supply something corresponding to the *Transcendental Doctrine of Method* in the first *Critique* than for any more cogent reason.

2. The fact that the opening words of the *Groundwork of the Metaphysics of Morals* have been quoted time and time again is no reason for not quoting them once more. 'It is impossible to conceive of anything in the world, or indeed out of it, which can be called good without qualification save only a good will.'[15] But though Kant begins his treatise in this dramatic way, he does not consider that he is giving a startling new piece of information. For in his opinion he is making explicit a truth which is present at least implicitly in ordinary moral knowledge. However, it is incumbent on him to explain what he means by saying that a good will is the only good without qualification.

The concept of an unqualified good can be explained without much difficulty. External possessions, such as wealth, can be misused, as everybody knows. Hence they are not good without qualification. And the same can be said about mental talents, such as quickness of understanding. A criminal can possess and misuse mental talents of a high order. We can also say the same of natural traits of character, such as courage. They can be employed or manifested in pursuing an evil end. But a good will cannot be bad or evil in any circumstances. It is good without qualification.

This statement, taken by itself, seems to be a mere tautology. For a good will is good by definition; and it is analytically true to say that a good will is always good. Kant must therefore explain what he means by a good will. He refers, indeed, in the first place to a will which is good in itself and not merely in relation to something else. We may say, for example, of a painful surgical treatment that it is good, not in itself, but in relation to the beneficial effect which it is designed to bring about. But the Kantian concept of a good will is the concept of a will which is always good in itself, by virtue of its intrinsic value, and not simply in relation to the production of some end, for example, happiness. We wish to know, however, when a will is good in itself, that is, when it has intrinsic value. According to Kant, a will cannot be said to be good in itself simply because it causes, for instance, good actions. For I may will, for instance, a good action which physical circumstances prevent me from performing. Yet my will can be none the less good. What makes it good? If we are to escape from mere tautology, we must give some content to the term 'good' when applied to the will and not content ourselves with saying that a good will is a good will or that a will is good when it is good.

To elucidate the meaning of the term 'good' when applied to the will, Kant turns his attention to the concept of duty which is for him the salient feature of the moral consciousness. A will which acts for the sake of duty is a good will. The matter has to be stated in this form if it is to be stated with accuracy. For the will of God is a good will, but it would be absurd to speak of God performing His duty. For the concept of duty or obligation involves the concept of at least the possibility of self-conquest, of having to overcome obstacles. And the divine will is not conceived as subject to any possible hindrance in willing what is good. Hence to be quite accurate we cannot say that a good will is a will which acts for the sake of duty; we have to say that a will which acts for the sake of duty is a good will. However, Kant calls a will such as the divine will, which is conceived as always and necessarily good, a 'holy will', thus giving it a special name. And if we prescind from the concept of a holy will and confine our attention to a finite will subject to obligation, we can permit ourselves to say that a good will is one which acts for the sake of duty. But the notion of acting for the sake of duty needs, of course, further elucidation.

3. Kant makes a distinction between actions which are in accordance with duty and acts which are done for the sake of duty. His own example serves to make clear the nature of this distinction. Let us suppose that a tradesman is always careful not to overcharge his customers. His behaviour is certainly in accordance with duty; but it does not necessarily follow that he behaves in this way for the sake of duty, that is, because it is his duty so to behave. For he may refrain from overcharging his customers simply from motives of pru-

dence; for example, on the ground that honesty is the best policy. Thus the class of actions performed in accordance with duty is much wider than the class of actions performed for the sake of duty.

According to Kant, only those actions which are performed for the sake of duty have moral worth. He takes the example of preserving one's life. 'To preserve one's life is a duty, and further, everyone has an immediate inclination to do so.'[16] These are the two presuppositions. Now, if I preserve my life simply because I have an inclination to do so, my action does not, in Kant's view, possess moral worth. To possess such worth my action must be performed because it is my duty to preserve my life; that is, out of a sense of moral obligation. Kant does not explicitly say that it is morally wrong to preserve my life because I desire to do so. For my action would be at least in accordance with duty and not incompatible with it, as suicide would be. But it has no moral value. On the one hand it is not a moral action; but on the other hand it can hardly be called an immoral action in the sense in which suicide is immoral.

This view may be incorrect; but Kant at any rate thinks that it represents the view which everyone who possesses moral convictions implicitly holds and which he will recognize as true if he reflects. Kant tends to complicate matters, however, by giving the impression that in his opinion the moral value of an action performed for the sake of duty is increased in proportion to a decrease in inclination to perform the action. In other words, he gives some ground for the interpretation that, in his view, the less inclination we have to do our duty, the greater is the moral value of our action if we actually perform what it is our duty to do. And this point of view leads to the strange conclusion that the more we hate doing our duty the better, provided that we do it. Or, to put the matter another way, the more we have to overcome ourselves to do our duty, the more moral we are. And, if this is admitted, it seems to follow that the baser a man's inclinations are, the higher is his moral value, provided that he overcomes his evil tendencies. But this point of view is contrary to the common conviction that the integrated personality, in whom inclination and duty coincide, has achieved a higher level of moral development than the man in whom inclination and desire are at war with his sense of duty.

However, though Kant sometimes speaks in a way which appears at first sight at least to support this interpretation, his main point is simply that when a man performs his duty contrary to his inclinations, the fact that he acts for the sake of duty and not simply out of inclination is clearer than it would be if he had a natural attraction to the action. And to say this is not necessarily to say that it is better to have no inclination for doing one's duty than to have such an inclination. Speaking of the beneficent man or philanthropist, he asserts, indeed, that the action of doing good to others has no moral worth if it is simply the effect of a natural inclination, springing from a naturally sympathetic temperament. But he does not say that there is anything wrong or undesirable in possessing such a temperament. On the contrary, actions arising from a natural satisfaction in increasing the happiness of others are 'proper and lovable'.[17] Kant may have been a rigorist in ethics; but his concern to bring out the difference between acting for the sake of duty and acting to satisfy one's natural desires and inclinations should not be taken to imply that he had no use for the ideal of a completely virtuous man who has overcome and transformed all desires which conflict with duty. Nor should it be taken to mean that in his opinion the truly virtuous man would be without any inclinations at all. Speaking of the commandment in the Gospels to love all men, he remarks that love as an affection ('pathological' love, as he puts it) cannot be commanded, but that beneficence for duty's sake ('practical' love) can be commanded, even if a man has an aversion towards beneficent action. But he certainly does not say that it is better to have an aversion towards beneficent action, provided that one performs such actions when it is one's duty to do so, than to have an inclination towards it. On the contrary, he explicitly asserts that it is better to do one's duty cheerfully than otherwise. And his moral ideal, as will be seen later, was the greatest possible approximation to complete virtue, to the holy will of God.

4. So far we have learned that a good will is manifested in acting for the sake of duty, and that acting for the sake of duty must be distinguished from acting out of mere inclination or desire. But we require some more positive indication of what is meant by acting for the sake of duty. And Kant tells us that it means acting out of reverence for law, that is, the moral law. 'Duty is the necessity of acting out of reverence for the law.'[18]

Now, by law Kant means law as such. To act for the sake of duty is to act out of reverence for law as such. And the essential characteristic (the form, we may say) of law as such is universality; that is to say, strict universality which does not admit of exceptions. Physical laws are universal; and so is the moral law. But whereas all physical things, including man as a purely physical thing, conform unconsciously and necessarily to physical law, rational beings, and they alone, are capable of acting in accordance with the idea of law. A man's actions, therefore, if they are to have moral worth, must be performed out of reverence for the law. Their moral worth is derived, according to Kant, not from their results, whether actual or intended, but from the maxim of the agent. And this maxim, to confer moral worth on actions, must be that of abiding by law, of obeying it, out of reverence for the law.

We are told, therefore, that the good will, the only good without qualification, is manifested in acting for the sake of duty; that duty means acting out of reverence for law; and that law is essentially universal. But this leaves us with a highly abstract, not to say empty, concept of acting for the sake of duty. And the question arises how it can be translated into terms of the concrete moral life.

Before we can answer this question, we must make a distinction between maxims and principles. A principle, in Kant's technical terminology, is a fundamental objective moral law, grounded in the pure practical reason. It is a principle on which all men would act if they were purely rational moral agents. A maxim is a subjective principle of volition. That is to say, it is a principle on which an agent acts as a matter of fact and which determines his decisions. Such maxims can be, of course, of diverse kinds; and they may or may not accord with the objective principle or principles of the moral law.

This account of the nature of maxims may seem to be incompatible with what has been said above about Kant's view that the moral worth of actions is determined by the agent's maxim. For if a maxim can be out of accord with the moral law, how can it confer moral worth on the actions prompted by it? To meet this difficulty we have to make a further distinction between empirical or material maxims and *a priori* or formal maxims. The first refer to desired ends or results while the second do not. The maxim which confers moral value on actions must be of the second type. That is to say, it must not refer to any objects of sensuous desire or to any results to be obtained by action; but it must be the maxim of obeying universal law as such. That is to say, if the subjective principle of volition is obedience to the universal moral law, out of reverence for the law, the actions governed by this maxim will have moral worth. For they will have been performed for the sake of duty.

Having made these distinctions, we can return to the question how Kant's abstract concept of acting for the sake of duty can be translated into terms of the concrete moral life. 'As I have robbed the will of all impulses (or inducements) which could arise for it from following any particular law, there remains nothing but the universal conformity of actions to law in general, which should serve the will as a principle. That is to say, *I am never to act otherwise than so that I can also will that my maxim should become a universal law.'*[19] The word 'maxim' must be taken here to refer to what we have called empirical or material maxims. Reverence for law, which gives rise to the formal maxim of acting in obedience to law as such, demands that we should bring all our material maxims under the form of law as such, this form being universality. We have to ask whether we could will that a given maxim should become a universal law. That is to say, could it assume the form of universality?

Kant gives an example. Let us imagine a man in distress, who can extricate himself from his plight only by making a promise which he has no intention of fulfilling. That is to say, he can obtain relief only by lying. May he do so? If he does act in this way, his maxim will be that he is entitled to make a promise with no intention of fulfilling it (that is, that he is entitled to lie) if only by this means can he extricate himself from a distressful situation. We may put the question in this form, therefore. Can he will that this maxim should become a universal law? The maxim, when universalized, would state that everyone may make a promise with no intention of keeping it (that is, that anyone may lie) when he finds himself in a difficulty from which he can extricate himself by no other means. According to Kant, this universalization cannot be willed. For it would mean willing that lying should become a universal law. And then no promises would be believed. But the man's maxim postulates belief in promises. Therefore he cannot adopt this maxim and at the same time will that it should become a universal law. Thus the maxim cannot assume the form of universality. And if a maxim cannot enter as a principle into a possible scheme of universal law, it must be rejected.

Far be it from me to suggest that this example is immune

from criticism. But I do not wish, by discussing possible objections, to distract attention from the main point which Kant is trying to make. It seems to be this. In practice we all act according to what Kant calls maxims. That is to say, we all have subjective principles of volition. Now, a finite will cannot be good unless it is motivated by respect or reverence for universal law. In order, therefore, that our wills may be morally good, we must ask ourselves whether we can will that our maxims, our subjective principles of volition, should become universal laws. If we cannot do so, we must reject these maxims. If we can do so, that is if our maxims can enter as principles into a possible scheme of universal moral legislation, reason demands that we should admit and respect them in virtue of our reverence for law as such.[20]

It is to be noted that up to this point Kant has been concerned with clarifying the idea of acting for the sake of duty. Further, in his opinion we have been moving in the sphere of what he calls the moral knowledge of common human reason. 'The necessity of acting from pure reverence for the practical law is that which constitutes duty, to which every other motive must give place, because it is the condition of a will being good *in itself*; and the worth of such a will is above everything. Thus, then, without leaving the moral knowledge of common human reason, we have arrived at its principle.'[21] Although men do not ordinarily conceive this principle in such an abstract form, yet it is known by them implicitly, and it is the principle on which their moral judgments rest.

The principle of duty, that I ought never to act otherwise than so that I can also will that my maxim should become a universal law, is a way of formulating what Kant calls the categorical imperative. And we can now turn our attention to this subject.

5. As we have seen, a distinction must be made between principles and maxims. The objective principles of morality may be also subjective principles of volition, functioning as maxims. But there may also be a discrepancy between the objective principles of morality on the one hand and a man's maxims or subjective principles of volition on the other. If we were all purely rational moral agents, the objective principles of morality would always govern our actions; that is to say, they would also be subjective principles of volition. In point of fact, however, we are capable of acting on maxims or subjective principles of volition which are incompatible with the objective principles of morality. And this means that the

latter present themselves to us as commands or imperatives. We thus experience obligation. If our wills were holy wills, there would be no question of command and no question of obligation. But inasmuch as our wills are not holy wills (though the holy will remains the ideal), the moral law necessarily takes for us the form of an imperative. The pure practical reason commands; and it is our duty to overcome the desires which conflict with these commands.

When defining an imperative, Kant makes a distinction between command and imperative.[22] 'The conception of an objective principle, in so far as it is necessitating for a will, is called a command (of reason), and the formula of the command is called an *imperative*. All imperatives are expressed by an *ought* and exhibit thereby the relation of an objective law of reason to a will which, by reason of its subjective constitution, is not necessarily determined by it.'[23] By speaking of the objective principle as being 'necessitating' (*nötigend*) for a will Kant does not mean, of course, that the human will cannot help obeying the law. The point is rather that the will does not necessarily follow the dictate of reason, with the consequence that the law appears to the agent as something external which exercises constraint or pressure on the will. In this sense the law is said to be 'necessitating' for the will. But the latter is not 'necessarily determined' by the law. Kant's terminology may be confusing; but he is not guilty of self-contradiction.

Now, there are three kinds of imperatives, corresponding to three different kinds or senses of good action. And as only one of these imperatives is the moral imperative, it is important to understand the Kantian distinction between the different types.

Let us first consider the sentence, 'If you wish to learn French, you ought to take these means'. Here we have an imperative. But there are two things to notice. First, the actions commanded are conceived as being good with a view to attaining a certain end. They are not commanded as actions which ought to be performed for their own sake, but only as a means. The imperative is thus said to be *hypothetical*. Secondly, the end in question is not one which everyone seeks by nature. A man may wish or not wish to learn French. The imperative simply states that *if* you wish to learn French, you ought to take certain means, that is, perform certain actions. This type of imperative is called by Kant a *problematic* hypothetical imperative or an imperative of skill.

There is no difficulty in seeing that this type of imperative is not the moral imperative. We have taken the example of learning French. But we might equally well have taken the example of becoming a successful burglar. 'If you wish to become a successful burglar, that is, if you wish to burgle and not to be found out, these are the means which you ought to take.' The imperative of skill, or the technical imperative as we might call it, has, in itself, nothing to do with morality. The actions commanded are commanded simply as useful for the attainment of an end which one may or may not desire to attain; and the pursuit may or may not be compatible with the moral law.

In the second place let us consider the sentence, 'You desire happiness by a necessity of nature; therefore you ought to perform these actions'. Here again we have a *hypothetical* imperative, in the sense that certain actions are commanded as means to an end. But it is not a problematic hypothetical imperative. For the desire of happiness is not an end which we set before ourselves or leave aside as we like, in the way that we can choose or not choose to learn French, to become successful burglars, to acquire the carpenter's art, and so on. The imperative does not say, '*if* you desire happiness': it *asserts* that you desire happiness. It is thus an *assertoric* hypothetical imperative.

Now, this imperative has been regarded in some ethical systems as a moral imperative. But Kant will not allow that any hypothetical imperative, whether problematic or assertoric, is the moral imperative. It seems to me that he is somewhat cavalier in his treatment of teleological ethical theories. I mean that he does not seem to give sufficient consideration to a distinction which has to be made between different types of teleological ethics. 'Happiness' may be regarded as a subjective state which is acquired by certain actions but which is distinct from these actions. In this case the actions are judged good simply as means to an end to which they are external. But 'happiness', if we follow, for instance, the customary way of translating Aristotle's[24] *eudaimonia*, may be regarded as an objective actualization of the potentialities of man as man (that is, as an activity); and in this case the actions which are judged good are not purely external to the end. However, Kant would probably say that we then have an ethic based on the idea of the perfection of human nature, and that, though this idea is morally relevant, it cannot supply the supreme principle of morality which he is seeking.

In any case Kant rejects all hypothetical imperatives, whether problematic or assertoric, as qualifying for the title of moral imperative. It remains, therefore, that the moral imperative must be *categorical*. That is to say, it must command actions, not as means to any end, but as good in themselves. It is what Kant calls an apodictic imperative. 'The categorical imperative, which declares an action to be objectively necessary in itself without reference to any purpose, that is, without any other end, is valid as an *apodictic* practical principle.'[25]

What is this categorical imperative? All that we can say about it purely *a priori*, that is, by considering the mere concept of a categorical imperative, is that it commands conformity to law in general. It commands, that is to say, that the maxims which serve as our principles of volition should conform to universal law. 'There is, therefore, only one categorical imperative, and it is this: *Act only on that maxim through which you can at the same time will that it should become a universal law*.'[26] But Kant immediately gives us another formulation of the imperative, namely to '*Act as if the maxim of your action were to become through your will a Universal Law of Nature*'.[27]

In the last section we met the categorical imperative expressed in a negative form. And in note 20 on page 243, I remarked that there is no question of deducing concrete rules of conduct from the concept of universal law as such. So here also we must remember that Kant does not intend to imply that concrete rules of conduct can be deduced from the categorical imperative in the sense in which the conclusion of a syllogism can be deduced from the premisses. The imperative serves, not as a premiss for deduction by mere analysis, but as a criterion for judging the morality of concrete principles of conduct. We might speak, however, of moral laws being derived in some sense from the categorical imperative. Suppose that I give money to a poor person in great distress when there is nobody else who has a greater claim on me. The maxim of my action, that is, the subjective principle of my volition, is, let us assume, that I will give alms to an individual who really needs such assistance when there is nobody else who has a prior claim on me. I ask myself whether I can will this maxim as a universal law valid for all, namely that one should give assistance to those who really need it when there is nobody else who has a prior claim on one. And I decide that I can so will. My maxim is thus morally justified. As for the moral law which I will, this is obviously not deducible by mere analysis from the categorical imperative. For it introduces ideas which are not contained in the latter. At the same time the law can be said to be derived from the categorical imperative, in the sense that it is derived through applying the imperative.

Kant's general notion, therefore, is that the practical or moral law as such is strictly universal; universality being, as it were, its form. Hence all concrete principles of conduct must partake in this universality if they are to qualify for being called moral. But he does not make it at all clear what precisely he means by 'being able' or 'not being able' to will that one's maxim should become a universal law. One would perhaps be naturally inclined to understand him as referring to the absence or presence of logical contradiction when one tries to universalize one's maxim. But Kant makes a distinction. 'Some actions are of such a nature that their maxims cannot, without contradiction, be even conceived as a universal law.'[28] Here Kant seems to refer to a logical contradiction between the maxim and its formulation as a universal law. In other cases, however, this 'intrinsic impossibility' is absent; 'but it is still impossible to *will* that the maxim should be raised to the universality of a law of nature, because such a will would contradict itself'.[29] Here Kant seems to refer to cases in which a maxim could be given the formulation of a universal law without logical contradiction, though we could not *will* this law because the will, as expressed in the law, would be in antagonism or, as Kant puts it, contradiction with itself as adhering steadfastly to some purpose or desire the attainment of which would be incompatible with the observance of the law.

A series of examples is, indeed, supplied. The fourth of these appears to be intended as an example of the second type of inability to will that one's maxim should become a universal law. A man enjoys great prosperity but sees that others are in misery and that he could help them. He adopts, however, the maxim of not concerning himself with the distress of others. Can this maxim be turned into a universal law? It can be done without logical contradiction. For there is no logical contradiction in a law that those in prosperity ought not to render any assistance to those in distress. But, according to Kant, the prosperous man cannot *will* this law without a contradiction or antagonism within his will. For his original maxim was the expression of a selfish disregard for others, and it was accompanied by the firm desire of himself obtaining help from others if he should ever be in a state of misery, a desire which would be negated by willing the universal law in question.

Kant's second example appears to be intended as an example of a logical contradiction being involved in turning one's maxim into a universal law. A man needs money, and he can obtain it only by promising to repay it, though he knows very well that he will be unable to do so. Reflection shows him that he cannot turn the maxim (when I am in need of money, I will borrow it and promise to repay it, though I know that I shall not be able to do so) into a universal law without contradiction. For the universal law would destroy all faith in promises, whereas the maxim presupposes faith in promises. From what he says Kant appears to have thought that the law itself would be self-contradictory, the law being that anyone who is in need and can obtain relief only by making a promise which he cannot fulfil may make such a promise. But it is difficult to see that this proposition is self-contradictory in a purely logical sense, though it may be that the law could not be *willed* without the inconsistencies to which Kant draws attention.

It may be said, of course, that we ought not to make heavy weather of concrete examples. The examples may be open to objection; but even if Kant has not given sufficient attention to their formulation, the theory which they are supposed to illustrate is the important thing. This would be an apt observation if the theory, in its abstract expression, were clear. But this does not seem to me to be the case. It seems to me that Kant has not properly clarified the meaning of 'being able' and 'not being able' to will that one's maxim should become a universal law. However, behind his examples we can see the conviction that the moral law is essentially universal, and that the making of exceptions for oneself from selfish motives is immoral. The practical reason commands us to rise above selfish desires and maxims which clash with the universality of law.

6. We have seen that according to Kant there is 'only one' categorical imperative, namely 'Act only on that maxim through which you can at the same time will that it should become a universal law'. But we have also seen that he gives another formulation of the categorical imperative, namely 'Act as if the maxim of your action were to become through your will a Universal Law of Nature'. And he gives further

formulations. There seem to be five in all; but Kant tells us that there are three. Thus he asserts that 'the three above-mentioned ways of presenting the principle of morality are at bottom so many formulas of the very same law, each of which involves the other two'.[30] By giving several formulations of the categorical imperative Kant does not, therefore, intend to recant what he has said about there being 'only one' such imperative. The different formulations are intended, he tells us, to bring an idea of the reason nearer to intuition, by means of a certain analogy, and thereby nearer to feeling. Thus the formulation 'Act as if the maxim of your action were to become through your will a Universal Law of Nature' makes use of an analogy between moral law and natural law. And elsewhere Kant expresses the formula in this way: 'Ask yourself whether you could regard the action which you propose to do as a possible object of your will if it were to take place according to a law of nature in a system of nature of which you were yourself a part.'[31] This formula[32] may be the same as the categorical imperative in its original form in the sense that the latter is its principle, as it were; but it is obvious that the idea of a system of Nature is an addition to the categorical imperative as first expressed.

Assuming, however, that the two formulations of the categorical imperative which have already been mentioned can be reckoned as one, we come to what Kant calls the second formulation or way of presenting the principle of morality. His approach to it is involved.

We have, Kant tells us, exhibited the content of the categorical imperative. 'But we have not yet advanced so far as to prove that there really is such an imperative, that there is a practical law which commands absolutely of itself and without any other impulses, and that the following of this law is duty.'[33] The question arises, therefore, whether it is a practically necessary law (that is, a law imposing obligation) for all rational beings that they should always judge their actions by maxims which they can will to be universal laws. If this is actually the case, there must be a synthetic *a priori* connection between the concept of the will of a rational being as such and the categorical imperative.

Kant's treatment of the matter is not easy to follow and gives the impression of being very roundabout. He argues that that which serves the will as the objective ground of its self-determination is the *end*. And if there is an end which is assigned by reason alone (and not by subjective desire), it will be valid for all rational beings and will thus serve as the ground for a categorical imperative binding the wills of all rational beings. This end cannot be a relative end, fixed by desire; for such ends give rise only to hypothetical imperatives. It must be, therefore, an end in itself, possessing absolute, and not merely relative, value. 'Assuming that there is something *the existence of which* has *in itself* absolute value, something which, *as an end in itself,* could be the ground of determinate laws, then in it and in it alone would lie the ground of a possible categorical imperative, that is, of a practical law.'[34] Again, if there is a supreme practical principle which is for the human will a categorical imperative, 'it must be one which, being derived from the conception of that which is necessarily an end for everyone because it is *an end in itself,* constitutes an *objective* principle of will, and can thus serve as a universal practical law'.[35]

Is there such an end? Kant postulates that man, and indeed any rational being, is an end in itself. The concept of a rational being as an end in itself can therefore serve as the ground for a supreme practical principle or law. 'The ground of this principle is: *rational nature exists as an end in itself.* . . . The practical imperative will thus be as follows: *So act as to treat humanity, whether in your own person or in that of any other, always at the same time as an end, and never merely as a means.*'[36] The words 'at the same time' and 'merely' are of importance. We cannot help making use of other human beings as means. When I go to the hairdresser's, for example, I use him as a means to an end other than himself. But the law states that, even in such cases, I must never use a rational being as a *mere* means; that is, as though he had no value in himself except as a means to my subjective end.

Kant applies this formulation of the categorical imperative to the same cases which he used to illustrate the application of the imperative as originally formulated. The suicide, who destroys himself to escape from painful circumstances, uses himself, a person, as a mere means to a relative end, namely the maintenance of tolerable conditions up to the end of life. The man who makes a promise to obtain a benefit when he has no intention of fulfilling it or when he knows very well that he will not be in a position to keep it, uses the man to whom he makes the promise as a mere means to a relative end.

We may note in passing that Kant makes use of this principle in his treatise *On Perpetual Peace.* A monarch who employs soldiers in aggressive wars undertaken for his own aggrandizement or for that of his country is using rational beings as mere means to a desired end. Indeed, in Kant's view, standing armies should be abolished in the course of time because hiring men to kill or to be killed involves a use of them as mere instruments in the hands of the State and cannot easily be reconciled with the rights of humanity, founded on the absolute value of the rational being as such.

7. The idea of respecting every rational will as an end in itself and not treating it as a mere means to the attainment of the object of one's desires leads us on to the 'idea of the will of every rational being as making universal law'.[37] In Kant's view, the will of man considered as a rational being must be regarded as the source of the law which he recognizes as universally binding. This is the principle of the autonomy, as contrasted with the heteronomy, of the will.

One of Kant's approaches to the autonomy of the will is more or less this. All imperatives which are conditioned by desire or inclination or, as Kant puts it, by 'interest' are hypothetical imperatives. A categorical imperative, therefore, must be unconditioned. And the moral will, which obeys the categorical imperative, must not be determined by interest. That is to say, it must not be heteronomous, at the mercy, as it were, of desires and inclinations which form part of a causally determined series. It must, therefore, be autonomous. And to say that a moral will is autonomous is to say that it gives itself the law which it obeys.

Now, the idea of a categorical imperative contains implicitly the idea of the autonomy of the will. But this autonomy can be expressed explicitly in a formulation of the imperative. And then we have the principle 'never to act on any other maxim than one which could, without contradiction, be also a universal law and accordingly always so to act that *the will could regard itself at the same time as making universal law through its maxim*'.[38] In the *Critique of Practical Reason*, the principle is expressed thus: 'So act that the maxim of your will could always at the same time be valid as a principle making universal law.'[39]

Kant speaks of the autonomy of the will as 'the supreme principle of morality'[40] and as 'the sole principle of all moral laws and of the corresponding duties'.[41] Heteronomy of the will, on the other hand, is 'the source of all spurious principles of morality';[42] and, far from being able to furnish the basis of obligation, 'is much rather opposed to the principle of obligation and to the morality of the will'.[43]

If we accept the heteronomy of the will, we accept the assumption that the will is subject to moral laws which are not the result of its own legislation as a rational will. And though reference has already been made to some of the ethical theories which, according to Kant, accept this assumption, it will clarify Kant's meaning if we refer to them briefly once again. In the *Critique of Practical Reason*[44] he mentions Montaigne as grounding the principles of morality on education, Mandeville as grounding them on the civil constitution (that is, on the legal system), Epicurus as grounding them on physical feeling (that is, pleasure), and Hutcheson as grounding them on moral feeling. All these theories are what Kant calls subjective or empirical, the first two referring to external empirical factors, the second two to internal empirical factors. In addition there are 'objective' or rationalistic theories; that is to say, theories which ground the moral law on ideas of reason. Kant mentions two types. The first, attributed to the Stoics and Wolff, grounds the moral law and obligation on the idea of inner perfection, while the second, attributed to Crusius, grounds the moral law and obligation on the will of God. All these theories are rejected by Kant. He does not say that they are all morally irrelevant; that is, that none of them has any contribution to make in the field of ethics. What he maintains is that none of them is capable of furnishing the supreme principles of morality and obligation. For instance, if we say that the will of God is the norm of morality, we can still ask why we ought to obey the divine will. Kant does not say that we ought not to obey the divine will, if it is manifested. But we must in any case first recognize obedience to God as a duty. Thus before obeying God we must in any case legislate as rational beings. The autonomy of the moral will is thus the supreme principle of morality.

Obviously, the concept of the autonomy of the morally legislating will makes no sense unless we make a distinction in man between man considered purely as a rational being, a moral will, and man as a creature who is also subject to desires and inclinations which may conflict with the dictates of reason. And this is, of course, what Kant presupposes. The will or practical reason, considered as such, legislates, and man, considered as being subject to a diversity of desires, impulses and inclinations, ought to obey.

In conceiving this theory of the autonomy of the will Kant was doubtless influenced to some extent by Rousseau. The latter, as we have seen, distinguished between the 'general will', which is always right and which is the real fount of moral laws, and the merely private will, whether taken separately or together with other private wills as 'the will of all'. And Kant utilized these ideas within the context of his own philosophy. Indeed, it is not unreasonable to suppose that the central position accorded by Kant in his ethical theory to the concept of the good will reflects, to some extent that is to say, the influence of his study of Rousseau.

8. The idea of rational beings as ends in themselves, coupled with that of the rational will or practical reason as morally legislating, brings us to the concept of a kingdom of ends (*ein Reich der Zwecke*). 'I understand by a *kingdom* the systematic union of rational beings through common laws.'[45] And because these laws have in view the relation of these beings to one another as ends and means, as Kant puts it, it can be called a kingdom of ends. A rational being can belong to this kingdom in either of two ways. He belongs to it as a *member* when, although giving laws, he is also subject to them. He belongs to it as a sovereign or supreme head (*Oberhaupt*) when, while legislating, he is not subject to the will of any other. Perhaps Kant can be interpreted as meaning that every rational being is both member and sovereign; for no rational being is, when legislating and as legislating, subject to the will of another. But it is also possible, and perhaps more likely, that *Oberhaupt* is to be taken as referring to God. For Kant goes on to say that a rational being can occupy the place of supreme head only if he is 'a completely independent being without want and without limitation of power adequate to his will'.[46]

This kingdom of ends is to be thought according to an analogy with the kingdom of Nature, the self-imposed rules of the former being analogous to the causal laws of the latter. It is, as Kant remarks, 'only an ideal'.[47] At the same time it is a possibility. It 'would be actually realized through maxims conforming to the rule prescribed by the categorical imperative for all rational beings, *if they were universally followed*'.[48] And rational beings ought to act as though they were through their maxims law-making members of a kingdom of ends. (Hence we have another variation of the categorical imperative.) The ideal of historical development is, we may say, the establishment of the kingdom of ends as an actuality.

9. Now, the categorical imperative states that all rational beings (that is, all rational beings who can be subject to an imperative at all) ought to act in a certain way. They ought to act only on those maxims which they can at the same time will, without contradiction, to be universal laws. The imperative thus states an obligation. But it is, according to Kant, a synthetic *a priori* proposition. On the one hand, the obligation cannot be obtained by mere analysis of the concept of a rational will. And the categorical imperative is thus not an analytic proposition. On the other hand, the predicate must be connected necessarily with the subject. For the categorical imperative, unlike a hypothetical imperative, is unconditioned and necessarily binds or obliges the will to act in a certain way. It is, indeed, a *practical* synthetic *a priori* proposition. That is to say, it does not extend our theoretical knowledge of objects, as is done by the synthetic *a priori* propositions which we considered when discussing the first *Critique*. It is directed towards action, towards the performance of actions good in themselves, not towards our knowledge of empirical reality. But it is none the less a proposition which is both *a priori*, independent of all desires and inclinations, and synthetic. The question arises, therefore, how is this practical synthetic *a priori* proposition possible?

We have here a question similar to that propounded in the first *Critique* and in the *Prolegomena to Any Future Metaphysics*. But there is a difference. As we saw, there is no need to ask *whether* the synthetic *a priori* propositions of mathematics and physics are possible, if we once assume that these sciences do contain such propositions. For the development of the sciences shows their possibility. The only pertinent question is *how* they are possible. In the case of a practical or moral synthetic *a priori* proposition, however, we have, according to Kant, to establish its possibility.

Kant's statement of the problem seems to me to be somewhat confusing. It is not always easy to see precisely what question he is asking. For he formulates it in different ways, and it is not always immediately evident that their meanings are equivalent. However, let us take it that he is asking for a justification of the possibility of a practical synthetic *a priori* proposition. In his terminology this means asking what is the 'third term' which unites the predicate to the subject or, perhaps more precisely, which makes possible a necessary connection between predicate and subject. For if the predicate cannot be got out of the subject by mere analysis, there must be a third term which unites them.

This 'third term' cannot be anything in the sensible world. We cannot establish the possibility of a categorical imperative by referring to anything in the causal series of phenomena. Physical necessity would give us heteronomy, whereas we are looking for that which makes possible the principle of autonomy. And Kant finds it in the idea of freedom. Obviously, what he does is to look for the necessary condition of the possibility of obligation and of acting for the sake of duty alone, in accordance with a categorical imperative; and he finds this necessary condition in the idea of freedom.

We might say simply that Kant finds 'in freedom' the condition of the possibility of a categorical imperative. But, according to him, freedom cannot be *proved*. Hence it is perhaps more accurate to say that the condition of the possibility of a categorical imperative is to be found 'in the idea of freedom'. To say this is not, indeed, to say that the idea of freedom is a mere fiction in any ordinary sense. In the first place the *Critique of Pure Reason* has shown that freedom is a negative possibility, in the sense that the idea of freedom does not involve a logical contradiction. And in the second place we cannot act morally, for the sake of duty, except under the idea of freedom. Obligation, 'ought', implies freedom, freedom to obey or disobey the law. Nor can we regard ourselves as making universal laws, as morally autonomous, save under the idea of freedom. Practical reason or the will of a rational being 'must regard itself as free; that is, the will of such a being cannot be a will of its own except under the idea of freedom'.[49] The idea of freedom is thus *practically* necessary; it is a necessary condition of morality. At the same time the *Critique of Pure Reason* showed that freedom is not logically contradictory by showing that it must belong to the sphere of noumenal reality, and that the existence of such a sphere is not logically contradictory. And as our theoretical knowledge does not extend into this sphere, freedom is not susceptible of theoretical proof. But the assumption of freedom is a practical necessity for the moral agent; and it is thus no mere arbitrary fiction.

The practical necessity of the idea of freedom involves, therefore, our regarding ourselves as belonging, not only to the world of sense, the world which is ruled by determined causality, but also to the intelligible or noumenal world. Man can regard himself from two points of view. As belonging to the world of sense, he finds himself subject to natural laws (heteronomy). As belonging to the intelligible world, he finds himself under laws which have their foundation in reason alone. 'And thus categorical imperatives are possible because the idea of freedom makes me a member of an intelligible world, in consequence of which, supposing that I were nothing else, all my actions *would* always conform to the autonomy of the will; but as I at the same time intuit myself as a member of the world of sense, my actions *ought* so to conform. And this *categorical* 'ought' implies a synthetic *a priori* proposition. . . .'[50]

The matter can be summed up thus in Kant's words. 'The question, therefore, how a categorical imperative is possible, can be answered to this extent, that one can assign the only presupposition on which it is possible, namely the idea of freedom; and one can also discern the necessity of this presupposition, which is sufficient for the *practical use* of reason, that is, for the conviction of the *validity of this imperative*, and hence of the moral law. But no human reason can ever discern how this presupposition itself is possible. However, on the presupposition that the will of an intelligence is free its *autonomy*, as the essential formal condition of its determination, is a necessary consequence.'[51] In saying here that no human reason can discern the possibility of freedom Kant is referring, of course, to positive possibility. We enjoy no intuitive insight into the sphere of noumenal reality. We cannot *prove* freedom, and hence we cannot *prove* the possibility of a categorical imperative. But we can indicate the condition under which alone a categorical imperative is possible. And the idea of this condition is a practical necessity for the moral agent. This, in Kant's view, is quite sufficient for morality, though the impossibility of proving freedom indicates, of course, the limitations of human theoretical knowledge.

10. What we have been saying about the practical necessity of the idea of freedom brings us naturally to the Kantian theory of the postulates of the practical reason. For freedom is one of them. The other two are immortality and God. The ideas, therefore, which Kant declared to be the main themes of metaphysics but which he also judged to transcend the limitations of reason in its theoretical use are here reintroduced as postulates of reason in its practical or moral use. And before we consider the Kantian theory of postulates in

general, it may be as well if we consider briefly each of the three particular postulates.

(i) There is no need to say much more about freedom. As we have seen, a theoretical proof that a rational being is free is, according to Kant, impossible for the human reason. None the less it cannot be shown that freedom is not possible. And the moral law compels us to assume it and therefore authorizes us to assume it. The moral law compels us to assume it inasmuch as the concept of freedom and the concept of the supreme principle of morality 'are so inseparably united that one might define practical freedom as independence of the will on anything but the moral law alone'.[52] Because of this inseparable connection the moral law is said to postulate freedom.

We must note, however, the difficult position in which Kant involves himself. As there is no faculty of intellectual intuition, we cannot observe actions which belong to the noumenal sphere: all the actions which we can observe, either internally or externally, must be objects of the internal or external senses. This means that they are all given in time and subject to the laws of causality. We cannot, therefore, make a distinction between two types of experienced actions, saying that these are free while those are determined. If, then, we assume that man, as a rational being, is free, we are compelled to hold that the same actions can be both determined and free.

Kant is, of course, well aware of this difficulty. If we wish to save freedom, he remarks, 'no other way remains than to ascribe the existence of a thing, so far as it is determinable in time, and therefore also its causality according to the law of *natural necessity*, to *appearance alone*, and to ascribe *freedom* to precisely *the same being as a thing in itself*'.[53] And he then asks, 'How can a man be called completely free at the same moment and in regard to the same action in which he is subject to an inevitable natural necessity?'[54] His answer is given in terms of time-conditions. In so far as a man's existence is subject to time-conditions, his actions form part of the mechanical system of Nature and are determined by antecedent causes. 'But the very same subject, being on the other hand also conscious of himself as a thing in itself, considers his existence also *in so far as it is not subject to time-conditions*, and he regards himself as determinable only through laws which he gives himself through reason.'[55] And to be determinable only through self-imposed laws is to be free.

In Kant's view this position is supported by the testimony of conscience. When I look on my acts which were contrary to the moral law precisely as past, I tend to attribute them to excusing causal factors. But the feeling of guilt remains; and the reason of this is that when the moral law, the law of my supersensible and supertemporal existence, is in question, reason recognizes no distinctions of time. It simply recognizes the action as mine, without reference to the time of its performance.

The statement, however, that man is noumenally free and empirically determined in regard to the very same actions is a hard saying. But it is one which, given his premisses, Kant cannot avoid.

(ii) Before we come directly to the second postulate of the practical reason, namely immortality, it is necessary to say something about Kant's conception of the *summum bonum*, a term which, literally translated, means the highest or supreme good. Indeed, without some understanding of what Kant has to say on this subject we cannot follow his doctrine either of the second postulate or of the third, namely that of God.

Reason, even in its practical function, seeks an unconditioned totality. And this means that it seeks the unconditioned totality of the *object* of practical reason or the will, to which object the name of *summum bonum* is given. This term is, however, ambiguous. It may mean the supreme or highest good in the sense of that good which is not itself conditioned. Or it may mean the perfect good in the sense of a whole which is not itself a part of a greater whole. Now, virtue is the supreme and unconditioned good. But it does not follow that it is the perfect good in the sense that it is the total object of the desires of a rational being. And in point of fact happiness must also be included in the concept of a perfect good. If, therefore, we understand by *summum bonum* the perfect good, it includes both virtue and happiness.

It is very important to understand Kant's view of the relation between these two elements of the perfect good. The connection between them is not logical. If the connection between them were logical or analytic, as Kant puts it, the endeavour to be virtuous, that is, to make one's will accord perfectly with the moral law, would be the same as the rational pursuit of happiness. And if this were what Kant meant to affirm, he would be contradicting his constantly repeated conviction that happiness is not and cannot be the ground of the moral law. The connection, therefore, between the two elements of the perfect good is synthetic, in the sense that virtue produces happiness, as a cause produces its effect. The *summum bonum* 'means the whole, the perfect good, in which, however, virtue as the condition is always the supreme good, because it has no condition above it; whereas happiness, while it is certainly pleasant to him who possesses it, is not of itself absolutely and in every respect good, but always presupposes morally right behaviour as its condition'.[56]

The truth of the proposition that virtue and happiness constitute the two elements of the perfect good cannot, therefore, be discovered by analysis. A man who is seeking his happiness cannot discover by analysis of this idea that he is virtuous. Nor can a virtuous man, whatever the Stoics may have said, discover that he is happy by analysing the idea of being virtuous. The two ideas are distinct. At the same time the proposition, though synthetic, is *a priori*. The connection between virtue and happiness is practically necessary, in the sense that we recognize that virtue ought to produce happiness. We cannot say, of course, that the desire of happiness must be the motive for pursuing virtue. For to say this would be to contradict the whole idea of acting for the sake of duty and would substitute heteronomy for autonomy of the will. But we must recognize virtue as the efficient cause of happiness. For the moral law, according to Kant, commands us to promote the *summum bonum*, in which virtue and happiness are related as conditions to conditioned, as cause to effect.

But how can we possibly hold that virtue necessarily produces happiness? The empirical evidence does not appear to warrant our making any such assertion. Even if it sometimes happens that virtue and happiness are actually found together, this is a purely contingent fact. We thus seem to arrive at an antinomy. On the one hand the practical reason demands a necessary connection between virtue and happiness. On the other hand the empirical evidence shows that there is no such necessary connection.

Kant's solution to this difficulty consists in showing that the assertion that virtue necessarily produces happiness is only conditionally false. That is to say, it is false only on condition that we take existence in this world to be the only sort of existence that a rational being can have, and if we take the assertion as meaning that virtue exercises in this sensible world a causality productive of happiness. The statement that the search for happiness produces virtue would be *absolutely* false; but the statement that virtue produces happiness is false, not absolutely, but only *conditionally*. It can, therefore, be true if I am justified in thinking that I exist, not only as a physical object in this sensible world, but also as a noumenon in an intelligible and supersensible world. And the moral law, being inseparably connected with the idea of freedom, demands that I should believe this. We must take it, therefore, that the realization of the *summum bonum* is possible, the first element, namely virtue (the supreme or highest good), producing the second element, happiness, if not immediately, yet at least mediately (through the agency of God).

(iii) The conception of existence in another world has already been referred to in what has just been said. But Kant actually approaches the postulate of immortality through a consideration of the first element of the perfect good, namely virtue.

The moral law commands us to promote the *summum bonum*, which is the necessary object of the rational will. This does not mean that the moral law commands us to pursue virtue because it causes happiness. But we are commanded by the practical reason to pursue virtue which causes happiness. Now, the virtue which we are commanded to strive after is, according to Kant, the complete accordance of will and feeling with the moral law. But this complete accordance with the moral law is holiness, and this is 'a perfection of which no rational being of the sensible world is capable at any moment of its existence'.[57] If, therefore, perfect virtue is commanded by reason in its practical use, and if at the same time it is not attainable by a human being at any given moment, the first element of the perfect good must be realized in the form of an indefinite, unending progress towards the ideal. 'But this endless progress is possible only on the supposition of the unending duration of the existence and personality of the same rational being, which is called the immortality of the soul.'[58] As, therefore, the attainment of the first element of the *summum bonum*, the pursuit of which is commanded by the moral law, is possible only on the supposition that the soul is immortal, immortality of the soul is a postulate of the pure practical reason. It is not demonstrable by reason in its theoretical use, which can show only that immortality is not logically impossible. But as the idea of immortality is inseparably connected with the moral law, immortality must be postulated. To deny it is, in the long run, to deny the moral law itself.

A variety of objections have been brought against Kant's doctrine about the second postulate. It has been objected, for instance, that he contradicts himself. On the one hand, the attainment of virtue must be possible; for it is commanded by the practical reason. If, therefore, it is not attainable in this life, there must be another life in which it is attainable. On the other hand, it is never attainable, either in this life or in any other. There is only unending progress towards an unattainable ideal. It seems, therefore, that the moral law commands the impossible. It has also been objected that we cannot regard the attainment of holiness as a command of the moral law. But, whatever may be the cogency of these objections, Kant himself laid considerable stress on the idea of the moral law commanding holiness as an ideal goal. In his opinion, denial of this command involves a degradation of the moral law, a lowering of standards to fit the weakness of human nature.

(iv) The same moral law which leads us to postulate immortality as the condition of obeying the command to attain holiness leads us also to postulate the existence of God as the condition for a necessary synthetic connection between virtue and happiness.

Happiness is described by Kant as 'the state of a rational being in the world with whom in the totality of his existence *everything goes according to his wish and will*'.[59] It depends, therefore, on the harmony of physical Nature with man's wish and will. But the rational being who is in the world is not the author of the world, nor is he in a position to govern Nature in such a way that a necessary connection is established in fact between virtue and happiness, the latter being proportioned to the former. If, therefore, there is an *a priori* synthetic connection between virtue and happiness, in the sense that happiness ought to follow and be proportioned to virtue as its condition, we must postulate 'the existence of a cause of the whole of Nature which is distinct from Nature and which contains the ground of this connection, namely of the exact harmony of happiness with morality'.[60]

Further, this being must be conceived as apportioning happiness to morality according to the conception of law. For happiness is to be apportioned to morality in the sense that it is to be apportioned according to the degree in which finite rational beings make the moral law the determining principle of their volition. But a being which is capable of acting according to the conception of law is intelligent or rational; and his causality will be his will. Hence the being which is postulated as the cause of Nature must be conceived as acting by intelligence and will. It must, in other words, be conceived as God. Further, we must conceive God as omniscient, as He is conceived as knowing all our inner states; as omnipotent, because He is conceived as capable of bringing into existence a world in which happiness is exactly proportioned to virtue; and so on with other attributes.

Kant reminds us that he is not now affirming what he denied in the first *Critique*, namely that the speculative reason can demonstrate the existence and attributes of God. The admission of God's existence is, of course, an admission by the reason; but this admission is an act of faith. We may speak of it as practical faith as it is connected with duty. We have a duty to promote the *summum bonum*. We can therefore postulate its possibility. But we cannot really conceive the possibility of the perfect good being realized except on the supposition that there exists a God. Hence, though the moral law does not directly enjoin faith in God, it lies at the basis of such faith.

(v) As Kant notes, the three postulates have this in common, that 'they all proceed from the principle of morality, which is not a postulate but a law'.[61] The question arises, however, whether they can be said to extend our knowledge. Kant answers, 'Certainly, but *only from a practical point of view*'.[62] And the customary statement of his view is that the postulates increase our knowledge, not from the theoretical, but only from the practical point of view. But it is by no means immediately clear what is meant by this. If Kant meant merely that it is pragmatically useful, in the sense of morally beneficial, to act as if we were free, as if we had immortal souls, and as if there were a God, his view, whether we agreed with it or not, would present no great difficulty, so far as understanding it was concerned. But in point of fact he appears to mean much more than this.

We are told, indeed, that inasmuch as neither free, immortal soul nor God are given as objects of intuition, 'there is, therefore, no extension of the knowledge *of given supersensible objects*'.[63] This seems to be pretty well a tautology. For if God and the soul are not given as objects, we obviously cannot know them as given objects. But we are also told that though God and the free, immortal soul are not given as objects of any intellectual intuition, the theoretical reason's knowledge of the supersensible is increased to this extent that it is compelled to admit 'that there are such objects'.[64] Further, given the practical reason's assurance of the existence of God and the soul, the theoretical reason can think these supersensible realities by means of the categories; and the latter, when so applied, are 'not empty but possess meaning'.[65] To be sure, Kant insists that the categories can be employed to conceive the supersensible in a definite manner 'only in so far as it is defined by such predicates as are necessarily connected with the pure practical purpose given *a priori* and with its possibility'.[66] But the fact remains that through the aid provided by the practical reason Ideas which for the speculative reason were simply regulative take on definite form and shape as ways of thinking supersensible realities, even if these realities are not given as objects of intuition but are affirmed because of their connection with the moral law.

It seems to me, therefore, to be arguable that what Kant is doing is to substitute a new type of metaphysics for the metaphysics which he rejected in the *Critique of Pure Reason*. In the case of the Ideas of a transcendental ego and of God the speculative reason is able to give body to them, as it were, thanks to the practical reason. And this is possible because the latter enjoys a position of primacy when the two co-operate.[67] 'If practical reason could not assume and think as given anything other than that which *speculative* reason can offer it from its own insight, then the latter would have the primacy. But if we suppose that practical reason has of itself original *a priori* principles with which certain theoretical positions are inseparably united, though they are at the same time withdrawn from any possible insight of the speculative reason (which they, however, must not contradict), then the question is, which interest is the superior (not which must give way, for they do not necessarily conflict). . . .'[68] That is to say, the question is whether the interest of speculative reason is to prevail, so that it obstinately rejects all that is offered from any other source than itself, or whether the interest of practical reason is to prevail, so that speculative reason takes over, as it were, the propositions offered it by the practical reason and tries 'to unite them with its own concepts'.[69] In Kant's opinion, the interest of practical reason should prevail. To be sure, this cannot be maintained if practical reason is taken as dependent on sensible inclinations and desires. For in this case speculative reason would have to adopt all sorts of arbitrary fancies. (Kant mentions Mohammed's idea of Paradise.) In other words, Kant does not wish to encourage mere wishful thinking. But if practical reason is taken as being the pure reason in its practical capacity, that is, as judging according to *a priori* principles; and if certain theoretical positions are inseparably connected with the exercise of pure reason in its practical function; then the pure reason in its theoretical capacity must accept these positions and attempt to think them consistently. If we do not accept this primacy of the practical reason, we admit a conflict within reason itself; for pure practical and pure speculative reason are fundamentally one reason.

That Kant is really engaged in creating a metaphysics based on the moral consciousness seems to me to be clear also from the fact that he appears to admit differences of degree in practical knowledge. The idea of freedom is so united with the concepts of moral law and duty that we cannot admit obligation and deny freedom. 'I ought' implies 'I can' (that is, I can obey or disobey). But we cannot say that the conception of the *summum bonum* or perfect good implies the existence of God in precisely the same way that obligation implies freedom. Reason cannot decide with absolute certainty whether the apportioning of happiness to virtue implies the existence of God. That is to say, it cannot exclude absolutely the possibility that a state of affairs which would render possible this apportioning might come about by the operation of natural laws without the supposition of a wise and good Creator. There is room, therefore, for choice; that is, for practical faith resting on an act of the will. True, we cannot 'demonstrate' freedom, and so it is in a sense an object of belief. But the fact remains that we cannot accept the existence of the moral law and deny freedom whereas it is possible to accept the existence of the moral law and doubt the existence of God, even if faith in God's existence is more in accordance with the demands of reason.

It would be misleading, therefore, to say simply that Kant rejects metaphysics. True, he rejects dogmatic metaphysics when it is considered either as an *a priori* construction based on *a priori* theoretical principles or as a kind of prolongation or extension of scientific explanation of phenomena. But even if he does not call the general theory of the postulates 'metaphysics', this is what it really amounts to. It is a metaphysics based on the moral consciousness of law and obligation. It does not provide us with an intuition of supersensible reality, and its arguments are conditional on the validity of the moral consciousness and on the Kantian analysis of moral experience. But there are, none the less, reasoned positions in regard to supersensible reality. And we can quite properly speak about a Kantian 'metaphysics'.

11. We have seen that morality, according to Kant, does not presuppose religion. That is to say, man does not need the idea of God to be able to recognize his duty; and the ultimate motive of moral action is duty for duty's sake, not obedience to the commands of God. At the same time morality leads to religion. 'Through the idea of the supreme good as object and final end of the pure practical reason the moral law leads to religion, that is, to the recognition of all duties as divine commands, *not as sanctions, that is, as arbitrary commands of an alien will which are contingent in themselves*, but as essential *laws* of every free will in itself, which, however, must be looked on as commands of the supreme Being, because it is only from a morally perfect (holy and good) and at the same time all-powerful will, and consequently only through harmony with this will, that we can hope to attain the highest good, which the moral law makes it our duty to take as the object of our endeavour.'[70] The moral law commands us to make ourselves worthy of happiness rather than to be happy or make ourselves happy. But because virtue should produce happiness, and because this completion of the *summum bonum* can be achieved only through divine agency, we are entitled to hope for happiness through the agency of a God whose will, as a holy will, desires that His creatures should be worthy of happiness, while, as an omnipotent will, it can confer this happiness on them. '*The hope* of happiness first begins with religion only.'[71]

This point of view reappears in *Religion within the Bounds of Pure Reason* (1793). Thus the preface to the first edition opens in this way. 'Morality, in so far as it is grounded in the concept of man as a being who is free but at the same time subjects himself through his reason to unconditional laws, needs neither the idea of another being above man for the latter to recognize his duty, nor any other motive than the law itself for man to fulfil his duty.'[72] At the same time, however, the question of the final result of moral action and of a possible harmonization between the moral and the natural orders cannot be a matter of indifference to the human reason. And in the long run 'morality leads inevitably to religion'.[73] For we cannot see any other way in which this harmonization could take place than through divine agency.

True religion, for Kant, consists in this, 'that in all our duties we regard God as the universal legislator who is to be reverenced'.[74] But what does it mean to reverence God? It means obeying the moral law, acting for the sake of duty. In other words, Kant attached little value to religious practices in the sense of expressions of adoration and prayer, whether public or private. And this attitude is summed up in the often-quoted words: 'Everything which, apart from a moral way of life, man believes himself capable of doing to please God is mere religious delusion and spurious worship of God.'[75]

This indifference to religious practices in the ordinary sense is coupled, of course, with an indifference to credal varieties as such. The word 'as such' are, I think, required. For some beliefs would be ruled out as incompatible with true morality, while others would be inacceptable to pure reason. But any idea of a unique revelation of religious truths, and still more of an authoritarian Church as custodian and accredited interpreter of revelation, is rejected by Kant. I do not mean that he rejected altogether the idea of a visible Christian Church, with a faith based on the Scriptures; for he did not. But the visible Church is for him only an approximation to the ideal of the universal invisible Church, which is, or would be, the spiritual union of all men in virtue and the moral service of God.

It is not my intention to discuss Kant's treatment of individual dogmas of Christianity.[76] But it is perhaps worth noting that he shows a strong tendency to strip away, as it were, the historical associations of certain dogmas and to find a meaning which fits in with his own philosophy. Thus he does not deny original sin: on the contrary, he affirms it against those who imagine that man is naturally perfect. But the ideas of an historical Fall and of inherited sin give place to the conception of a fundamental propensity to act out of mere self-love and without regard to the universal moral laws, a propensity which is an empirical fact and of which we cannot provide an ultimate explanation, though the Bible does so in picture-language. In this way Kant affirms the dogma in the sense that he verbally admits it, while at the same time he interprets it rationalistically in such a way that he is able to deny on the one hand the extreme Protestant doctrine of the total depravity of human nature and on the other the optimistic theories of the natural perfection of man. This tendency to retain Christian dogmas while giving a rationalistic account of their content becomes much more evident with Hegel. But the latter, with his reasoned distinction between the ways of thinking characteristic of religion and of philosophy, produced a much more profound philosophy of religion than that of Kant.

We can say, therefore, that Kant's interpretation of religion was moralistic and rationalistic in character. At the same time this statement can be misleading. For it may suggest that in the content of true religion as Kant understands it every element of what we may call piety towards God is missing. But this is not the case. He does, indeed, show scant sympathy with mystics; but we have already seen that for him religion means looking on our duties as divine commands (in the sense at least that the fulfilment of them fits into the end which is willed by the holy will of God as the final end of creation). And in the *Opus Postumum* the conception of consciousness of duty as a consciousness of the divine presence comes to the fore. To be sure, it is impossible to know how Kant would have systematized and developed the various ideas contained in the notes which form this volume, if he had had the opportunity to do so. But it appears that though the idea of the moral law as the one valid path to faith in God was retained intact, Kant was inclined to lay greater stress on the immanence of God and on an awareness of our moral freedom and of moral obligation as an awareness of the divine presence.

12. It cannot be denied, I think, that there is a certain grandeur in Kant's ethical theory. His uncompromising exaltation of duty and his insistence on the value of the human personality certainly merit respect. Moreover, a great deal of what he says finds a genuine echo in the moral consciousness. Thus, however much particular moral convictions may differ in different people, the conviction that cases arise when in some sense at least consequences are irrelevant and the moral law must be obeyed, whatever the consequences may be, is a common feature of the moral consciousness. If we have any moral convictions at all, we all feel, to use popular language, that the line must be drawn somewhere, even if we do not all draw it in the same place. The maxim *Fiat*

iustitia, ruat coelum can easily be understood in terms of the ordinary man's moral outlook. Again, Kant rightly drew attention to the universal character of the moral law. The fact that different societies and different individuals have had somewhat different moral ideas does not alter the fact that the moral judgment makes, as such, a universal claim. When I say that I ought to do this or that, I imply at least that anyone else in precisely the same situation ought to act likewise; for I am saying that it is the right thing to do. Even if one adopts an 'emotive' theory of ethics, one must allow for this universal claim of the moral judgment. The statement that I ought to perform action X is obviously, in this as in other respects, of a different type from the statement that I like olives, even if the former is held to be the expression of an emotion or of an attitude rather than of the application of a supreme principle of reason.[77]

At the same time, even if Kant's ethical theory reflects to some extent the moral consciousness, it is open to serious objections. It is easy to understand how Hegel among others criticized Kant's account of the supreme principle of morality on the ground of formalism and abstractness. Of course, from one point of view objections against Kant's ethical theory on the ground of formalism and 'emptiness' are beside the mark. For in pure, as distinct from applied, ethics he was engaged precisely in ascertaining the 'formal' element in the moral judgment, prescinding from the empirically given 'matter'. And what else, it may be pertinently asked, could the formal element possibly be but formalistic? Again, what is the value of the charge of emptiness when the categorical imperative, though applicable to empirically given material, was never intended to be a premiss for the deduction of concrete rules of conduct by sheer analysis? The categorical imperative is meant to serve as a test or criterion of the morality of our subjective principles of volition, not as a premiss for analytic deduction of a concrete moral code. True; but then the question arises whether the Kantian principle of morality is really capable of serving as a test or criterion. We have already noted the difficulty that there is in understanding precisely what is meant by speaking of a rational agent as 'being able' or 'not being able' to will that his maxims should become universal laws. And it may well be that this difficulty is connected with the abstractness and emptiness of the categorical imperative.

Some philosophers would object to Kant's rationalism, to

the idea, that is to say, that the moral law rests ultimately on reason and that its supreme principles are promulgated by the reason. But let us assume that Kant was right in his view that the moral law is promulgated by reason. The question then arises whether, as he thought, the concept of duty possesses an absolute primacy or whether the concept of the good is primary, the concept of duty being subordinate to it. And, apart from any other consideration, it is arguable that the second of these theories is better able to serve as a framework for interpreting the moral consciousness. True, any teleological theory of ethics which takes the form of the utilitarianism of, for example, Bentham, lays itself open to the charge of changing the specifically moral judgment into a non-moral empirical judgment, and so of explaining morals by explaining it away. But it does not follow that this must be true of every teleological interpretation of morals. And the question whether it does or does not follow can hardly be regarded as having been finally settled by Kant.

As for Kant's philosophy of religion, it stands in certain obvious ways under the influence of the Enlightenment. Thus in interpreting the religious consciousness Kant attaches too little importance to the historical religions; that is, to religion as it has actually existed. Hegel afterwards attempted to remedy this defect. But, generally considered, the Kantian philosophy of religion is clearly a feature of his attempt to reconcile the world of Newtonian physics, the world of empirical reality governed by causal laws which exclude freedom, with the world of the moral consciousness, the world of freedom. The theoretical reason, of itself, can tell us only that it sees no impossibility in the concept of freedom and in the idea of supra-empirical, noumenal reality. The concept of the moral law, through its inseparable connection with the idea of freedom, gives us a practical assurance of the existence of such a reality and of our belonging to it as rational beings. And theoretical reason, on the basis of this assurance, can attempt to think noumenal reality so far as the practical reason warrants our assuming it. But, so far as we can see, it is God alone who is capable of achieving the ultimate harmonization of the two realms. If, therefore, the 'interest' of practical reason should prevail, and if the moral law demands, at least by implication, this ultimate harmonization, we are justified in making an act of faith in God, even if reason in its theoretical function is incapable of demonstrating that God exists.

But though we are entitled to turn to religion and to hope from God the creation of a state of affairs in which happiness will be apportioned to virtue, it is obvious that we are left here and now with a juxtaposition of the realm of natural necessity and that of freedom. Inasmuch as reason tells us that there is no logical impossibility in the latter, we can say that the two are logically compatible. But this is hardly enough to satisfy the demands of philosophical reflection. For one thing, freedom finds expression in actions which belong to the empirical, natural order. And the mind seeks to find some connection between the two orders or realms. It may not, indeed, be able to find an objective connection in the sense that it can prove theoretically the existence of noumenal reality and show precisely how empirical and noumenal reality are objectively related. But it seeks at least a subjective connection in the sense of a justification, on the side of the mind itself, of the transition from the way of thinking which is in accordance with the principles of Nature to the way of thinking which is in accordance with the principles of freedom.

To find, however, Kant's treatment of this subject we have to turn to the third *Critique*, namely the *Critique of Judgment*.

Chapter Fifteen

KANT (6): AESTHETICS AND TELEOLOGY

The mediating function of judgment – The analytic of the beautiful – The analytic of the sublime – The deduction of pure aesthetic judgments – Fine art and genius – The dialectic of the aesthetic judgment – The beautiful as a symbol of the morally good – The teleological judgment – Teleology and mechanism – Physico-theology and ethico-theology.

1. At the end of the last chapter mention was made of the need for some principle of connection, at least on the side of the mind, between the world of natural necessity and the world of freedom. Kant refers to this need in his introduction to the *Critique of Judgment*.[1] Between the domain of the concept of Nature or sensible reality and the domain of the concept of freedom or supersensible reality there is a gulf of such a kind that no transition from the first to the second is possible by means of the theoretical use of reason. It appears, therefore, that there are two sundered worlds, of which the one can have no influence on the other. Yet the world of freedom must have an influence on the world of Nature, if the principles of practical reason are to be realized in action. And it must, therefore, be possible to think Nature in such a way that it is compatible at least with the possibility of the attainment in it of ends in accordance with the laws of freedom. Accordingly, there must be some ground or principle of unity which 'makes possible the transition from the way of thinking which is in accordance with the principles of the one (world) to the way of thinking which is in accordance with the principles of the other'.[2] In other words, we are looking for a connecting link between theoretical philosophy, which Kant calls the philosophy of Nature, and practical or moral philosophy which is grounded on the concept of freedom. And Kant finds this connecting link in a critique of judgment which is 'a means to unite in one whole the two parts of philosophy'.[3]

To explain why Kant turns to a study of judgment in order to find this connecting link, reference must be made to his theory of the powers or faculties of the mind. In a table given at the end of the introduction to the *Critique of Judgment*[4] he distinguishes three powers or faculties of the mind.[5] These are the cognitive faculty in general, the power of feeling pleasure and displeasure, and the faculty of desire. This suggests at once that feeling mediates in some sense between cognition and desire. He then distinguishes three particular cognitive powers, namely understanding (*Verstand*), judgment (*Urteilskraft*), and reason (*Vernunft*). And this suggests that judgment mediates in some sense between understanding and reason, and that it bears some relation to feeling.

Now, in the *Critique of Pure Reason* we have considered the *a priori* categories and principles of the understanding, which exercise a 'constitutive' function and make possible a knowledge of objects, of Nature. We also considered the Ideas of pure reason in its speculative capacity, which exercise a 'regulative' and not a constitutive function. In the *Critique of Practical Reason* it has been shown that there is an *a priori* principle of pure reason in its practical employment, which legislates for desire (*in Ansehung des Begehrungsvermögens*).[6] It remains, therefore, to inquire whether the power of judgment, which is said by Kant to be a mediating power between the understanding and the reason, possesses its own *a priori* principles. If so, we must also inquire whether these principles exercise a constitutive or a regulative function. In particular, do they give rules *a priori* to feeling; that is, to the power of feeling pleasure and displeasure? If so, we shall have a nice, tidy scheme. The understanding gives laws *a priori* to phenomenal reality, making possible a theoretical knowledge of Nature. The pure reason, in its practical employment, legislates with regard to desire. And judgment legislates for feeling, which is, as it were, a middle term between cognition and desire, just as judgment itself mediates between understanding and reason.

In the technical terms of the critical philosophy, therefore, the problem can be stated in such a way as to throw into relief the similarity of purpose in the three *Critiques*. Has the power of judgment its own *a priori* principle or principles? And, if so, what are their functions and field of application? Further, if the power or faculty of judgment is related, in regard to its *a priori* principles, to feeling in a manner analogous to the ways in which understanding is related to cognition and reason (in its practical employment) to desire, we can see that the *Critique of Judgment* forms a necessary part of the critical philosophy, and not simply an appendage which might or might not be there.

But what does Kant mean by judgment in this context? 'The faculty of judgment in general', he tells us, 'is the power of thinking the particular as being contained in the universal.'[7] But we must distinguish between determinant and reflective judgment. 'If the universal (the rule, the principle, the law) is given, then the faculty of judgment which subsumes the particular under it is *determinant*, this being true also when the faculty as a transcendental faculty of judgment gives *a priori* the conditions under which alone the particular can be subsumed under the universal. But if only the particular is given, for which the faculty of judgment is to find the universal, then judgment is merely *reflective*.'[8] In considering the *Critique of Pure Reason* we saw that there are, according to Kant, *a priori* categories and principles of the understanding which are ultimately given in the structure of this faculty. And judgment simply subsumes particulars under these 'universals' as under something given *a priori*. This is an example of *determinant* judgment. But there are obviously many general laws which are not given but have to be discovered. Thus the empirical laws of physics are not given *a priori*. Nor are they given *a posteriori* in the sense in which particulars are given. We know *a priori*, for instance, that all phenomena are members of causal series; but we do not know particular causal laws *a priori*. Nor are they given to us *a posteriori* as objects of experience. We have to discover the general empirical laws under which we subsume particulars. This is the work of *reflective* judgment, the function of which, therefore, is not merely subsumptive; for it has to find the universal, as Kant puts it, under which the particulars can be subsumed. And it is with this reflective judgment that we are concerned here.

Now, from our point of view at least empirical laws are contingent. But the scientist is always trying to subsume more particular under more general empirical laws. He does not leave his laws alongside one another, so to speak, without endeavouring to establish relations between them. He aims at constructing a system of interrelated laws. And this means that he is guided in his inquiry by the concept of Nature as an intelligible unity. The *a priori* principles of science are grounded in our understanding. But 'the special empirical laws . . . must be considered . . . as if (*als ob*) an understanding which is not ours had given them for our powers of cognition, to make possible a system of experience according to special laws of nature'.[9] Kant adds that he does not intend to imply that the scientist must presuppose the existence of God. What he means is that the scientist presupposes a unity of Nature of such a kind as would obtain if Nature were the work of a divine mind; if, that is to say, it were an intelligible system adapted to our cognitive faculties. The idea of God is here employed simply in its regulative function. And Kant's point is really simply this, that all scientific inquiry is guided by the at least tacit assumption that Nature is an intelligible unity, 'intelligible' being understood in relation to our cognitive faculties. It is on this principle that reflective judgment proceeds. It is an *a priori* principle in the sense that it is not derived from experience but is a presupposition of all scientific inquiry. But it is not an *a priori* principle in precisely the same sense that the principles considered in the *Transcendental Analytic* are *a priori*. That is to say, it is not a necessary condition for there being objects of experience at all. Rather is it a necessary *heuristic* principle which guides us in our study of the objects of experience.

The concept of Nature as unified through the common ground of its laws in a superhuman intelligence or mind which adapts the system to our cognitive faculties is the concept of the purposiveness or finality of Nature. 'Through this concept Nature is represented as though an intelligence contained the ground of the unity of the manifold of Nature's empirical laws. The purposiveness of Nature is thus a special *a priori* concept which has its ultimate source in the faculty of reflective judgment.'[10] And the principle of the purposiveness or finality of Nature is, Kant maintains, a transcendental principle of the faculty or power of judgment. It is transcendental because it concerns possible objects of empirical knowledge in general and does not itself rest on empirical observation. Its transcendental character becomes evident, according to Kant, if we consider the maxims of judgment to which it gives rise. Among the examples given[11] are 'Nature takes the shortest way' (*lex parsimoniae*) and 'Nature makes no leaps' (*lex continui in natura*). Such maxims are not empirical generalizations; rather are they *a priori* rules or maxims which guide us in our empirical investigation of Nature. And they rest on the general *a priori* principle of the purposiveness or finality of Nature; that is, of the latter's being adapted to our cognitive faculties in respect of the ultimate unity of its empirical laws.

The validity of this *a priori* principle of judgment is subjective rather than objective. In Kantian terminology it does not prescribe to or legislate for Nature considered in itself. It is not a constitutive principle in the sense of a necessary condition for there being any objects at all. And it does not entail the proposition that there is, in an ontological sense, finality in Nature. We cannot deduce from it *a priori* that there actually are final causes operating in Nature. It legislates for the reflective judgment, telling it to regard Nature as though it were a purposive whole, adapted to our cognitive faculties. And if we say that the principle makes Nature possible, we mean that it makes possible an empirical knowledge of Nature in regard to its empirical laws, not that it makes Nature possible in the same sense in which the categories and principles of the understanding make it possible. Of course, the principle is, in a real sense, empirically verified. But in itself it is *a priori*, not the result of observation; and, as an *a priori* principle, it is a necessary condition, not of objects themselves, which are considered as already given, but of the employment of reflective judgment in investigating these objects. Kant is not, therefore, enunciating a metaphysical dogma, namely that there are final causes operating in Nature. He is saying that, because reflective judgment is what it is, all empirical inquiry into Nature involves from the start regarding Nature *as though* it embodied a system of empirical laws which are unified through their common ground in an intelligence other than ours and which are adapted to our cognitive faculties.

Of course, we cannot regard Nature as purposive without attributing purposiveness or finality to Nature. Kant is quite well aware of this fact. 'But that the order of Nature in its particular laws, in this at least possible variety and heterogeneity which transcend our power of comprehension, is yet really adapted to our power of cognition, is, as far as we can discern, a contingent fact. And the discovery of this order is a task of the understanding, a task which is carried out with a view to a necessary end of the understanding, namely the unification of the principles of Nature. And the power of judgment must, then, attribute this end to Nature, because the understanding cannot prescribe any law to Nature in this respect.'[12] But the *a priori* attribution to Nature of finality or purposiveness does not constitute an *a priori* dogma about Nature in itself; it is an attribution with a view to our knowledge. In other words, the *a priori* principle of judgment is, as has already been said, a heuristic principle. If we then find in our empirical investigation that Nature fits in with this principle, this is, as far as we can see, a purely contingent fact. That it *must* fit, is an *a priori* assumption, a heuristic principle of judgment.

Now, the finality or purposiveness of Nature can be represented in two ways. In the first place the finality of a given object of experience can be represented as an accordance of the form of the object with the cognitive faculty, without, however, any reference of the form to a concept with a view to determinate knowledge of the object. The form of the object is considered as the ground of a pleasure which comes from the representation of the object. And when we judge that the representation is necessarily accompanied by this pleasure and that, as a consequence, the representation should be pleasurable for all (and not merely for the particular subject who happens here and now to perceive the form of the object), we have an aesthetic judgment. The object is called beautiful, and the faculty of judging universally on the basis of the pleasure which accompanies the representation is called taste.

In the second place the finality of a given object of experience can be represented as an 'accordance of its form with the possibility of the thing itself, according to a concept of the thing which precedes and contains the ground of its form'.[13] In other words, the thing is represented, in respect of its form, as fulfilling an end or purpose of Nature. And when we judge that this is the case, we have a teleological judgment.

A *Critique of Judgment*, therefore, must pay attention to both the aesthetic and the teleological judgment, distinguishing them carefully. The former is purely subjective, not in the sense that there is no universal claim in the judgment (for there is), but in the sense that it is a judgment about the accordance of the form of an object, whether a natural object or a work of art, with the cognitive faculties on the basis of the feeling caused by the representation of the object and not with reference to any concept. Kant can say, therefore, that the faculty of judging aesthetically is 'a special power of judging things according to a rule, but not according to concepts'.[14] The teleological judgment, however, is objective in the sense that it judges that a given object fulfils a conceived purpose or end of Nature, and not that it is the ground of certain feelings in the subject. And Kant tells us that the power of making such judgments is 'not a special power but simply reflective judgment in general. . . .'[15]

Finally, reflective judgment's *a priori*, regulative concept of the purposiveness of Nature serves as a connecting link between the domain of the concept of Nature on the one hand and the domain of the concept of freedom on the other. For although it neither constitutes Nature, in the sense that the categories and principles of the understanding constitute Nature, nor legislates with a view to action, as does the *a priori* principle of pure practical reason, it enables us to think Nature as not being entirely alien, as it were, to the realization of ends. Works of art are phenomenal expressions of the noumenal realm of value; and the beauty which aesthetic appreciation of such works enables us to see in natural objects enables us to regard Nature itself as a phenomenal manifestation of the same noumenal reality, which Kant sometimes calls the 'supersensible substrate'.[16] And the concept of the purposiveness of Nature, which finds expression in the teleological judgment, enables us to conceive the possibility of an actualization of ends in Nature in harmony with the latter's laws.

Kant also puts the matter in this way. A study of the *a priori* principles of the understanding shows that we know Nature only as phenomenon. But at the same time it implies that there is a noumenal reality or 'supersensible reality'. Understanding, however, leaves the latter completely undetermined. As we saw when we considered the concepts of phenomenon and noumenon in connection with the first *Critique*, the term *noumenon* must be taken in its negative sense. Judgment, in virtue of its *a priori* principle for judging Nature, leads us to consider noumenal reality on the 'supersensible substrate', as well within as outside us, as determinable by means of the intellectual faculty. For it represents Nature as being a phenomenal expression of noumenal reality. And reason, by its *a priori* practical law, determines noumenal reality, showing us how we should conceive it. 'And thus the faculty of judgment makes possible the transition from the domain of the concept of Nature to that of the concept of freedom.'[17]

This section has been devoted to lines of thought which are outlined by Kant in his introduction to the *Critique of*

Judgment. The main body of the work falls into two parts, the first dealing with aesthetic, the second with teleological judgment. And it is, of course, in these two parts that the main interest of the work lies. But once one turns to the detailed treatment of, for instance, the aesthetic judgment, one is tempted to consider it simply as Kant's aesthetic theory, that is, purely for its own sake, as though it were an isolated part of his philosophy. For this reason it seemed to me appropriate to dwell at some length on the lines of thought which, however involved they may be, at any rate serve to show that the third *Critique* was for Kant an integral part of his system and not a combination of two monographs dealing with subjects interesting in themselves but without intrinsic relation to the first two *Critiques*.

2. Following the usage of English writers on aesthetic, Kant called the judgment which pronounces a thing to be beautiful the judgment of taste (*das Geschmacksurteil*). The word 'taste' immediately suggests subjectivity; and we have already seen that in Kant's view the ground of this judgment is subjective. That is to say, a representation is referred by the imagination to the subject itself, to the feeling of pleasure or displeasure. The ground of our judgment that a thing is beautiful or ugly is the way in which our power of feeling is affected by the representation of the object. In modern language we might say that for Kant the judgment of taste is an emotive proposition, expressing feeling and not conceptual knowledge. As Kant observes, conceptual knowledge about a building is one thing; appreciation of its beauty is another.

But though the ground of the judgment of taste is subjective, what we actually say is obviously something about the thing, namely that it is beautiful. The ground for the statement consists in feeling; but when I say that an object is beautiful I am not simply making a statement about my private feelings. For such a statement would be an empirically verifiable (in principle at least) psychological judgment. It would not be a judgment of taste as such. The latter arises only when I pronounce a thing to be beautiful. There is room, therefore, for an analytic of the beautiful (*Analytik des Schönen*), even though beauty cannot be regarded as an objective quality of an object without relation to the subjective ground of the judgment that the object is beautiful.

Kant's analytic of the beautiful takes the form of a study of what he calls four 'moments' of the judgment of taste. Rather oddly perhaps these four moments are correlated with the four logical forms of judgment, namely quality, quantity, relation and modality. I say 'rather oddly perhaps', because the judgment of taste is not itself a logical judgment, even though, according to Kant, it involves a reference or relation to the understanding. However, the study of each moment of the judgment of taste results in a partial definition of the beautiful. We are given, as it were, four complementary elucidations of the meaning of the term 'beautiful'. And Kant's discussion of the theme is of some interest for its own sake, quite apart from the correlation of the four moments with the four logical forms of judgment.

Consideration of the judgment of taste from the standpoint of quality leads us to the following definition of the beautiful. 'Taste is the power of judging of an object or of a way of representing it through an *entirely disinterested* satisfaction or dissatisfaction. The object of such a satisfaction is called *beautiful*.'[18] By saying that aesthetic appreciation is 'entirely disinterested' (*ohne alles Interesse*) Kant does not mean, of course, that it is boring: he means that it is contemplative. In terms of the theory of taste the aesthetic judgment implies that the object which is called beautiful causes satisfaction without reference to desire, to the appetitive faculty. A simple example is sufficient to convey an idea of what Kant means. Suppose that I look at a painting of fruit and say that it is beautiful. If I mean that I should like to eat the fruit, were it real, thus relating it to appetite, my judgment would not be a judgment of taste in the technical sense, that is, an aesthetic judgment; and I should be misusing the word 'beautiful'. The aesthetic judgment implies that the form of the thing is pleasing precisely as an object of contemplation, without any reference to appetite or desire.

Kant distinguishes between the pleasant (*das Angenehme*), the beautiful (*das Schöne*) and the good (*das Gute*) as designating three relations in which representations can stand to the feelings of pleasure and displeasure or pain. The pleasant is that which gratifies inclination or desire, and it is experienced by animals as well as by men. The good is the object of esteem: it is that to which objective worth is attributed. And it concerns all rational beings, including rational beings, if there are any, which are not human beings; that is, which have no bodies. The beautiful is that which simply pleases, without any intrinsic reference to inclination or desire. It is experienced only by rational beings, but not by all. That is to say, it involves sense-perception and so concerns only those rational beings which possess bodies.

Further, the aesthetic judgment, according to Kant, is indifferent to existence. If to take the simple example given above, I relate the painted fruit to my appetite or desire, I am interested in its existence, in the sense that I wish that the fruit were real, so that I could eat it. But if I contemplate it aesthetically, the fact that the fruit is represented fruit and not existent, eatable fruit is entirely irrelevant.

Finally, Kant points out that when he speaks of the aesthetic judgment as entirely disinterested, he does not mean to say that it cannot or that it ought not to be accompanied by any interest. In society men certainly have an interest in communicating the pleasure which they feel in aesthetic experience. And Kant calls this an empirical interest in the beautiful. But interest, though it may accompany or be combined with the judgment of taste, is not its determining ground. Considered in itself, the judgment is disinterested.

Turning to the study of the judgment of taste according to quantity, we find Kant defining the beautiful as 'that which pleases universally, without a concept'.[19] And we can consider these two characteristics separately.

The fact, already established, that the beautiful is the object of an entirely disinterested satisfaction implies that it is the object, or ought to be the object, of a universal satisfaction. Suppose that I am conscious that my judgment that a given statue is beautiful is entirely disinterested. This means that I am conscious that my judgment is not dependent on any private conditions peculiar to myself. In pronouncing my judgment I am 'free', as Kant puts it, neither impelled by desire on the one hand nor dictated to by the moral imperative on the other.[20] And I therefore believe that I have reason for attributing to others a satisfaction similar to that which I experience in myself; for the satisfaction is not grounded in the gratification of my private inclinations. Accordingly, I speak of the statue as if beauty were an objective characteristic of it.

Kant distinguishes, therefore, in respect to universality, between a judgment concerning the pleasant and a judgment concerning the beautiful. If I say that the taste of olives is pleasant, I am quite prepared for someone to say, 'Well, you may find it pleasant, but I find it unpleasant'. For I recognize that my statement was based on private feeling or taste, and that *de gustibus non est disputandum*. But if I say that a certain work of art is beautiful, I tacitly claim, according to Kant, that it is beautiful for all. I claim, that is to say, that the judgment is based, not upon purely private feelings, so that it has validity only for myself, but upon feelings which I either attribute to others or demand of them. We must distinguish, therefore, between the judgment of taste in Kant's technical use of the term and judgments which we might normally be inclined to call judgments of taste. In making the former judgment we claim universal validity, but in the second class of judgments we do not. And it is only the first type of judgment which is concerned with the beautiful.

Naturally, Kant does not mean to imply that when someone calls a statue beautiful, he necessarily believes that all, as a matter of fact, judge it to be beautiful. He means that by making the judgment a man claims that others should recognize the statue's beauty. For, being conscious that his judgment is 'free' in the sense mentioned above, he either attributes to others a satisfaction similar to his own or claims that they should experience it.

What sort of claim or demand is this? We cannot prove logically to others that an object is beautiful. For the claim of universal validity which we make on behalf of an aesthetic judgment does not have any reference to the cognitive faculty, but only to the feeling of pleasure and pain in every subject. In Kant's terminology, the judgment does not rest upon any concept: it rests upon feeling. We cannot, therefore, make good our claim to the universal validity of the judgment by any process of logical argument. We can only persuade others to look again, and to look with more attention, at the object, confident that in the end their feelings will speak for themselves and that they will concur with our judgment. When we make the judgment, we believe that we speak, as it were, with a universal voice, and we claim the assent of others; but they will give this assent only on the basis of their own feelings, not in virtue of any concepts which we adduce. 'We may now see that in the judgment of taste nothing is postulated but such a *universal* voice in respect of the satisfaction without the intervention of concepts.'[21] We can draw attention as much as we like to different features of the object to persuade others that it is beautiful. But the assent, if it comes, is the result of a certain satisfaction which is at last felt and does not rest on concepts.

But what is this satisfaction or pleasure of which Kant is

speaking? He tells us that it is not emotion (*Rührung*), which is 'a sensation in which pleasantness is produced only by means of a momentary checking and a consequent more powerful outflow of the vital force'.[22] Emotion in this sense is relevant to the experience of sublimity, but not to that of beauty. But to say that the satisfaction or state of pleasure which is the determining ground of the judgment of taste is not emotion is not to explain what it is. And we can ask the question in this form. What is the object of the satisfaction or pleasure of which Kant is speaking? For if we know what arouses it, what it is satisfaction at or in, we shall know of what kind of satisfaction or pleasure he is speaking.

To answer this question, we can turn to Kant's study of the third moment of the judgment of taste, corresponding to the category of relation. His discussion of this third moment results in the following definition. '*Beauty* is the form of the *purposiveness* of an object, so far as this is perceived *without any representation of a purpose*.'[23] But as the meaning of this definition is not perhaps immediately evident, some explanation is required.

The fundamental idea is not difficult to grasp. If we look at a flower, say a rose, we may have the feeling that it is, as we say, just right; we may have the feeling that its form embodies or fulfils a purpose. At the same time we do not represent to ourselves any purpose which is achieved in the rose. It is not merely that if someone asked us what purpose was embodied in the rose we should be unable to give any clear account of it: we do not conceive or represent to ourselves any purpose at all. And yet in some sense we *feel*, without concepts, that a purpose is embodied in the flower. The matter might perhaps be expressed in this way. There is a sense of meaning; but there is no conceptual representation of what is meant. There is an awareness or consciousness of finality; but there is no concept of an end which is achieved.

There can, of course, be a concept of purpose, which accompanies the experience of beauty. But Kant will not allow that a judgment of taste is 'pure' if it presupposes a concept of a purpose. He distinguishes between what he calls 'free' and 'adherent' beauty. If we judge that a flower is beautiful, we have, most probably, no concept of a purpose which is achieved in the flower. The beauty of the latter is then said to be free; and our judgment of taste is said to be pure. But when we judge that a building, say a church, is beautiful, we may have a concept of a purpose which is achieved and perfectly embodied in the building. The beauty of the latter is then said to be adherent, and our judgment is said to be impure, in the technical sense that it is not simply an expression of a feeling of satisfaction or pleasure but involves a conceptual element. An aesthetic judgment is pure only if the person who makes it has no concept of a purpose or if he abstracts from the concept, supposing that he has one, when he makes the judgment.

Kant insists upon this point because he wishes to maintain the special and unique character of the aesthetic judgment. If the latter involved a concept of objective purposiveness, of perfection, it would be 'just as much a cognitive judgment as the judgment by which something is pronounced good'.[24] But in point of fact the determining ground of the aesthetic judgment is not a concept at all, and consequently it cannot be a concept of a definite purpose. 'A judgment is called aesthetic precisely because its determining ground is not a concept but the feeling (of the inner sense) of that harmony in the play of the mental powers, so far as it can be experienced in feeling.'[25] Kant admits that we can and do form standards of beauty and that, in the case of man, we form an ideal of beauty which is at the same time a visible expression of moral ideas. But he insists that 'judgment according to such a standard can never be purely aesthetic, and that judgment according to an ideal of beauty is not a mere judgment of taste'.[26]

The fourth partial definition of beauty, derived from a consideration of the judgment of taste according to the modality of the subject's satisfaction in the object, is this. 'The *beautiful* is that which without any concept is recognized as the object of a *necessary* satisfaction.'[27]

This necessity is not a theoretical objective necessity. For if it were, I should know *a priori* that everyone will assent to my judgment of taste. And this is certainly not the case. I claim universal validity for my judgment; but I do not know that it will be admitted in fact. Nor is this necessity a practical necessity; that is, the result of an objective law telling us how we ought to act. It is what Kant calls *exemplary*; 'that is, necessity of the assent of *all* to a judgment which is regarded as an example of a universal rule which one cannot state'.[28] When I say that something is beautiful, I claim that all ought to describe it as beautiful; and this claim presupposes a universal principle, of which the judgment is an example. But the principle cannot be a logical principle. It must be regarded, therefore, as a common sense (*ein Gemeinsinn*). But this is not common sense (*sensus communis*) according to the ordinary usage of the term. For the latter judges by concepts and principles, however indistinctly represented. Common sense in the aesthetic understanding of the term refers to 'the effect resulting from the free play of our cognitive powers'.[29] In passing an aesthetic judgment we presuppose that a certain similar satisfaction will arise or should arise from their interplay in all who perceive the object in question.

What right have we got to presuppose this common sense? We cannot prove its existence; but it is presupposed or assumed as the necessary condition of the communicability of aesthetic judgments. According to Kant, judgments, along with the conviction which accompanies them, must admit of universal communicability. But aesthetic judgments cannot be communicated by concepts and by appeal to a universal logical rule. Hence 'common sense' is the necessary condition of their communicability. And this is our ground for presupposing such a common sense.

In general, it must be understood that in his 'analytic of the beautiful' Kant is not concerned with giving rules or hints for educating and cultivating aesthetic taste. He expressly disclaims any such intention in his preface to the *Critique of Judgment.* He is concerned first and foremost with the nature of the aesthetic judgment, with what we can say about it *a priori;* that is, with its universal and necessary features. In the course of his discussion he obviously draws attention to ideas which, whether we accept them or not, are worthy of consideration. The 'disinterestedness' of the aesthetic judgment and the notion of purposiveness without any concept of a purpose are cases in point. But the fundamental question is probably whether the aesthetic judgment expresses feeling, in the sense that the latter is the only determining ground of the pure judgment of taste, or whether it is in some sense a cognitive judgment. If we think that Kant's account of the matter is too subjectivist and that the aesthetic judgment does in fact express objective knowledge of a kind for which he does not allow, we must, of course, be prepared to state what this knowledge is. If we cannot do so, this is at least a prima facie ground for thinking that Kant's account was on the right lines. But on this matter the reader must form his own opinion.

3. Edmund Burke's *Philosophical Inquiry into the Origin of Our Ideas of the Sublime and the Beautiful* (1756) was regarded by Kant as the most important work in this line of

research which had appeared. But though he followed Burke in distinguishing between the beautiful and the sublime,[30] he looked on the English writer's treatment as being 'purely empirical' and 'physiological'[31] and considered that what was needed was a 'transcendental exposition' of aesthetic judgments. Having already considered Kant's study of the judgment of taste in the sense of a judgment about the beautiful, we can now turn to the analytic of the sublime. But I propose to deal with this theme in a more cursory way.

The beautiful and the sublime (*das Erhabene*) have some common features. For instance, both cause pleasure; and the judgment that something is sublime no more presupposes a determinate concept than does the judgment that an object is beautiful. But there are at the same time considerable differences between the beautiful and the sublime. For example, the former is associated with quality rather than with quantity, the latter with quantity rather than with quality. Natural beauty, as we have seen, has to do with the form of an object; and form implies limitation. The experience of the sublime, however, is associated with formlessness, in the sense of absence of limitation, provided that this absence of limits is represented together with totality. (Thus the overpowering grandeur of the tempestuous ocean is felt as limitless, but the absence of limits is also represented as a totality.) Kant is thus enabled to associate beauty with the understanding, the sublime with the reason. Aesthetic experience of the beautiful does not, as we have seen, depend on any determinate concept. Nevertheless, it involves a free interplay of the faculties; in this case imagination and understanding. The beautiful as definite is felt as adequate to the imagination, and the imagination is considered as being in accord, in regard to a given intuition, with the understanding, which is a faculty of concepts. The sublime, however, does violence to the imagination; it overwhelms it, as it were. And it is then represented as being in accord with the reason, considered as the faculty of indeterminate ideas of totality. The sublime, in proportion as it involves absence of limits, is inadequate to our power of imaginative representation; that is to say, it exceeds and overwhelms it. And in so far as this absence of limits is associated with totality, the sublime can be regarded as the 'exhibition', as Kant puts it, of an indefinite idea of the reason. Another difference is that whereas the pleasure produced by the beautiful can be described as a positive joy, prolonged in quiet contemplation, the sublime must be said to cause wonder and awe rather than positive joy. And the experience of it is associated with emotion in the sense alluded to in the last section, namely a momentary checking and a consequent more powerful outflow of the vital force. Finally, the beautiful, though distinct from the charming, can be linked with it. But charm (*Reiz*) and the sublime are incompatible.

From the fact, or supposed fact, that the sublime is experienced as doing violence to the imagination and as being out of accord with our power of representation Kant draws the conclusion that it is only improperly that natural objects are called sublime. For the term indicates approval. And how can we be said to approve what is experienced as in some sense hostile to ourselves? "Thus the wide tempestuous ocean cannot be called sublime. The sight of it is terrible; and one must have one's mind already filled with many sorts of Ideas, if through such a sight it is to be attuned to a sentiment which is itself sublime because by it the mind is incited to abandon the realm of sense and to occupy itself with Ideas which involve a higher purposiveness.'[32] There are many natural objects which can properly be called beautiful. But, properly speaking, sublimity belongs to our feelings or sentiments rather than to the objects which occasion them.

Kant distinguishes between the mathematical and the dynamical sublime, according as to whether the imagination refers the mental movement involved in the experience of the sublime to the faculty of cognition or to that of desire. The mathematical sublime is said to be 'that which is absolutely great'[33] or '*that in comparison with which all else is small*'.[34] Among examples Kant gives that of St. Peter's at Rome. The dynamical sublime is experienced, for example, when we are confronted with the spectacle of the terrible physical power of Nature but when at the same time we find in our mind and reason a superiority to this physical might.[35]

4. According to Kant, pure judgments of taste (that is, judgments about the beauty of natural objects) stand in need of a deduction, in the sense of justification. The aesthetic judgment demands *a priori* that in representing a given object all should feel the peculiar kind of pleasure (arising from the interplay of imagination and understanding) which is the determining ground of the judgment. As the latter is a particular judgment made by a particular subject, and as its determining ground is subjective (not an objective cognition of a thing), what is the justification of the claim to universal

validity? We cannot justify it by logical proof. For the judgment is not a logical judgment. Nor can we justify it by appealing to a factual universal consent. For, quite apart from the fact that people by no means always agree in their aesthetic judgments, the claim on or demand for universal consent is made *a priori*. It is an essential feature of the judgment as such, and it is thus independent of the empirical facts concerning common assent, or the lack of it, to the judgment. The justification, therefore, can take the form neither of a logical deduction nor of an empirical induction, aiming to establish the truth of the judgment when viewed as claiming universal validity.

Kant's way of dealing with the matter amounts to assigning the conditions under which the claim to universal assent can be justified. If the aesthetic judgment rests on purely subjective grounds, on, that is to say, the pleasure or displeasure arising from the interplay of the powers of imagination and understanding in regard to a given representation, and if we have a right to presuppose in all men a similar structure of the cognitive powers and of the relations between them, then the claim to universal validity on the part of the aesthetic judgment is justified. But the judgment does rest on purely subjective grounds. And communicability of representations and of knowledge in general warrants our presupposing in all men similar subjective conditions for judgment. Therefore the claim to universal consent is justified.

It does not seem to me that this deduction[36] carries us much further. No deduction is required, Kant tells us, in the case of judgments about the sublime in Nature. For it is only improperly that the latter is called sublime. The term refers to our sentiments rather than to the natural phenomena which occasion them. In the case of the pure judgment of taste, however, a deduction is required; for an assertion is made about an object in respect of its form, and this assertion involves an *a priori* claim to universal validity. And fidelity to the general programme of the critical philosophy demands a deduction or justification of such a judgment. But what we are actually told in the course of the deduction amounts to little more than the statements that the claim to universal validity is warranted if we are justified in presupposing in all men a similarity of the subjective conditions of judgment, and that communicability justifies this presupposition. It is perhaps true that this fits into the general pattern of the critical philosophy, inasmuch as the possibility of the aesthetic judgment, considered as a synthetic *a priori* proposition, is referred to conditions on the part of the subject. But one might have expected to have heard some more about conditions on the part of the object. True, the determining grounds of the judgment of taste are, according to Kant, subjective. But, as we have seen, he allows that natural objects can properly be called beautiful, whereas sublimity is only improperly predicated of Nature.

5. So far we have been concerned with the beauty of natural objects.[37] We must now turn to the subject of art. Art in general 'is distinguished from Nature as making (*facere*), from acting or operating (*agere*), and the product or result of the former from the product or result of the latter as work (*opus*) from effect (*effectus*)'.[38] Fine art (*die schöne Kunst*), as distinguished from merely pleasing art (*die angenehme Kunst*), is 'a kind of representation which has its end in itself, but which none the less, although it has no purpose external to itself, promotes the culture of the mental powers with a view to social communication'.[39]

According to Kant, it pertains to a product of fine art that we should be conscious that it is art and not Nature. But at the same time the purposiveness of its form must seem to be as free from the constraint of arbitrary rules as though it were a product of Nature. Kant does not mean, of course, that no rules should be observed in the production of a work of art. He means that their observance should not be painfully apparent. The work of art, to be a work of art, should appear to possess the 'freedom' of Nature. However, whether it is a question of natural beauty or of a work of art, we can say: *'That is beautiful which pleases in the mere act of judging it* (not in sensation, nor by means of a concept).'[40]

Fine art is the work of genius, genius being the talent or natural gift which gives the rule to art. The latter presupposes rules by means of which a product is represented as possible. But these rules cannot have concepts as their determining grounds. Hence the artist, if he is a true artist or genius, cannot devise his rules by means of concepts. And it follows that Nature itself, as operating in the artist (by the harmony of his faculties), must give the rule to art. Genius, therefore, can be defined as 'the inborn mental disposition (*ingenium*) *through which* Nature gives the rule to art'.[41]

It would be out of place to deal here at length with Kant's ideas about art and genius. It is sufficient to mention two points. First, among the faculties which Kant attributes to genius is spirit (*Geist*), which he describes as the animating principle of the mind. It is 'the faculty of presenting aesthetical Ideas',[42] an aesthetical Idea being a representation of the imagination which occasions much thought although no concept is adequate to it, with the consequence that it cannot be made fully intelligible by language. An aesthetical Idea is thus a counterpart of a rational Idea, which, conversely, is a concept to which no intuition or representation of the imagination can be adequate.

The second point which we can note is Kant's insistence on the originality of genius. 'Everyone is agreed that Genius is entirely opposed to the spirit of imitation.'[43] It follows that genius cannot be taught. But it does not follow that genius can dispense with all rules and technical training. Originality is not the only essential condition for genius considered as productive of works of art.

6. We have had occasion to notice Kant's passion for architectonic. This is apparent in the *Critique of Judgment* as well as in the first two *Critiques*. And just as he supplies a deduction of the pure judgment of taste, so also does he supply a short *Dialectic of the Aesthetic Judgment*.[44] This contains the statement of an antinomy and its solution.

The antinomy is as follows. '*Thesis:* The judgment of taste is not based upon concepts; for otherwise it would admit of dispute (would be determinable by proofs). *Antithesis:* The judgment of taste is based upon concepts; for otherwise, in spite of its diversity, we could not quarrel about it (we could not claim for our judgment the necessary assent of others).'[45]

The solution of the antinomy consists in showing that the thesis and antithesis are not contradictory, because the word 'concept' is not to be understood in the same sense in the two propositions. The thesis means that the judgment of taste is not based upon *determinate* concepts. And this is quite true. In the antithesis we mean that the judgment of taste is based upon an *indeterminate* concept, namely that of the supersensible substrate of phenomena. And this also is true. For, according to Kant, this indeterminate concept is the concept of the general ground of the subjective purposiveness of Nature for the judgment; and this is required as a basis for the claim to universal validity on behalf of the judgment. But the concept does not give us any knowledge of the object; nor can it supply any proof of the judgment. Hence thesis and antithesis can both be true, and so compatible; and then the apparent antinomy disappears.

7. The fact that the judgment of taste rests in some sense on the indeterminate concept of the supersensible substrate of phenomena suggests that there is some link between aesthetics and morals. For the aesthetic judgment presupposes, indirectly, this indeterminate concept; and reflection on the moral law gives to the idea of the supersensible or intelligible a determinate content. It is not surprising, therefore, to find Kant saying that 'the beautiful is the symbol of the morally good',[46] and that 'taste is at bottom a power of judging of the sensible illustration of moral ideas (by means of a certain analogy involved in our reflection upon both of these)'.[47]

What does Kant understand by a symbol? His own example is an apt illustration of his meaning. A monarchical State can be represented by a living body if it is governed by laws which spring from the people,[48] and by a machine (such as a hand-mill) if it is governed according to the individual, absolute will of an autocrat. But the representation is in both cases only *symbolic*. The former type of State is not in actual fact like a body; nor does the latter type bear any literal resemblance to a hand-mill. At the same time there is an analogy between the rules according to which we reflect upon the type of State and its causality on the one hand and the representative symbol and its causality on the other. Thus Kant bases his idea of symbolism on analogy. And the question arises, what are the points of analogy between the aesthetic and the moral judgments, or between the beautiful and the morally good, which justify our looking on the former as a symbol of the latter?

There is an analogy between the beautiful and the morally good in the fact that both please *immediately*. That is to say, there is a similarity between them in the fact that they both please immediately; but there is at the same time a difference. For the beautiful pleases in reflective intuition, the morally good in the concept. Again, the beautiful pleases apart from any interest; and though the morally good is indeed bound up with an interest, it does not precede the moral judgment but follows it. So here too there is an analogy rather than a strict similarity. Further, in the aesthetic judgment the imagination is in harmony with the understanding; and this harmony is analogous to the moral harmony of the will with itself according to the universal law of the practical reason. Lastly, there is an analogy between the claim to universality on the part of the subjective principle in the judgment of taste and the claim to universality on the part of the objective principle of morality.

Kant's way of talking may sometimes suggest a moralizing of aesthetic experience. Thus we are told that 'the true propaedeutic for the foundation of taste is the development of moral ideas and the culture of the moral feeling; for it is only when sensibility is brought into agreement with this that genuine taste can take a definite invariable form'.[49] But Kant does not wish to reduce the aesthetic to the moral judgment. As we have seen, he insists on the special characteristics of the former. The point which he wishes to make is that aesthetic experience forms a connecting link between the sensible world as presented in scientific knowledge and the supersensible world as apprehended in moral experience. And it is primarily with this point in mind that he draws attention to analogies between the beautiful and the morally good.

8. We have seen that the judgment of taste is concerned with the form of the purposiveness of an object, so far as this purposiveness is perceived without any representation of a purpose. It is thus in some sense a teleological judgment. In Kant's terminology it is a formal and subjective teleological judgment. It is formal in the sense that it is not concerned with explaining the existence of anything. Indeed, it is not, of itself, concerned with existing things. It is concerned primarily with representations. And it is subjective in the sense that it refers to the feeling of the person who makes the judgment. That is to say, it asserts a necessary connection between the representation of an object as purposive and the pleasure which accompanies this representation.

Besides the subjective formal teleological judgment there is also the objective formal teleological judgment. This is to be found, according to Kant, in mathematics. One of his examples is the following. In so simple a figure as the circle, he remarks, there is contained the ground for the solution of a number of geometrical problems. For instance, if one wishes to construct a triangle, given the base and the opposite angle, the circle is 'the geometrical place for all triangles which conform to this condition'.[50] And the judgment about the suitability of the circle for this purpose is a teleological judgment; for it states 'purposiveness'. It is a formal teleological judgment, because it is not concerned with existing things and with the causal relationship. In pure mathematics nothing is said 'of the existence, but only of the possibility of things'.[51] But it is an objective, and not a subjective, judgment because there is no reference to the feelings or desires of the person making the judgment.

In addition to formal teleological judgments there are also material teleological judgments, which refer to existing things. And these judgments too can be either subjective or objective. They are subjective if they state human purposes; objective if they are concerned with purposes in Nature. The second part of the *Critique of Judgment* deals with the fourth class; that is, with objective, material teleological judgments. And when Kant speaks simply about the 'teleological judgment', it is this sort of judgment which he has in mind.

But there is a further distinction to be made. When we assert that there is purposiveness or finality in Nature, we may be referring either to relative (also called outer or external) or to inner finality. If, for example, we were to say that reindeer exist in the north in order that Eskimos should have meat to eat, we should be asserting a case of relative or outer finality or purposiveness. We should be saying that the natural purpose of the reindeer is to serve something external to itself. If, however, we were to say that the reindeer is a natural purpose in itself, meaning that it is an organic whole in which the parts are mutually interdependent, existing for the whole of which they are parts, we should be asserting a case of inner finality. That is, the natural purpose or end of the reindeer is stated to lie in itself, considered as an organic whole, and not in a relation to something external and other than itself.

Now, let us consider the first judgment, namely that reindeer exist for the sake of human beings. This purports to be an explanation of the existence of reindeer. It is different, however, from a causal explanation. For a causal explanation (in accordance with the schematized category of causality) would merely tell us *how* reindeer come to exist. It would not tell us *why* they exist. The relative teleological judgment purports to supply an answer to the question *why*. But the answer could, at best, be only *hypothetical*. That is to say, it assumes that there must be human beings in the far north. But no amount of study of Nature will show us that there must be human beings in the far north. It is, indeed, psychologically understandable that we should be inclined to think that reindeer should exist for the Eskimos and grass for the sheep and the cows; but, as far as our knowledge is concerned, we might just as well say that human beings are capable of existing in the far north because there happen to be reindeer there, and that sheep and cows are able to live in certain places and not in others because there happens to be appropriate food in the first place and not in the second. In other words, apart from any other possible objections against the assertion of outer finality in Nature, our judgments could never be absolute. We could never be justified in saying absolutely that reindeer exist for men and grass for sheep and cows. The judgments may possibly be true; but we cannot know that they are true. For we cannot see any necessary connections which would establish their truth.

Judgments about inner finality, however, are absolute teleological judgments. That is to say, they assert of some product of Nature that it is in itself a purpose or end of Nature (*Naturzweck*). In the case of relative finality we say, equivalently, that one thing exists with a view to some other thing if this other thing embodies a purpose of Nature. But in the case of inner finality we say that a thing embodies a purpose of Nature because the thing is what it is, and not because of its relation to something else. The question arises, therefore, what are the requisite conditions for making this judgment?

'I should say in a preliminary fashion that a thing exists as a purpose of Nature *when it is cause and effect of itself*, although in a twofold sense.'[52] Kant takes the example of a tree. It is not merely that the tree produces another member of the same species: it produces itself as an individual. For in the process which we call growth it receives and organizes matter in such a way that we can regard the whole process as one of self-production. Further, there is a relation of mutual interdependence between a part and the whole. The leaves, for instance, are produced by the tree; but at the same time they conserve it, in the sense that repeated defoliation would eventually kill the tree.

Trying to define more accurately a thing considered as a purpose of Nature, Kant observes that the parts must be so related to one another that they produce a whole by their causality. At the same time the whole can be regarded as a final cause of the organization of the parts. 'In such a product of Nature each part not only exists *by means of* all the other parts but is also regarded as existing *for the sake* of the others and of the whole, that is, as an instrument (organ).'[53] This is not, however, a sufficient description. For a part of a watch can be regarded as existing for the sake of the others and of the whole. And a watch is not a product of Nature. We must add, therefore, that the parts must be regarded as reciprocally producing each other. It is only a product of this kind which can be called a purpose of Nature; for it is not only organized but also a self-organizing being. We regard it as possessing in itself a formative power (*eine bildende Kraft*), which is not present in an artificial production or machine such as a watch. A watch possesses a moving power (*eine bewegende Kraft*), but not a formative power.

We have, therefore, a principle for judging of internal purposiveness in organized beings. 'This principle, which is at the same time a definition, is as follows: *An organized product of Nature is one in which everything is reciprocally end and means*. In it nothing is in vain, without purpose, or to be ascribed to a blind mechanism of Nature.'[54] This principle is derived from experience in the sense that its formulation is occasioned by observation of organic beings. But at the same time 'on account of the universality and necessity which it predicates of such purposiveness'[55] it cannot rest merely on empirical grounds. It must be grounded on an *a priori* principle, the Idea of a purpose of Nature, which is a regulative (and not constitutive) Idea. And the principle quoted above can be called, Kant tells us, a maxim for the employment of this regulative Idea in judging the inner purposiveness of organized beings.

The question arises, however, whether we can be content with a dichotomy in Nature. Internal finality or purposiveness can be said to be verified for us only in self-organizing beings. For, whatever may be the case absolutely speaking, we at least are not in a position to give an adequate explanation of such beings in terms of merely mechanical causality, by working, that is to say, with the schematized category of causality. But this is not the case with inorganic beings, where we do not seem to require the concept of finality. Are we, therefore, to be content with making a split, as it were, in Nature, using the concept of final causality in the case of certain types of beings and not using it in other cases?

According to Kant, we cannot remain content with such a dichotomy. For the Idea of finality, of a purpose of Nature, is a regulative Idea for judgment's interpretation of Nature. And we are thus led to the view of Nature as a system of ends, a view which in turn leads us to refer Nature, as empirically given in sense-perception, to a supersensible substrate. Indeed, the very Idea of a natural purpose takes us beyond the sphere of sense-experience. For the Idea is not given in mere sense-perception; it is a regulative principle for judging what is perceived. And we naturally tend to unify the whole of Nature in the light of this Idea. 'If we have once discovered in Nature a power of bringing forth products which can be thought by us only according to the concept of final causes, we go further and are entitled to judge that those things too belong to a system of ends which do not . . . necessitate our seeking for any principle of their possibility beyond the mechanism of causes working blindly. For the first Idea, as regards its ground, already brings us beyond the world of sense; because the unity of the supersensible principle must be regarded as valid in this way not merely for certain species of natural beings, but for the whole of Nature as a system.'[56]

It is important to understand, of course, that the principle of finality in Nature is for Kant a regulative Idea of reflective judgment, and that the maxims to which it gives rise are heuristic principles. We must not confuse natural science and theology. Thus we should not introduce the concept of God into natural science in order to explain finality. 'Now, to keep itself strictly within its limits, physics abstracts from the question whether ends in Nature (*Naturzwecke*) are *intentional or unintentional*; for this would mean intruding itself into alien territory (namely that of metaphysics). It is enough that there are objects which are *explicable* as regards their internal form, or even intimately *knowable* solely by means of natural laws which we cannot think except by taking the Idea of ends as a principle.'[57] The Idea of a purpose of Nature, so far as natural science is concerned, is a useful, indeed inevitable, heuristic principle. But though teleology leads naturally to theology, in the sense that a teleological view of Nature leads naturally to the assumption that Nature is the work of an intelligent Being acting for a purpose, this does not mean that the existence of God can be regarded as a conclusion which is demonstrable on the basis of natural science. For the regulative Idea of reflective judgment and the maxims which govern its employment are subjective principles. On the side of the mind, the teleological judgment helps us to bridge the gulf between the phenomenal and noumenal spheres; but it cannot form the basis for a dogmatic metaphysics.

9. As we have seen, Kant concentrates on what he calls inner purposiveness or finality; that is, on the finality manifested within an organic being through the relations of the

parts to one another and to the whole. A purely mechanistic explanation is insufficient in the case of such beings.

But the situation is not, of course, as simple as this statement of Kant's position might suggest. On the one hand the categories are constitutive in regard to experience. And though this does not tell us anything about noumenal or supersensible reality, it appears to tell us that all phenomena must be explicable in terms of mechanical causality, or at least that they must be considered to be explicable in this way. On the other hand consideration of organic beings leads us to use the idea of finality in interpreting them. As Kant puts it, the understanding suggests one maxim for judging corporeal things, while reason suggests another. And these two maxims of judgment appear to be mutually incompatible. There thus arises an antinomy, or at least an apparent antinomy, which Kant discusses under the general heading of *Dialectic of Teleological Judgment*.

The antinomy is first stated as follows. '*The first maxim* of judgment is the *proposition:* All production of material things and their forms can be judged to be possible only according to merely mechanical laws. *The second maxim* is the *counter-proposition:* Some products of material Nature cannot be judged to be possible according to merely mechanical laws. (To judge them requires a quite different law of causality, namely that of final causes.)'[58]

Kant remarks that if we turn these maxims into constitutive principles of the possibility of objects, we are, indeed, faced with a contradiction. For we shall have the following statements. '*Proposition:* All production of material things is possible according to merely mechanical laws. *Counter-proposition:* Some production of material things is not possible according to merely mechanical laws.'[59] And these two statements are clearly incompatible. But judgment does not provide us with constitutive principles of the possibility of objects. And no *a priori* proof of either statement can be given. We must return, therefore, to the antinomy as first stated, where we have two maxims for judging material objects according to the empirical laws of Nature. And it is Kant's contention that the two maxims do not in fact contradict one another.

The reason why they do not contradict one another is this. If I say that I must judge the production of material things to be possible according to merely mechanical laws (that is, without introducing the idea of purpose or finality), I do not say that the production of material things is only possible in this way. I say that I ought to consider them as being possible only in this way. In other words, I lay down the principle that in the scientific investigation of Nature I must push, as it were, mechanistic explanation as far as it will go. And this does not prevent me from judging that in regard to certain material things I cannot provide an adequate explanation in terms of mechanical causality, and that I have to introduce the idea of final causality. I do not thereby assert dogmatically that organic beings cannot possibly be produced by the operation of mechanical causal laws. I say rather that I do not see how the general principle of explaining the production of material things in terms of mechanical causality can be applied in this case, and that I find myself driven to consider such beings as ends, as embodying purposes of Nature, even if the Idea of a purpose of Nature is not altogether clear to me.

Kant notes that in the history of philosophy there have appeared different ways of explaining purposiveness in Nature. He groups them under two general headings, idealism and realism. The former maintains that such purposiveness is undesigned, while the latter holds that it is designed. Under the heading of idealism Kant includes both the system of the Greek atomists, according to which everything is due to the working of the laws of motion, and the system of Spinoza, according to which purposiveness in Nature arises fatalistically, as it were, from the character of infinite substance. Under realism he includes both hylozoism (the theory, for example, of a world-soul) and theism.

The names are oddly chosen. I mean, it is odd to call the philosophies of Democritus and Epicurus 'idealism'. But the main point to be noticed is that according to Kant theism is by far the most acceptable system of explanation. Epicurus tries to explain purposiveness in Nature through blind chance; but in this way 'nothing is explained, not even the illusion in our teleological judgment'.[60] Spinoza's system leads to the conclusion that all is purposive; for all follows necessarily from Substance, and this is what purposiveness is made to mean. But to say that a thing is purposive simply because it is a thing is tantamount to saying that nothing is purposive. It is true, Kant remarks, that Spinoza's doctrine of the original Being is not easy to refute; but this is because it is not understandable in the first place. As for hylozoism, 'the possibility of a living matter cannot even be thought; for its concept involves a contradiction, because lifelessness, *inertia*, constitutes the essential character of matter'.[61] We are left, therefore, with theism which is superior to all other grounds of explanation in that it refers purposiveness in Nature to an original Being acting intelligently.

But though theism is superior to all other explanations of finality in Nature, it cannot be proved. 'What now in the end does even the most complete teleology prove? Does it prove that there is such an intelligent Being? No; it proves nothing more than that according to the constitution of our cognitive powers, and in the consequent combination of experience with the highest principles of reason, we can form for ourselves absolutely no concept of the possibility of such a world except by thinking a supreme cause of it *working by design*. Objectively, therefore, we cannot assert the proposition that there is an intelligent original Being; but only subjectively for the use of our faculty of judgment in its reflection upon the purposes in Nature, which cannot be thought according to any other principle than that of the designing (intentional) causality of a highest cause.'[62]

Once more, therefore, the Idea of purpose in Nature (*Naturzweck*) is a regulative principle, giving rise to heuristic maxims of judgment. These are found useful, even inevitable, in judging of organic beings. And we are led naturally, first to the concept of the whole of Nature as a system of ends, secondly to the concept of an intelligent cause of Nature. But we are dealing here with the implications of a subjective regulative Idea, not with objective proof. At the same time it cannot be shown that final causality is impossible in Nature. True, we cannot understand in a positive way how mechanical and final causality can be ultimately reconciled; how things can be subject, as it were, to two kinds of causal law at the same time. But the possibility remains that they are reconciled in the 'supersensible substrate' of Nature, to which we have no access. And theism provides us with the best framework for thinking the universe, though the objective truth of theism, is not capable of being theoretically demonstrated.

10. Towards the close of the *Critique of Judgment* Kant discusses once more the deficiencies of a theology based on the idea of purposiveness or finality in Nature (physico-theology, as he calls it). As we saw when considering his criticism of speculative metaphysics, an argument for the existence of God which is based on empirical evidence of design or purpose in Nature can bring us, at best, only to the con-

cept of a designer, an architect of Nature. It could not bring us to the concept of a supreme cause of the existence of the universe. Nor could it serve to determine any attribute of the suprahuman designer save intelligence. In particular, it could not serve to determine the moral attributes of this Being. Kant now adds that the physico-theological argument could, at best, bring us to the concept of 'an artistic understanding (*Kunstverstand*) for scattered purposes'.[63] That is to say, reflection on certain types of material beings (organisms) would bring us to the concept of a suprahuman intelligence which manifests itself in these beings. But it would not bring us to the concept of a divine wisdom (*Weisheit*)[64] which created the whole universe for one supreme final end. For one thing, the physico-theological argument is based on empirical data; and the universe as a whole is not an empirical datum. We could not refer the 'scattered' purposes which we find in Nature to the unity of a common final end.

If, however, we approach the matter from a different point of view, namely from the point of view of the moral consciousness, the situation is different. As we saw in *Chapter Fourteen*, the moral law demands that we should postulate the existence, not simply of a suprahuman intelligence, but of God, the supreme, infinite cause of all finite things. And we must conceive God as creating and sustaining the universe for a final end. What can this end be? According to Kant, it must be man. 'Without man the whole creation would be a mere desert, in vain and without final purpose.'[65] But 'it is only as a moral being that we recognize man as the purpose of creation'.[66] We must look on the end or purpose of creation as a moral purpose, as the full development of man as a moral being in a realized kingdom of ends and as consequently involving human happiness in the final harmonization of the physical and moral orders.

We might, therefore, be inclined to say that in Kant's view 'moral theology' (or ethico-theology) complements and supplies for the deficiencies of physico-theology. And he does sometimes speak in this way. But he also insists that moral theology is quite independent of physico-theology, in the sense that it does not presuppose the latter. Indeed, physical theology is said to be 'a misunderstood physical teleology, only serviceable as a preparation (propaedeutic) for theology'.[67] It can be called theology only when it invokes the aid of the principles of moral theology. In itself, it does not merit the name of theology. For it could just as well, or better, lead to a 'demonology', the indefinite conception of a suprahuman power or powers. In other words, Kant, while retaining his respect for the physico-theological argument for the existence of God once again lays all the emphasis on the moral argument.

The moral argument, however, 'does not supply any *objectively*-valid proof of the existence of God; it does not prove to the sceptic that there is a God, but that, if he wishes to think in a way consonant with morality, he must admit the *assumption* of this proposition under the maxims of his practical reason'.[68] We cannot demonstrate the existence or attributes of God. It is a matter of practical faith, not of theoretical cognition.

This faith is free: the mind cannot be compelled to assent by any theoretical proof. But it is worth noting that Kant does not intend to say that this moral faith is irrational. On the contrary, 'faith (as *habitus*, not as *actus*) is the moral way of thinking (*Denkungsart*) of Reason as to belief in that which is unattainable by theoretical knowledge'.[69] To have theoretical knowledge of God we should have to employ the categories of the understanding. But though these can be used to think God analogically or symbolically, their employment cannot give us knowledge of Him. For they give knowledge of objects only by means of their function as constitutive principles of experience. And God is not a possible object of experience for Kant. At the same time belief in God is grounded in reason in its practical or moral employment. It cannot, therefore, be called irrational.

It may seem that Kant's return to the subject of philosophical theology at the close of the *Critique of Judgment* is a case of superfluous repetition. But though it certainly involves repetition, it is not really superfluous. For it re-emphasizes his view that while the aesthetic and teleological judgments enable us to conceive Nature as a possible field for final causality, it is only the practical reason which enables us to give determinate shape, as it were, to the noumenal reality which is vaguely implied by aesthetic experience and by experience of 'objective' finality in certain products of Nature.

Chapter Sixteen

KANT (7): REMARKS ON THE OPUS POSTUMUM

The transition from the metaphysics of Nature to physics – Transcendental philosophy and the construction of experience – The objectivity of the Idea of God – Man as person and as microcosm.

1. The *Critique of Judgment* appeared in 1790. From 1796 until 1803, the year before his death, Kant was engaged in preparing material for a work dealing with the transition from the metaphysics of Nature to physics. For in his opinion this was required to fill a gap in his philosophy. The manuscripts which he left behind him were at length published by Adickes as the *Opus Postumum*[1] or *Posthumous Work* of Kant. As might be expected in what amounts to a collection of notes comprising material for a systematic work, there is a great deal of repetition. Further, while some points are comparatively developed, others remain undeveloped. Again, it is by no means always easy either to elucidate the meaning of Kant's statements or to harmonize apparently divergent points of view. In other words, the commentator is not infrequently unable to decide with any certainty how Kant would have developed his thought if he had had the opportunity to do so, which ideas he would have discarded and which he would have retained, or how precisely he would have reconciled points of view which for us at least it is difficult to reconcile. And study of the chronology of the notes has not done away with these difficulties of interpretation. Hence any account of the movement of Kant's mind as revealed in the *Opus Postumum* is bound by the nature of the case to be largely problematic and conjectural. But this does not mean, of course, that the work is of no interest, or that it can simply be dismissed as an old man's jottings.

The metaphysics of Nature presents us with the concept of matter as that which is subject to motion in space (*das Bewegliche im Raum*)[2] and with its laws so far as these are determinable *a priori*. Physics, however, is concerned with

'the laws of the moving forces of matter in so far as they are
given in experience'.[3] At first sight it might appear that no
special bridge or transition from the one to the other is required. But Kant is not of this opinion. For experience[4] is
not something which is simply given; it is constructed. And
physics, considered as concerned with the laws of the moving
forces of matter as given in experience, presupposes something corresponding to a schematism of the *a priori* concepts
of the metaphysics of Nature, a schematism which will form
a bridge between the latter and empirical representations.
'The transition from the one science to the other must have
(involve) certain mediating concepts (*Zwischenbegriffe*)
which are given in the former and applied to the latter, and
which belong both to the territory of the one and to that of
the other. Otherwise this progress would be, not a regular
transition (*ein gesetzmäsziger Uebergang*), but a leap
(*Sprung*), in which one does not know where one is going
to arrive, and after which, when one looks back, one does not
really see the point of departure.'[5]

What Kant appears to be looking for is a schema of physics,
in the sense of anticipations of the empirical investigation of
Nature. Mere empirical observation of the moving forces of
matter cannot be called physics, if physics is a science. As a
science physics involves system, not a mere aggregation of
observations. And systematization takes place according to
a priori principles which give us, as it were, guiding lines in
empirical investigation. 'From empirical intuition we can take
nothing but what we ourselves have put there for physics.'[6]
Thus 'there must be *a priori* principles according to which
the moving forces are co-ordinated in relation to one another
(that is, according to the formal element), while the moving
forces in themselves (according to the material element, the
object) are considered empirically'.[7] Some definite truths are,
indeed, deducible *a priori*; but we also have problematical
anticipations of the empirical investigation of Nature, in the
sense that we know that this or that must be the case, though
empirical verification alone can tell us which is the case.

Kant aims, therefore, at elaborating a 'schematism of the
faculty of judgment for the moving forces of matter'.[8] The
metaphysics of Nature, providing us with the concept of matter as that which is subject to motion in space, has a natural
tendency towards physics, that is, towards grounding a systematic empirical doctrine of Nature. But for this to be possible we require a mediating concept. And this is provided

by the concept of matter in so far as it has moving forces. This concept is partly empirical, inasmuch as it is on the basis of experience that the subject conceives moving forces of matter. But it is also partly *a priori*; for the relations of the moving forces to one another imply *a priori* laws, such as those of attraction and repulsion. The concept of matter in so far as it has moving forces is thus adapted to act as a mediating concept (*Zwischenbegriff*) between the purely *a priori* and the purely *a posteriori* or empirical. And Kant proposes to consider the moving forces of matter in a characteristic manner: 'The moving forces of matter are best divided according to the arrangement of the categories; according to their quantity, quality, relation and modality.'[9]

From one point of view, therefore, the *Opus Postumum* is a programme for working out the transition from the metaphysics of Nature to physics. But this transition falls under the general heading, so to speak, of the subject's construction of experience. Indeed, in his manuscripts Kant gives so much emphasis to this idea that he has appeared to some readers to be adumbrating a purely idealist system. And I wish now to say something about this topic.

2. In the *Opus Postumum* the Ideas of pure reason occupy a prominent place. According to Kant, the system of Ideas is the foundation of the possibility of the whole of experience. 'Transcendental philosophy is the system of synthetic knowledge by *a priori* concepts.'[10] If we took this proposition by itself, we might be inclined to interpret it as referring simply to the system of the categories and of the *a priori* principles of the understanding. But this is not precisely what Kant has in mind. The word 'system', which signifies a 'complete system of the possibility of the absolute whole of experience',[11] is the system of the Ideas of pure reason. 'Transcendental philosophy is pure philosophy (mixed neither with empirical nor with mathematical elements) in a system of the Ideas of the speculative and moral-practical reason, in so far as this constitutes an unconditioned whole.'[12] And this system is made possible 'through the positing of three objects, God, the World and the Idea of Duty':[13] or, we can say, through the positing of God, the World 'and Man in the world, as subject to the principles of duty'.[14] Or, inasmuch as man is in the world, we can say that 'the totality of beings is God and the World'.[15] Transcendental philosophy is thus said to be 'the doctrine of God and the World'.[16] Again, 'highest point of view of the transcendental philosophy

in the two mutually related Ideas, *God and the World*.[17]
In the Idea of God we think the totality of supersensible or
noumenal reality, and in the Idea of the World we think the
totality of sensible reality. Each Idea contains a 'maximum',
and we can say that 'there is one God and one World'.[18]

These two Ideas together form the Idea of the Universe.
'The totality of things, *universum*, comprising God and the
World.'[19] Apart from God and the World there can be nothing. But while these two Ideas are mutually related, the relation is not one of simple coordination. The World is thought
as subordinate to God, the sensible to the supersensible, the
phenomenal to the noumenal. God and the World as *'entia
non coordinata, sed subordinata'*.[20] Further, the relation between them is synthetic, not analytic. That is to say, it is
man, as thinking subject, who thinks and relates these Ideas.
'God, the World, and the subject which links together both
objects, the thinking being in the World. God, the World,
and that which unites both in one system, the thinking immanent principle of man (*mens*) in the World.'[21] Again,
'God, the World and I, the thinking being in the World,
which links them together. God and the World are the two
objects of transcendental philosophy, and (subject, predicate
and copula) that is the thinking Man; the subject which
binds them together in one proposition'.[22]

Kant does not mean that the Ideas of God and the World
are conceptual apprehensions of objects given in experience.
In a certain sense, of course, God and the World are thought
as objects, that is, as objects of thought; but they are not
given as objects. The Ideas are the thinking of pure reason as
it constitutes itself as thinking subject. They are 'not mere
concepts but laws of thinking which the subject prescribes to
itself. Autonomy.'[23] By thinking these Ideas the subject gives
itself an object and constitutes itself as conscious. 'The first
act of reason is consciousness.'[24] But 'I must have objects of
my thought and apprehend them; for otherwise I am not conscious of myself (*cogito, sum*: it should not run, *ergo*). It is
autonomia rationis purae. For without this I should be without ideas . . . like a beast, without knowing that I am.'[25]
The Ideas supply the material, as it were, for the subject's
construction of experience. 'These representations are not
mere concepts but also Ideas which provide the material (*den
Stoff*) for synthetic *a priori* laws by means of concepts.'[26]
God and the World are not 'substances outside my ideas but
the thinking whereby we make for ourselves objects through

synthetic *a priori* cognitions and are, subjectively, self-creators (*Selbstschöpfer*) of the objects we think'.[27]

The construction of experience can thus be represented as a process of what Kant calls self-positing, self-making, self-constituting, and so on. From the Idea of the World downwards, so to speak, there is a continuous process of schematization which is at the same time a process of objectification. And this process is the work of the self-positing noumenal subject. The categories are said to be acts by which the subject posits itself and constitutes itself as object for the sake of possible experience. And space and time, repeatedly affirmed to be pure subjective intuitions and not things or objects of perception, are said to be primitive products of imagination, self-made intuitions. The subject constitutes or posits itself as object, that is to say, both as the empirical ego and as the object which affects the empirical ego. We can thus speak of the subject as affecting itself.

The transition, therefore, from the metaphysics of Nature to physics, with which the *Opus Postumum* professedly deals, can be seen in the light of this general scheme. For it has to be shown that the possible types of moving forces in Nature and the possible types of quality experienced by the subject in its reaction to these forces are derivable, by a process of schematization, from the self-positing of the subject. At least this has to be shown if it is held that it is the subject itself which constructs experience.

Kant does not attempt to conceal the fact that this theory of the construction of experience through the self-positing of the subject is in some sense an idealist view. 'The transcendental philosophy is an idealism; inasmuch as the subject constitutes itself.'[28] Moreover, this philosophy bears a marked resemblance, at least at first sight, to that of Fichte, who published his *Basis of the Entire Theory of Science* in 1794. And the resemblance becomes all the more striking when we find Kant interpreting the thing-in-itself as a way in which the subject posits itself or makes itself its own object. 'The object in itself (*Noumenon*) is a mere *Gedankending* (*ens rationis*), in the representation of which the subject posits itself.'[29] It is 'the mere representation of its own (the subject's) activity'.[30] The subject projects, as it were, its own unity, or its own activity of unification, in the negative idea of the thing-in-itself. The concept of the thing-in-itself becomes an act of the self-positing subject. The thing-in-itself is 'not a real thing';[31] it is 'not an existing reality but merely a principle',[32] 'the principle of the synthetic *a priori* knowledge of the manifold of sense-intuition in general and of the law of its co-ordination'.[33] And this principle is due to the subject in its construction of experience. The distinction between appearance and thing-in-itself is not a distinction between objects but holds good only for the subject.

At the same time the resemblances between Kant's theory of the construction of experience, as outlined or at least hinted at in the *Opus Postumum*, and Fichte's subjective transcendental idealism[34] do not justify a dogmatic assertion that in his old age Kant abandoned the doctrine of the thing-in-itself and derived the whole of reality from the self-positing of the noumenal subject. For to make such an assertion would be to over-emphasize the use of certain terms and to press certain statements at the expense of others. For example, passages occur in the *Opus Postumum* which appear simply to reaffirm the doctrine about the thing-in-itself which is to be found in the *Critique of Pure Reason*. Thus we are told that though the thing-in-itself is not given as an existing object, and indeed cannot be so given, it is none the less 'a *cogitabile* (and, indeed, as *necessarily thinkable*) which cannot be given but must be thought. . . .'[35] The idea of the thing-in-itself is correlative to that of appearance. Indeed, on one or two occasions Kant seems to go further in a realistic direction than one would expect. 'If we take the world as appearance, it proves precisely the existence (*Dasein*) of something which is not appearance.'[36] He also seems to imply on occasion that the thing-in-itself is simply the thing which appears when considered apart from its appearing. And as for the use of the word 'idealism' for transcendental philosophy, this does not seem to involve any new or revolutionary point of view. For transcendental philosophy is, as we have seen, the system of the Ideas of pure reason. And when Kant emphasizes in the *Opus Postumum* the problematic (not assertoric) character of these Ideas, he is not departing from the doctrine of the *Critiques*.

The fact of the matter seems to be that in the *Opus Postumum* Kant attempts to show that within the framework of the critical philosophy he can answer the objections of those who consider the theory of the thing-in-itself to be inconsistent and superfluous. It is indeed arguable in the effort to reformulate his views in such a way as to answer his critics and to show that his philosophy contained within itself all that was valid in the development of Fichte and others Kant went a considerable way towards transforming his system into one of pure transcendental idealism. But to admit this is not the same thing as to admit that he ever definitely repudiated or abandoned the general point of view which is characteristic of the *Critiques*. And I do not believe that he did so.

3. Turning to the Idea of God, we can note in the first place that Kant distinguishes carefully between the question what is meant by the term 'God', that is, what is the content of the Idea of God, and the question whether God exists, that is, whether there is a being which possesses the attributes comprised in the Idea of God.

'God is not the world-soul. . . . The concept of God is that of a Being as supreme cause of the things in the world and as a person.'[37] God is conceived as the supreme Being, the supreme intelligence, the supreme good, who possesses rights and is a person. Again, 'a Being for which all human duties are at the same time his commands is God'.[38] Man thinks God according to the attributes which make him (man) a being in the noumenal sphere; but in the Idea of God these attributes are raised, as it were, to the maximum or absolute degree. Man, for instance, is free; but his being involves receptivity, and his freedom is not absolute. God, however, is conceived as supreme spontaneity and freedom, without receptivity and without limitation. For while man is finite and a mixed being, in the sense that he belongs both to the noumenal and to the phenomenal spheres, God is conceived as infinite noumenal reality. The World is conceived as the totality of sensible reality; but it is conceived as subordinate to the creative power of God and to his purposeful and holy will. As we have seen, the relation between the Ideas of God and the World is not one of co-ordination: it is a relation of subordination, in the sense that the World is conceived as dependent on God.

Now, some statements in the *Opus Postumum*, if they are taken in isolation, that is to say, naturally tend to suggest that Kant has abandoned any notion of there being a God independently of the Idea of God. Thus while the Idea of God is said to be necessary, in the sense that it is inevitably thought by pure reason as an ideal, it is said to represent 'a thought thing[39] (*ens rationis*)'.[40] Indeed, 'the concept of such a Being is not the concept of a substance, that is, of a thing which exists independently of any thought, but the Idea (auto-creation, *Selbstgeschöpf*), thought-thing, *ens rationis*, of a reason which constitutes itself as an object of thought, and which produces, according to the principles of transcendental philosophy, *a priori* propositions and an Ideal, in regard to which there is no question of asking whether such an object exists; for the concept is transcendent'.[41]

At first sight at least this last quotation states clearly and explicitly that the Idea of God is a man-made ideal, a creation of thought, and that there is no extramental divine Being which corresponds to the Idea. Elsewhere, indeed, in the *Opus Postumum* Kant appears to be looking for a simpler and more immediate moral argument for God's existence than the argument already advanced in the second *Critique*. And this fact obviously militates against the view that in his old age Kant abandoned any belief in God as an objective reality, especially when there is other evidence to show that he retained this belief up to his death. It is true, indeed, that the *Opus Postumum* consists very largely of jottings, of ideas which occurred to Kant and which were noted for further consideration; and it is not really surprising if in a series of such notes there appear divergent lines of thought which we are not in a position to harmonize or reconcile. At the same time, however, it must be remembered that the ideas expressed in the passages mentioned in the last paragraph can be paralleled, to a great extent at least, in the *Critiques*, and that in the *Critiques* Kant also puts forward a justification of belief in God. Hence even if the divergence of views is sharper in the *Opus Postumum* than in the *Critiques*, it is not a novel phenomenon.

In the *Critique of Pure Reason* Kant had already made it clear that in his opinion the Idea of God, considered as the creation of pure reason, is that of a 'transcendental Ideal'. It does not express any intuition of God; nor can we deduce God's existence from the Idea. And these views reappear in the *Opus Postumum*. We enjoy no intuition of God. 'We see Him as in a mirror; never face to face.'[42] Hence it is impossible to deduce God's existence from the Idea of God:[43] this Idea is a creation of pure reason, a transcendental Ideal. Further, though we think of God as infinite substance, He is not and cannot be a substance; for He transcends the categories of the human understanding. Hence, if we once presuppose this point of view, we cannot sensibly ask whether there is a divine Being corresponding to the Idea of God, at least in so far as the Idea involves thinking of God in terms of the categories. This conclusion substantially repeats the doctrine of the first *Critique*. But, as we have seen, Kant went on in the second *Critique* to offer a moral or practical justification for belief in God. And in the *Opus Postumum* he offers some suggestions for following out or developing this line of thought.

In the second *Critique* Kant justified belief in God as a postulate of the practical reason. We arrive, or can arrive, at belief in God through reflection on the demands of the moral law in regard to the synthesis of virtue with happiness. In the *Opus Postumum* he appears to be concerned with finding a more immediate transition from consciousness of the moral law to belief in God. And the categorical imperative is represented as containing within itself the precept of looking on all human duties as divine commands. 'In the moral-practical reason lies the categorical imperative to regard all human duties as divine commands.'[44] Again, 'To see all in God. The categorical imperative. The knowledge of my duties as divine commands, enunciated through the categorical imperative.'[45] Thus 'the concept of God is the concept of an obligation-imposing subject outside myself'.[46] The categorical imperative is for us the voice of God; and God is manifested in the consciousness of moral obligation, through the moral law.

To be sure, Kant insists that this is not a proof of God's existence as a substance existing outside the human mind. He also insists that nothing is added to the force of the moral law by regarding it as a divine command, and that if a man does not believe in God the obliging force of the categorical imperative is not thereby taken away.'[47] And it is easy to understand that those who concentrate their attention on such statements are inclined to draw the conclusion that the word 'God' became for Kant simply a name for the categorical imperative itself or a name for a purely subjective projection of a voice speaking through the moral law. But, as we have seen, on Kant's premises there could not possibly be a proof of God's existence as a particular substance. And unless Kant is prepared to reject the doctrine of the second *Critique* about the autonomy of the will, he is bound to say that the moral force of the categorical imperative does not depend on our regarding it as the expression of a divine command. But it does not necessarily follow that God is for him no more than a name for the categorical imperative. What follows is that the only access we have to God is through the moral consciousness. No theoretical demonstration of God's existence is possible. This is, indeed, the doctrine of the

Critique; but in the *Opus Postumum* Kant seems to be seeking a more immediate connection between consciousness of
obligation and belief in God. 'Freedom under laws: duties as
divine commands. There is a God.'[48]

It is perhaps in the light of this desire to find a more immediate justification of belief in God that we should interpret the passages in the *Opus Postumum* which at first sight
appear to amount to a statement of the *a priori* or ontological
argument for God's existence. Kant tells us, for example,
that 'the idea (*Gedanke*) of Him is at the same time belief
in Him and in His personality'.[49] Again, 'the mere Idea
(*Idee*) of God at the same time a postulate of His existence.
To think Him and to believe in Him is an identical proposition.'[50] And if we were to connect these statements with the
statement that 'a necessary being is one the concept of which
is at the same time a sufficient proof of its existence',[51] we
might be inclined to suppose that Kant, after having rejected
the ontological argument in the *Critique of Pure Reason*,
came to accept it in the *Opus Postumum*. But it is most un-
likely that he did anything of the kind. He seems to be speaking, not of a theoretical demonstration, such as the ontological argument purported to be, but of a 'sufficient proof' for
the moral consciousness, that is, from the purely practical or
moral point of view. 'The principle of fulfilling all duties as
divine commands in religion, proves the freedom of the human will . . . and is at the same time, in relation to practical
pure principles of reason, a proof of the existence of God as
the one God.'[52] It is not that I first have an idea of the divine
essence, from which I deduce God's existence. It is rather
that through consciousness of the categorical imperative I
rise to the idea of God as speaking to me through and in the
moral law. And to have this idea of God and to believe in
Him are one and the same thing. That is to say, to conceive
God as immanent to me, as morally commanding subject, is
to conceive Him as existing. But this awareness of God as
immanent in the moral consciousness is a 'sufficient proof' of
His existence only for this consciousness.

If this interpretation is on the right lines (and one is
scarcely in a position to dogmatize on this matter), we can
say perhaps that Kant is giving or suggesting a moral equivalent of or analogue to the ontological argument. The latter
was thought by its defenders to be a theoretical demonstration of God's existence of such a kind that, once properly
understood, it compels assent. Kant does not admit that

there is any such argument. But there is something analogous to it. To conceive God as morally commanding subject, immanent in the moral consciousness, and to have a religious belief in Him are one and the same thing. But this does not mean that from a purely abstract idea of a supreme moral legislator one can deduce theoretically the existence of this divine legislator in such a way as to compel the mind's assent. It means rather that within and for the moral consciousness itself the idea of the law as the voice of a divine legislator is equivalent to belief in God's existence. For to have this idea of God is, for the moral consciousness, to postulate His existence. This may not be a very convincing line of argument. For it is arguable that in the long run it amounts to the tautology that to believe in God is to believe in Him. But it is evident at least that Kant is seeking a more immediate approach to belief in God based on the moral consciousness than the one already developed in the second *Critique*. How he would have developed his new approach, if he had had the opportunity of doing so, we cannot, of course, say.

4. We have seen that the synthesis between the Ideas of God and the World is effected by man, the thinking subject. This is possible because man is himself a mediating being; and the concept of man is a mediating concept or idea. For man has a foot, so to speak, in both camps. He belongs to both the supersensible and the sensible, the noumenal and the phenomenal spheres; and through the moral consciousness the sensible is subordinated to the supersensible. The human reason can thus think the totality of supersensible being in the Idea of God and the totality of sensible being in the Idea of the World; and it synthesizes these Ideas by positing a relation between them whereby the Idea of the World is subordinated to the Idea of God.

That man belongs to the sensible order or sphere is evident. That is to say, it is evident that he belongs to the class of physical organic beings. And, as such, he is subject to the laws of determined causality. But his moral life manifests his freedom; and, as free, he belongs to the noumenal order or sphere. 'Man (a being in the world, *ein Weltwesen*) is at the same time a being which possesses freedom, a property which is outside the causal principles of the world but which nevertheless belongs to man.'[53] And to possess freedom is to possess spirit. 'There is thus a being above the world, namely the *spirit* of man.'[54] And to be free in virtue of a spiritual principle is to be a person. 'The living corporeal being is

besouled (*animal*). If it is a person, it is a human being.'[55]
Man is a person in that he is a free, self-conscious, moral
being.

Does this mean that man is split, as it were, into two elements? It obviously means that we can distinguish between
man as noumenon and man as phenomenon. 'Man in the
world belongs to the knowledge of the world; but man as
conscious of his duty in the world is not phenomenon but
noumenon; and he is not a thing but a person.'[56] But though
man possesses this dual nature, there is a unity of consciousness. 'I (the subject) am a person, not merely conscious of
myself, but also as object of intuition in space and time, and
so as belonging to the world.'[57] I possess 'the consciousness
of my existence in the world in space and time'.[58] This
unity, which is at the same time a unity of two principles, is
manifested in the moral consciousness. 'There is in me a
reality which, different from me in the causal relation of
efficacity (*nexus effectivus*), acts on me (*agit, facit, opera-
tur*). This reality, which is free, that is, independent of the
natural law in space and time, directs me interiorly (justifies
or condemns me); and I, man, am myself this reality. . . .'[59]
Moreover, my freedom can translate itself into action within
the world. 'There is in man an active but supersensible principle which, independent of Nature and of natural causality,
determines phenomena and is called freedom.'[60]

If Kant had developed his theory of the construction of
experience, he might, indeed, have derived the empirical ego
and man as a phenomenal being from the self-positing of
the noumenal ego with a view to moral self-realization. But
to say this is to say that there are grounds in the Kantian
philosophy for the development of the position adopted by
Fichte. And the latter, indeed, always maintained that his
own system was a consistent development of the inner tendencies of Kantianism. As it is, however, we are presented rather
with the metaphysical concept of man as the microcosm
which thinks the macrocosm, namely the Universe. The
Universe, as thought by man in the regulative Ideas of God
and the World, is a projection of man's dual nature. Neither
Idea represents a given object. And from the regulative Idea
of God as the transcendental Ideal we cannot deduce God's
existence as a substance. So far as His existence can be spoken
of as given or manifested, it is manifested only to the moral
consciousness in its awareness of obligation. But, as we have
seen, this leaves the problem of God's objective existence in

suspense. Is the reality corresponding to the term 'God' simply the supersensible principle in man himself, the noumenal ego? Or it is a Being distinct from man, which is known only in and through the awareness of obligation? For my part I think that the second view represents Kant's conviction. But it cannot be said that the jottings which form the *Opus Postumum* make the answer very clear. Rather does the work illustrate the tendency of Kantianism to transform itself into a system of transcendental idealism, subordinating being to thought or, rather, ultimately identifying them. I do not think that Kant himself ever took this decisive step. But the tendency to do so is implicit in his writings, even if Kant did not take kindly to Fichte's suggestions that he should eliminate the element of realism in his system or, as Fichte put it, the element of 'dogmatism'. It is, however, inappropriate to interpret the Kantian philosophy simply in terms of its relation to the speculative idealism which succeeded it. And, if we take it by itself, we can see in it an original attempt to solve the problem of reconciling the two realms of necessity and freedom, not by reducing the one to the other, but by finding the meeting-point in the moral consciousness of man.

Chapter Seventeen

CONCLUDING REVIEW

Introductory remarks – Continental rationalism – British empiricism – The Enlightenment and the science of man – The philosophy of history – Immanuel Kant – Final remarks.

1. In the preface to the present volume I remarked that the fourth, fifth and sixth volumes of this *History*, which together cover the philosophy of the seventeenth and eighteenth centuries, form a trilogy. That is to say, they can be regarded as one whole. At the beginning of Volume 4 there was an introductory chapter relating to the matter covered in all three volumes. And I promised to supply a common concluding review at the end of Volume 6.

The purpose of this concluding review is not to give a synopsis of the different philosophies discussed in the trilogy, but to attempt some discussion of the nature, importance and value of the chief styles of philosophizing or philosophical movements in the seventeenth and eighteenth centuries. It will be necessary to confine the discussions to certain selected themes. Further, though reference will, of course, be made to individual philosophers, it will sometimes be necessary to treat complex movements of thought, comprising philosophies which differ from one another in important respects, as though they represented homogeneous styles of philosophizing or even homogeneous systems. In other words, I propose to indulge in discussion of ideal types, as it were, and in generalizations which stand in need of considerable qualification. This procedure may not, indeed, be desirable in itself, but it seems to me to be a legitimate way of drawing attention to certain features of philosophical thought in the period in question, provided, of course, that the different philosophies are treated separately elsewhere.

2. In the introduction to the fourth volume attention was drawn to Descartes' desire to overcome the revived scepticism of the Renaissance which included scepticism about the possibility of solving metaphysical problems and attaining

truth in metaphysics. And we saw that he looked to mathematics as a model of clear and certain reasoning. He wished to give to philosophy a clarity and certainty analogous to the clarity and certainty of mathematics and to distil, as it were, from mathematical method a method which would enable the mind to proceed in an orderly way from step to step without confusion or error.

It is easily understandable that Descartes looked to mathematics as a model of reasoning when one remembers his own mathematical studies and talents and the contemporary advances in this subject. And there is nothing exceptional in this instance of philosophical thought being influenced by extra-philosophical factors. For although philosophy has a continuity of its own, in the sense that we can give an intelligible account of its historical development, this continuity is not absolute, as though philosophy pursued a completely isolated path, without connection with other cultural factors. It can be influenced by other factors in various ways. It can be influenced, for instance, in respect of the concept of the proper method to be employed. Descartes' tendency to look to mathematics as providing a model of method is a case in point. Another example would be modern attempts to interpret metaphysics as hypotheses of wider generality than those of the particular sciences, an interpretation which reflects the influence of an extra-philosophical model, namely the hypothetico-deductive method of modern physics. Again, philosophy can be influenced by extra-philosophical factors in respect of its subject-matter or of the emphasis placed on a certain theme or themes. In the Middle Ages philosophy was powerfully influenced by theology, 'the queen of the sciences'. In the first decades of the nineteenth century we can see the consciousness of historical development, which found expression in the growth of historical science, reflected in the system of Hegel. Marxism obviously showed the influence of the increasing consciousness of the part played by economic factors in the history of civilization and culture. The philosophy of Bergson owed much not only to the scientific hypothesis of evolution but also to the studies of psychologists and sociologists. The thought of Whitehead was influenced by the transition from classical to modern physics. Again, philosophy can be influenced by extra-philosophical factors in regard to the formulation of its problems. For instance, the problem of the relation between soul and body is a classical and a recurrent problem; but the rise of the particular sciences has affected the ways in which the problem has presented itself to different philosophers. The advance of mechanics led to the problem presenting itself to seventeenth-century philosophers in one light, while modern developments in psychology have given a rather different colouring, so to speak, to the problem in the eyes of later thinkers. In one sense we can speak of the same problem, of a 'perennial' problem; but in another sense we can speak of different problems, namely in the sense that different relevant factors which affect our conception and formulation of the basic problem have to be taken into consideration.

To speak in this way is simply to recognize empirical facts: it is not to proclaim the theory that truth is relative. It is, indeed, foolish to deny the historical data to which adherents of the theory of relativism appeal in support of their thesis. But it does not necessarily follow that acknowledgment of the historical data entails acceptance of the thesis that systems of philosophy must be judged simply and solely in terms of their historical contexts and situations, and that no absolute judgments about the truth or falsity of the propositions comprised in them are possible. We can hardly deny that in the course of its development philosophy (that is, the minds of philosophers) has been influenced by extra-philosophical factors. But it is still open to us to discuss, without reference to these factors, whether the propositions enunciated by philosophers are true or false.

Returning to Descartes' admiration for the mathematical model of method, we can recall that other leading rationalist philosophers of the pre-Kantian modern period were also influenced by this model, Spinoza, for example. But what is called 'rationalism'[1] in the history of seventeenth-century philosophy does not consist simply in a preoccupation with method. It is natural to think of philosophy as capable of increasing our knowledge of reality.[2] This is a spontaneous expectation; and any doubt about philosophy's capacity in this respect follows, rather than precedes, the expectation. It is understandable, therefore, that the signal success of the application of mathematics in physical science from the time of the Renaissance onwards should incline some philosophers to think that the application in philosophy of a method analogous to that of mathematics would enable them not only to systematize what was already known or to give the form of knowledge, so to speak, to propositions which were true but which had not been logically demonstrated, but also to increase our knowledge through the deduction of unknown or unrecognized truths. The idea of using mathematics for the advance of physical science was not, of course, new. Roger Bacon, for instance, had already insisted on the need for this use in the thirteenth century. But at the same time it is not until the Renaissance that we can really speak of the signal or striking success of the application in physics. It was natural, therefore, that some post-Renaissance thinkers should look to the application in philosophy of a method analogous to that of mathematics to increase the scope of our knowledge of reality. In other words, the rationalists were concerned not only with methodology but also with using the appropriate method to discover new truths, to increase our positive knowledge of reality.

Now, if we put together the idea of giving to philosophy a method analogous to that of mathematics and the idea of deducing from fundamental propositions or from already demonstrated propositions other propositions which give us new factual information about reality, we obtain the idea of a deductive system of philosophy which will be akin to mathematics in its deductive form but different from it in the sense that the system of philosophy will give us truths about existent reality. I do not intend to imply that this distinction would have been universally admitted by Renaissance and post-Renaissance thinkers. Galileo, for example, thought of mathematics, not as a purely formal science exhibiting the implications of freely-chosen definitions and axioms, but as opening to us the very heart of Nature, as enabling us to read the book of Nature. However, it is clear that a proposition about, say, the properties of a triangle, does not tell us that there are triangular objects, whereas the great rationalist philosophers of the pre-Kantian modern period thought of themselves as concerned with existent reality.

Now, the successful application of mathematics in physical science naturally suggested that the world is intelligible or 'rational'. Thus for Galileo God had written the book of Nature in mathematical characters, as it were. And, indeed, if philosophy is to be a deductive system and at the same time to give us certain factual information about the world, it is obviously necessary to assume that the world is of such a kind that it is possible for philosophy to do this. In practice this means that the causal relation will be assimilated to the relation of logical implication. And we find among the rationalist philosophers the tendency to make this assimilation.

Now, let us assume that the world is a rational system in the sense that it has an intelligible structure which can be reconstructed by the philosopher through a process of deduction. Philosophy can then be represented as the unfolding of reason itself, in such a way that the systematic development of philosophical knowledge discloses to us the objective structure of reality. But if the system of reality can be reconstructed by a deductive process which represents the self-unfolding of reason, it is not unnatural to postulate a theory of ideas which are at least virtually innate. For the self-unfolding of reason will mean the development of a philosophical system by the mind from its own resources, so to speak. And the system will be prefigured in the mind in the form of ideas which are virtually present from the start, even though experience may be the occasion of them becoming actual. I do not mean to imply that a deductive system of philosophy necessarily entails a theory of innate ideas. But if it is represented as an unfolding of the mind itself, and if this description signifies anything more than the development of the logical implications of certain definitions and axioms which are either freely chosen or derived in some way from experience, some version of the theory of innate ideas seems to be required. And the theory of virtually innate ideas obviously fits in very much better with the concept of the self-unfolding of mind or reason than would a theory of actual innate ideas.

If philosophy is to rest on virtually innate ideas, and if its conclusions are to be certainly true to reality, it is clear that these ideas must represent real insights into objective essences. Further, we shall require some assurance that in the process of philosophical deduction we are treating of existent reality, and not simply with the realm of possibility. We can understand, therefore, the fondness of the rationalist metaphysicians for the ontological argument for the existence of God. For, if it is valid, it permits an immediate inference from the idea to the existence of the ultimate reality, God or the absolutely perfect and necessary being.

How is this argument of use in a deductive reconstruction of the structure of reality? In this way. If we press the analogy between the development of a deductive system of mathematics and the construction of a philosophical system, we are driven to start in philosophy with a proposition expressing the existence of the ultimate being (a proposition taken as analogous to the fundamental axioms in mathematics) and to deduce finite being by assimilating the causal relation to that of logical implication. We require, therefore, to be assured of the existence of the primary metaphysical principle or ultimate being. And the ontological argument, passing directly from the idea of this being to its existence, fits in much better with the demands of a purely deductive system than does an *a posteriori* argument which explicitly infers the existence of God from the existence of finite being. For we wish to pass, in logical language, from principle to conclusion rather than from conclusion to principle.

The foregoing account of rationalism is, of course, a description of an ideal type, of what might be called pure or ideal rationalism. And it cannot be applied without qualification to the great systems of pre-Kantian continental philosophy. Of the three leading rationalist systems which were discussed in Volume 4 it is that of Spinoza which approximates most closely to the description. Descartes, as we saw, did not start with the ultimate reality but with the existence of the finite ego as thinking subject. And he did not think that the existence of the world can be deduced from the existence of God. As for Leibniz, he distinguished between necessary truths or truths of reason and contingent truths or truths of fact. He tended, indeed, to present this distinction as being relative to our finite knowledge; but he made it none the less. And he did not maintain that the creation of the monads which actually exist is logically deducible from the divine essence by a process of reasoning based on the principle of non-contradiction. To explain the transition from the order of necessary essences to that of contingent existences he invoked the principle of perfection or of the best rather than the principle of non-contradiction.

But though the description of rationalism which I have given above cannot be applied without qualification to all those systems which are generally labelled systems of rationalist metaphysics, it represents a tendency which is present in them all. And in my introductory remarks to this chapter I gave notice that for the purpose of discussing different styles of philosophizing I should make use of ideal types and indulge in generalizations which, in their application to particular instances, would stand in need of qualification.

It is scarcely necessary, I think, to discuss at length the theory of innate ideas. For it seems to me that in its main lines at least Locke's criticism of the theory as a superfluous hypothesis is clearly justified. If the theory of virtually innate ideas meant merely that the mind possesses the capacity of forming certain ideas, all ideas could be called innate. But in this case there would be no point in so describing them. The theory can have point only if certain ideas cannot be derived from experience, while other ideas can be so derived. But what is meant by the derivation of ideas from experience? If, of course, experience is reduced to the reception of impressions (in Hume's sense), and if ideas are thought of as automatic effects or as photographic representations of impressions, it becomes very difficult, if not impossible, to explain certain ideas as derived from experience. We have no impression, for instance, of absolute perfection or of absolute infinity. But if we once allow for the constructive activity of the mind, it does not seem to be any longer necessary to suppose that an idea of absolute perfection, for instance, is either imprinted by God or innate. If, indeed, the idea were equivalent to an intuition of absolute perfection, we could not explain its origin in terms of the mind's synthesizing activity based on experience of finite and limited perfection. But there does not appear to be any adequate reason for saying that we possess intuitions of absolute perfection and absolute infinity. And we can give an empirical explanation of the origin of such ideas, provided that we do not understand derivation from experience as meaning photographic representation of the immediate data of sense-perception and introspection. It is not that the theory of innate ideas states a logical impossibility. It is rather that it appears to constitute a superfluous hypothesis to which the principle of economy or Ockham's razor can be profitably applied. The theory can, of course, be transformed in the way that Kant subsequently transformed it in his theory of *a priori* categories, which were moulds of concepts, as it were, rather than concepts or ideas in the ordinary sense. But once it has been transformed in this way it can no longer perform its original function of forming a basis for a metaphysical system in the sense in which the pre-Kantian rationalists understood metaphysics.

Rejection of the theory of innate ideas must, of course, entail rejection of the rationalist ideal if this is taken to be the ideal of deducing a system of reality simply from the resources of the mind itself without recourse to experience. For this ideal would involve the theory of virtually innate ideas. But rejection of this theory does not necessarily entail the rejection of the ideal of a deductive metaphysics as such. For we might be able to arrive at the fundamental principles of such a metaphysics on the basis of experience. That is to say, experience might be the occasion of our seeing the truth of certain fundamental metaphysical propositions. Take the proposition, 'everything which comes into being does so through the agency of an extrinsic cause'. The ideas of coming into being and of causality are obtained through experience: they are not innate ideas.[3] Further, the ideas are distinct. The idea, that is to say, of being caused is not obtained by mere analysis of the idea of coming into being, in a sense which would make it true to say that the proposition in question is a tautology. Hence the proposition is synthetic. But if, as I believe to be the case, the proposition expresses an insight into an objective necessary connection, it is not a synthetic *a posteriori* proposition, in the sense of an empirical generalization which might prove to admit of exceptions. On the contrary, it is a synthetic *a priori* proposition, not in the sense that it is innate but in the sense that its truth is logically independent of empirical verification.[4] And if there are a number of propositions of this type, it may very well be possible to give to general metaphysics or ontology the form of a deductive science.

It certainly does not follow, however, that from propositions of the type mentioned we can deduce existential propositions. The proposition, 'everything which comes into being does so through the agency of an extrinsic cause', states that if anything comes into being it does so through the agency of an extrinsic cause. It does not state that there is anything which comes into being, has done so or will do so. Nor can we deduce from the proposition the conclusion that there is, has been or will be anything of this kind. More accurately, from two propositions, neither of which is an existential proposition, we cannot logically deduce an existential conclusion. We may, for instance, be able to deduce a proposition or propositions which will be true of any finite being, if there is any finite being; but we cannot deduce that there is in fact a finite being. In other words, if we once grant that there can be synthetic *a priori* propositions, it follows that we can deduce a scheme of reality in the sense of a body of propositions which will be true of existent things if there are any existent things. But we cannot deduce that this condition is in fact fulfilled. We remain within the sphere of possibility.

Further, from propositions which state what must be true of every existent thing we can deduce only similar propositions. That is to say, from necessary propositions we cannot deduce contingent propositions, the opposite of which is possible. And this holds good whether we confine necessary propositions to those of formal logic and pure mathematics or whether we admit metaphysical principles which are necessarily true. In other words, if we start with premisses belonging to general metaphysics or ontology and proceed deductively, we remain within the sphere of general metaphysics or ontology. From such premisses we cannot deduce the true propositions which belong to the body of a particular science. We can, of course, apply metaphysical principles which are necessarily true of, say, every finite thing to particular classes of finite things. But this is not the same as deducing the propositions of chemistry or botany or medicine from metaphysical premisses. If we assume that the proposition that everything which comes into being does so through the agency of an extrinsic cause is a necessarily true metaphysical proposition, it follows that if there is such a thing as cancer of the lung it will have a cause or causes. But it certainly does not follow that we can deduce from metaphysics what the causes are.

I do not intend to imply that Descartes, for instance, believed that we can in fact start with general metaphysical truths and then deduce logically all the truths of natural science, dispensing with experiment or observation, hypothesis and empirical verification. But the tendency of rationalism was to assimilate the whole body of true propositions to a mathematical system in which all conclusions are logically implied by the fundamental premisses. And in so far as the rationalists entertained the ideal of such an assimilation, they were indulging in a vain dream.

Now, it has been said above that from two premisses neither of which is an existential proposition we cannot deduce an existential conclusion. But the question arises whether we can start with an existential proposition and deduce other existential propositions in such a way that from the existence of the ultimate ontological principle we can deduce the existence of dependent, finite being. In other words, can we start with the affirmation of the existence of the absolutely perfect and infinite being and deduce the existence of finite being?

To do this, we should have to be able to demonstrate one of two things. We should have to be able to show either that the meaning of the term 'infinite being' contains as part of itself the meaning of the term 'finite being' or that the nature of infinite being is such that it must necessarily cause (that is, create) finite being. In the first case we should have a monistic philosophy. To assert the existence of infinite being would be to assert the existence of finite being, the latter being comprised in some way within the former. If we had already demonstrated the existence of infinite being, by the ontological argument for example, we should only have to analyse the term 'infinite being' to show that finite being exists. In the second case we should not necessarily have a monistic philosophy; but finite being, even if distinct from God, would proceed from Him by a necessity of the divine nature.

As for the first alternative, the term 'infinite being' is used in contradistinction to the term 'finite being', and it comprises the latter within its meaning only in the sense that it involves the negation of finitude. Affirmation of the existence of infinite being involves the negation that this being is finite, not that finite being exists as its modification. Some might perhaps wish to claim that the term 'infinite being', taken in contradistinction to 'finite being', is vacuous; and that to give it content we must understand it as meaning the infinite complex of finite beings. But in this case the assertion that infinite being exists would be equivalent to the assertion that the number of finite beings is infinite. And it would be as idle to talk about deducing the existence of finite being from that of infinite being as it would be to talk about deducing the existence of tea-cups from the statement that the number of tea-cups is infinite. In the present context we are concerned with the deduction of finite being from that of infinite being when the existence of the latter is already known. But if to assert the existence of infinite being were to assert that the number of finite beings is infinite, how could we possibly be said to know that there is infinite being unless we knew that there was an infinite number of finite beings? And in this case the question of deducing their existence would not arise.

As for the second alternative, namely that of showing that God creates by a necessity of His nature, what basis could we possibly have for such an assertion? If we understand by God, an absolutely perfect and infinite being, to affirm God's existence is to affirm the existence of a being which is by nature self-sufficient. That is to say, the creation of finite being cannot add anything to God which would otherwise be lacking. And in this case it does not appear that there could be any conceivable grounds for asserting the necessity of creation. It is significant that Leibniz, when trying to explain divine creation, had recourse to the idea of moral rather than of metaphysical necessity. But if we once understand by God the absolutely perfect being, there does not seem to be any ground for speaking of creation as 'necessary' in any sense of the word.

Of course, if we were discussing theism and pantheism as such, we should have to consider the whole theme of the relation of the finite to the infinite. But we have been discussing a specific point, namely the deduction of finite from infinite being when the existence of the latter is taken as known. And this question implies a distinction between finite and infinite, for it is a question of deducing the existence of the finite from that of the infinite. If, therefore, the term 'infinite being' is analysed in such a way that it means simply an infinite number of finite beings, the problem of deduction, as originally understood, simply disappears. All that is required is an analysis of 'infinite being', and the analysis dissolves the problem. The original question no longer possesses any significance. If, however, we maintain the distinction which is essential for the significance of the problem (that is, the distinction between the infinite and the finite), there seems to be no conceivable ground for a deduction of the existence of finite being from that of infinite being. And it is with this deduction alone that we have been concerned, not with the problems which arise when we proceed the other way round and infer the existence of the infinite from the existence of the finite.

To sum up these critical reflections in dogmatic form. In the first place, from premisses which state what must be true of anything if there is anything, we cannot deduce the conclusion that there is something. In the second place, from premisses which state what must necessarily be true of anything we cannot deduce conclusions which are in fact true but which could conceivably be false. In the third place, we cannot begin with the affirmation of infinite being and deduce the existence of finite being. We cannot, therefore, construct a purely deductive metaphysics according to the model of a mathematical system, if we mean by a purely deductive metaphysics one in which the affirmation of the being that is first in the ontological order corresponds to the fundamental premisses of a mathematical system and in which the deduction of the existence of the world of finite beings corresponds to the deduction of conclusions in the mathematical system.

Obviously, these critical comments affect the systems of Descartes, Spinoza and Leibniz only in so far as they approximate to what I have called the ideal type of rationalism. And they do this in varying degrees. It is not my intention to deny that these philosophers said anything which was true or interesting. At the very least these philosophers present us with interesting outlooks on the world. And they raise important philosophical problems. Further, they offer programmes, as it were, for subsequent research. Thus Spinoza's description of the awareness or feeling of freedom as ignorance of determining causes can be interpreted, when we look back, as an invitation to the development of depth psychology. And Leibniz' dream of an ideal symbolic language has an obvious importance in the fields of logic and linguistic analysis. But all this does not alter the fact that the history of pre-Kantian continental rationalism has helped to show that metaphysical philosophy cannot take a form suggested by a close analogy with the deductive form of pure mathematics.

3. When we turn our attention to British empiricism, we are turning to a movement of thought which has a much greater significance for contemporary philosophy than pre-Kantian continental rationalism can be said to have. Hume is a living thinker in a sense in which Spinoza is not. The empiricism of the seventeenth and eighteenth centuries has, indeed, been developed; and the language in which it is now expressed is somewhat different from that employed by the classical empiricists. In particular, emphasis is now placed on logical rather than on psychological considerations. But the fact remains that empiricism exercises a powerful influence in modern thought, especially, of course, in England, whereas the influence exercised by pre-Kantian rationalist philosophers on the more metaphysically-minded thinkers of today does not proceed from their approximation to what I have called rationalism as an ideal type but from other aspects of their thought.

In discussing classical British empiricism one is faced with a difficulty analogous to that with which one is faced in attempting to discuss rationalism as such. For those philosophers of the seventeenth and eighteenth centuries who are traditionally classed as empiricist differed very considerably in their views. If one interprets empiricism in the light of its point of departure, namely Locke's theory that all ideas

are derived from experience, then we must obviously include
Locke as an empiricist. But if one interprets the movement
in the light of its point of arrival in the philosophy of Hume,
we shall have to admit that the philosophies of Locke and
Berkeley, while containing empiricist elements, are not purely
empiricist systems. But this difficulty is, of course, unavoidable if we propose to discuss empiricism as a set of doctrines
and as an ideal type rather than as an historical movement.
And as in this section I intend to concern myself with empiricism as represented principally by Hume, I remark in
advance that I am perfectly well aware that my comments
are relevant much more to Hume's thought than to that of
either Locke or Berkeley.

Hume's empiricism can, of course, be regarded under different aspects. It can be regarded as a psychological doctrine
about the origin and formation of ideas, or as an epistemological doctrine concerning the nature, scope and limits of human knowledge. We can consider it as a logical theory of the
different types of propositions or as an essay in conceptual
analysis, that is, in the analysis of concepts such as mind,
body, cause and so on. But all these different aspects are
unified by Hume himself in his idea of the science of human
nature, the study of man in his cognitive and reasoning activities and in his moral, aesthetic and social life. As we saw
when considering Hume's thought in Volume 5, he envisaged
an extension of 'experimental philosophy' to what he called,
using the term in a wide sense, 'moral subjects'. A study of
man is not, as such, a mark of empiricism. Man was studied
by the rationalists as well, not to speak of Greek, mediaeval
and Renaissance philosophers. But, as has just been mentioned, it was Hume's aim to apply to his subject-matter the
method of 'experimental philosophy'. And this meant for
him restricting oneself to the evidence offered by observation.
True, we ought to endeavour to find the simplest and fewest
causes which will explain phenomena. But in doing this we
must not go beyond phenomena in the sense of appealing to
occult entities, to unobserved substances. There may be occult causes; but even if there are, we cannot have anything
to do with them in the experimental science of man. We
must try to find general laws (the principle of the association of ideas, for example) which will correlate phenomena
and permit verifiable prediction. But we ought not to expect
or pretend to discover ultimate causes which transcend the

phenomenal level. And any hypothesis which purports to do so should be rejected.

In other words, Hume's plan is to extend to philosophy in general the methodological limitations of Newtonian physics. It is therefore not unreasonable to say that just as continental rationalism was influenced by the model of mathematical deduction, so was the empiricism of Hume influenced by the model of Newtonian physics. This is, indeed, made quite clear by Hume himself in his introduction to the *Treatise of Human Nature*. It is thus possible to look on both rationalism and empiricism as experiments, on rationalism as an experiment to see how far the mathematical model was applicable in philosophy, and on empiricism as an experiment in applying in philosophy the methodological limitations of classical physics.[5]

The feature of Hume's actual procedure which immediately strikes the reader is probably reductive analysis. By this term I understand analysis of the complex into the simple or relatively simple and of wholes into constituent parts. There was, indeed, nothing novel in the use of reductive analysis as such. Without going further back we can recall Locke's reduction of complex to simple ideas and Berkeley's analysis of material things as clusters of phenomena or, as he put it, 'ideas'. But Hume applied this method of investigation in a much more radical way than his predecessors had done. We have only to think of his analysis of causality and of the self.

We cannot say, of course, that Hume's philosophy was all analysis and no synthesis. For one thing he tried to reconstruct the complex out of its elements. Thus he tried to show, for example, how our complex idea of the causal relation arises. For another thing he performed an activity of synthesis in the sense of giving a general picture of, say, the extent of human knowledge and of the nature of moral experience. But metaphysical synthesis of the traditional type was excluded. It was excluded by his methodological limitations, and it was excluded by the results of his analysis. Given his analysis of causality, for example, he could not synthesize the multiplicity of phenomenal objects by relating them, as effects to cause, to a One which transcended the objects to be synthesized. Locke and Berkeley were able to proceed on these lines; but not Hume. Hence while it would be incorrect to say that there is no synthesis at all in the developed empiricism of Hume, we can legitimately say that in comparison with the rationalist systems it is an analytic philosophy. That is to say, its obvious feature is reductive analysis rather than synthesis as this would be understood by the rationalist metaphysicians.

We can put the matter in this way. Hume was concerned with analysing the meanings of terms such as 'cause', 'self', 'justice', and so on. He was not concerned with deducing the existence of one thing from that of another. In fact, his empiricism did not permit any such deduction. Hence any metaphysical synthesis of the rationalist type was excluded. The emphasis was necessarily placed on analysis. And we can say that a fully empiricist philosophy must be a predominantly analytic philosophy. In the philosophies of Locke and Berkeley analysis, though obviously present, is less predominant than in the philosophy of Hume. And the reason is that their philosophies are only partly empiricist.

There is, of course, no fault to be found with analysis as such. Nor can we reasonably object to a philosopher devoting himself primarily to analysis if he chooses to do so. Quite apart from the fact that metaphysical syntheses constructed without careful analysis of terms and propositions are likely to be houses of cards, it is quite natural that different philosophers should have different bents of mind. Further, the fact that the results of Hume's analysis exclude metaphysical syntheses of the traditional type can hardly be taken to prove without more ado that there must be flaws in his analysis. For the empiricist at least would comment that it is a case of so much the worse for metaphysics.

But though there can be no valid objection to analysis as such, it may be possible to object to the assumption or assumptions which are implicit in a given philosopher's practice of analysis. And it seems to me that Hume's practice of reductive analysis is guided by a mistaken assumption, namely that the real constituents of human experience are atomic, discrete 'perceptions'. Once Hume has assumed or, as he believes, shown that all ideas are derived from impressions[6] and that these impressions are 'distinct existences', it remains only to apply this assumption to the analysis of those ideas which seem to be of importance or interest. And if in the process of application we come upon cases where the general principle fails to work, inasmuch as it leads to insuperable inconsistencies, doubt is inevitably cast upon the validity of the general principle.

Hume's analysis of the self seems to be a case in point.

The self is resolved into distinct 'perceptions'. But Hume himself admits that we have a propensity to substitute the notion of identity for that of related objects (that is, distinct perceptions), and that this propensity is so great that we are apt to imagine something substantial connecting the perceptions. And it appears to follow that that which has to be reconstructed out of distinct perceptions must be something to which we can reasonably attribute such a propensity. Yet this is precisely what cannot be done. If the self consists, as Hume says it does, of a series or bundle of perceptions, there is nothing of which it can reasonably be said that it has a propensity to imagine something substantial connecting the perceptions. Hume, indeed, sees the difficulty. He admits his perplexity and openly confesses that he does not know how to correct his opinions or to render them consistent. But this admission really shows that his phenomenalistic analysis of the self will not do. And this conclusion casts doubt upon the general assumption that the ultimate constituents of human experience are atomic, discrete impressions.

It may be objected that it is incorrect to speak of an 'assumption'. Reductive analysis is a method, not an assumption, and Hume shows, to his own satisfaction at least, that it can be successfully applied to ideas such as those of causality and the self. One may think perhaps that the application in the case of the self, for instance, is not successful. But this is no reason for speaking of an assumption.

It is true, of course, that Hume attempts to show in concrete cases that we can analyse the meanings of words such as 'self' in terms of distinct 'perceptions'. And in this sense it is true to say that he does not simply assume that it can be done. But he certainly assumes as a working hypothesis that our ideas can be explained in terms of discrete impressions. And he does this because he tacitly assumes, again as a working hypothesis, that the ultimate constituents of human experience are atomic, discrete impressions which are the empirical data from which our interpretation of the world is constructed. He takes it that we can reduce our interpretation of the world to the empirical data which are the direct objects of consciousness, and that these data are 'impressions'. But in carrying out this empiricist reduction he forgets the self which enters experience as subject, in order to concentrate on the immediate objects of introspection. This procedure can perhaps be associated with the endeavour to apply the method of 'experimental philosophy' to 'moral subjects'. But its results, in the case of analysis of the self, show the limitations of the method.

In general, we have to be careful not to confuse the results of abstraction with the ultimate data of experience. Perceiving is a form of experiencing. And it may be that within perception we can distinguish by abstraction something corresponding to what Hume calls impressions. But it does not follow that impressions are the actual constituents, as it were, of perception, so that we can reconstruct the total experience simply in terms of impressions. Still less does it follow that what we perceive consists of impressions. It may sound naïve to say that in perceiving we must distinguish between subject, object and act of perceiving. It may seem to some to be no more than a reflection of language, that is, of the subject-verb-object type of proposition. But if one eliminates the subject, it is the subject which performs the elimination. And if we eliminated the object as distinct from the perceiving, we should end in solipsism.

It seems to me that the lines of criticism which I have suggested are applicable not only to Hume's philosophy but also to certain modern versions of his empiricism. Some empiricists have tried to avoid giving the impression that their phenomenalistic analysis is a piece of metaphysics, an ontological theory. Thus according to the theory of 'logical constructions' it is possible, in principle at least, to translate sentences about the mind into other sentences which do not contain the word 'mind' but mention psychical phenomena or events instead, in such a way that if the original sentence is true (or false) the equivalent sentences are true (or false), and *vice versa*. Similarly, a sentence about a table could, in principle at least, be translated into sentences in which the word 'table' would not occur but in which sense-data would be mentioned instead, there being a relation of truth-equivalence between the original sentence and its translation. A table is then said to be a 'logical construction' out of sense-data, and a mind a 'logical construction' out of psychical phenomena or events. Phenomenalism is thus put forward as a logical or linguistic and not as an ontological theory. But it seems to be doubtful whether this ingenious attempt to avoid having to admit that phenomenalism is a rival metaphysical theory to a non-phenomenalistic theory is successful. And in any case it can be asked how, given this analysis of mind, the construction of the 'logical construction' is possible. Further, if the analysis of physical objects such as tables implies that we perceive sense-data (and it is difficult to see how this implication can be successfully avoided), it is arguable that solipsism is the necessary consequence, unless one is willing to hold the strange theory of unattached sense-data, so to speak.

The objection may be raised that, whether my criticism of Hume is valid or not, it does not really touch the most important feature of his empiricism, namely its logical theory. The older empiricists certainly approached philosophy from a psychological angle. Thus Locke began by inquiring into the origin of our ideas. And this was a psychological question. Hume followed him in this path by tracing the origin of almost all ideas to impressions. But though such psychological questions are of importance if we are considering the history of empiricism, the permanent value of classical empiricism consists primarily in its contribution to logical theory. And it is this aspect of Hume's thought which should be stressed. It is the aspect which links him most closely with modern empiricism.

As regards Hume's link with modern empiricism, this is, I think, quite true. As we saw when considering Hume's philosophy in Volume 5, he made a distinction between demonstrative reasoning, which concerns the 'relations between ideas' and which is found, for example, in pure mathematics, and moral reasoning, which concerns 'matters of fact' and in which logical demonstration has no place. When we argue, for instance, from an effect to its cause, our conclusions may be more or less probable; but its truth is not, and cannot be, demonstrated. For the contrary of a matter of fact is always conceivable and possible: it never involves a logical contradiction. In pure mathematics, however, where we are concerned with the relations between ideas and not with matters of fact, affirmation of the contrary of the conclusion of a demonstration involves a contradiction.

Hume is here concerned with two kinds of reasoning; and his conclusion is that reasoning about matters of fact cannot amount to demonstration. We cannot, for example, demonstrate the existence of one thing from the existence of another. We may, indeed, feel certain about the truth of our conclusion; but if we prescind from states of feeling and attend to the logical aspect of the matter, we must admit that conclusions attained by reasoning about matters of fact cannot be certain.

In modern empiricism this point of view is retained; but

the emphasis is placed on a distinction between two types of proposition. A proposition which, in Hume's language, states a relation between ideas, is said to be analytic and to be true *a priori*. That is to say, its truth is logically independent of empirical verification. A proposition which, in Hume's language, concerns a matter of fact, is said to be synthetic. Its truth cannot be known from the proposition alone but only by empirical verification. It is empirical verification which shows whether the proposition is true or false. The contrary of the proposition is always logically possible; hence no amount of empirical verification can give it more than a very high degree of probability.

This classification of propositions excludes, of course, the possibility of any necessarily true existential propositions. But, as interpreted by the empiricists, it excludes also all propositions which, while not affirming the existence of any thing, purport to be both informative about reality and true *a priori* in the sense that their truth cannot be empirically refuted, even in principle. Take, for example, the statement that everything that comes into being or begins to exist does so through the agency of a cause. In Hume's opinion the truth of this statement is not seen by intuition. For the contrary is conceivable. Nor is its truth demonstrable. It is, therefore, an empirical generalization, an hypothesis which may be generally verified but which, in principle at least, admits of empirical refutation. And I suppose that if Hume were alive today, he would look on what is called 'infra-atomic indeterminacy' as constituting empirical confirmation of his assessment of the logical status of the principle of causality.

In the language of modern empiricism, therefore, there are analytic propositions, which are in some sense 'tautologies', and synthetic *a posteriori* propositions or empirical hypotheses; but there are no synthetic *a priori* propositions. All candidates for this class turn out in the end to be either tautologies, open or concealed, or empirical generalizations, which may enjoy a very high degree of probability but the truth of which cannot be known by analysis of the proposition itself.

The problem of synthetic *a priori* propositions is too complicated to be discussed here. But it may be as well to draw attention to the following points. Let us assume that the phenomena which are grouped under the title of infra-atomic indeterminacy can be so interpreted that the principle of causality can still be offered as a candidate for the rank of synthetic *a priori* proposition. And let us take it that the principle of causality states that anything which comes into being or begins to exist does so through the agency of a cause.[7] In one sense the empiricist is quite right when he says that denial of this proposition involves no logical contradiction. That is to say, there is no verbal contradiction between the propositions 'X comes into being' and 'X has no cause'. If there were a verbal contradiction, the principle of causality, as stated above, would be an analytic proposition in the sense in which the empiricist understands the term. It is thus possible to understand the meanings of the English (or French or German, etc.) words used in stating the principle of causality and yet not to see any necessary connection between coming into being and being caused. We can hardly claim that nobody who denies this necessary connection understands the English words employed in the statement of the principle. We should have, I think, to be able to show that there is a deeper level of understanding than what is ordinarily meant by understanding the meanings of certain words.[8] It might then be claimed that though the empiricist's position cannot be assailed at the level of reflection on which he stands, its inadequacy can be seen when one passes to the level of metaphysical insight.

These remarks obviously do not answer the question whether there are or are not synthetic *a priori* propositions. They are designed rather to indicate what must be shown if we claim that there are. It may, indeed, occur to the reader that there is another way of tackling the empiricist position, namely by denying that the propositions of pure mathematics, for example, are purely formal in the sense of being 'tautological'. In other words, it might be claimed that the propositions of pure mathematics are in some sense about reality, even though they are not existential propositions. But if we wish to claim that they are synthetic *a priori* propositions and not analytic propositions in the sense in which the empiricist uses the term, we must be prepared to explain in what sense they are informative about reality.

To return to Hume. Given his classification of propositions, it is clearly impossible to construct an *a priori* deductive system of metaphysics, the propositions of which will be infallibly true of reality. Nor, given his analysis of causality, can we start with the data of experience and infer the existence of God by a causal argument in the way that both Locke and Berkeley thought that we could. But it may appear at first sight that it is still possible to regard metaphysical theories as hypotheses which may enjoy varying degrees of probability.

It is true, of course, that Hume discussed some metaphysical problems. And he seems to have been willing to say that it is more probable that there is some cause of order in the universe which bears a remote analogy to human intelligence than that there is no such cause. At the same time it seems to me to follow from his general premises that terms which are used to denote metaphysical entities are void of meaning when used in this context. For ideas are derived from impressions. And if we think that we have an idea because we use a certain word, and if at the same time we cannot indicate, even in principle, the impression or impressions from which this idea is derived, we are forced to conclude that we have no such idea. And in this case the term or word is vacuous. True, Hume allowed for possible exceptions from the general rule that ideas follow impressions. But he certainly did not make this concession in favour of metaphysics. And though it is only in a rhetorical passage that he dismisses metaphysics as meaningless nonsense, I am inclined to think that this passage represents the conclusion to which Hume's premises logically lead, at least if we press the assertion that ideas are faint images of impressions. And in this case metaphysical theories can hardly be genuine hypotheses.

It seems arguable, therefore, that the empiricism of Hume, if it is developed to the conclusions which are implicitly contained in it, leads to the rejection of metaphysics as so much verbiage. And this development has taken place in the present century at the hands of the neopositivists or logical positivists or radical empiricists, according to whom metaphysical statements can possess no more than 'emotive' significance.[9] So once more we have a link between Hume's philosophy and modern radical empiricism.

It may be objected that this line of interpretation amounts to treating Hume's thought as a kind of preparation for neopositivism, and that this treatment is defective on several counts. In the first place his contemporary relevance lies rather in the emphasis he gave to philosophical analysis in general than in his anticipations of neopositivism in particular, which, in its original dogmatic form at least, has proved to be a passing phase. In the second place a treatment of Hume as a preparation for later thinkers, whether positivists or not, necessarily fails to do justice to his own interpretation of human experience. Whether one agrees or not with what he says, his account of the scope and limitations of human knowledge, his examination of man's affective, moral and aesthetic life and his political theory, which together constitute his attempt to develop a science of man, are only obscured if one persists in treating his thought in function of later philosophical developments.

These objections are, I think, well-founded. At the same time a treatment of Hume's philosophy in the light of later empiricism does help to bring into relief his contemporary relevance. And it is important to do this, even if one confines oneself to a particular aspect of his contemporary relevance. Hume's empiricism suffers from several grave defects. For instance, his atomization of experience is, in my opinion, a fundamental mistake; his theory of ideas is not, I think, tenable; and it might well be claimed that Kant, in his insistence on the transcendental unity of apperception as a basic condition of human experience, was in a sense more 'empirical' than Hume. But the defects of Hume's philosophy do not diminish its historical importance. And though in some respects his thought falls into older patterns,[10] his concentration on analysis is certainly not the least of his titles to be considered a living thinker.

4. In the introduction to Volume 4 we noted that Hume's idea of a science of man represents very well the spirit of the eighteenth-century Enlightenment. And in considering the French Enlightenment in the present volume we saw how philosophers such as Condillac endeavoured to develop Locke's psychological and epistemological theories and to give an empirical account of the genesis and growth of man's mental life; how writers such as Helvétius developed theories of man's moral life; how Montesquieu studied the structure and growth of societies; how Rousseau and others produced their political theories; how the physiocrats began the study of economics; and how thinkers such as Voltaire, Turgot and Condorcet sketched theories of historical development in the light of the ideals of the Age of Reason. All such studies, psychological, ethical, social, political, historical and economic, can be grouped together under the general title of the scientific study of man.

In pursuing this study the philosophers whom we are accustomed to consider as typical representatives of the Enlightenment were concerned to free it from theological and metaphysical presuppositions. This is, I think, one of the salient features of the thought of the period. The aim is not so much to deduce a comprehensive system from self-evident principles as to understand the empirical data by correlating them under empirically verified laws. Thus Condillac was concerned with giving an empirical account of the development of man's mental life, and Montesquieu endeavoured to group the diverse data in the development of different societies under universal laws. In general, Locke's empirical approach exercised a widespread influence. And there is thus a very considerable difference between the atmosphere, so to speak, of the great systems of continental rationalism and the thought of the eighteenth-century Enlightenment. The atmosphere of the former is that of deduction, of the latter that of induction. It is true that this statement, like other such rash generalizations, stands in need of qualification. For instance, one would hardly think immediately of empirical induction on hearing the name of Wolff, the hero of the German *Aufklärung*. At the same time the generalization does at any rate draw attention, even if in an over-simplified manner, to a real difference in spirit and atmosphere.

This difference can be illustrated by a reference to moral theory. The moral theory of Spinoza formed an integral part of a deductively-expounded grandiose system; and it was closely associated with metaphysical doctrines. But when we turn to the moral theories of Hume in England or of Helvétius and the Encyclopaedists in France, we find their authors insisting on the autonomy of the moral consciousness and on the separation of ethics from theology.

Similarly, while the idea of the social compact or contract in political theory is not derived from study of the empirical data but constitutes an attempt to give a rational justification of political authority and of the restriction of individual liberty in organized society, we do not find that the political theorists of the eighteenth century are much given to deducing society and authority from metaphysical and theological doctrines. They are concerned rather with the observed needs of man. And it is this approach, of course, which enables Hume to substitute for the more rationalist idea of the social contract the empirical idea of felt utility.

This is not to say, indeed, that the men of the Enlightenment had no presuppositions of their own. As we saw, they assumed a theory of progress according to which progress consists in the advancing rationalization ot man, this rationalization involving man's emancipation from religious superstition and from irrational forms of government, ecclesiastical or civil. In their opinion the fruits of progress were best represented by themselves, the enlightened free-thinkers of the Parisian *salons*; and further progress would consist in the spread of the ideas for which they stood and in the refashioning of society according to the ideals of the Enlightenment. Once a reform of the social structure had taken place, men would advance in morality and virtue. For the moral state of man is largely dependent on his environment and on education.

It may be objected that the theory of progress as maintained by the men of the Enlightenment was an empirical generalization rather than a presupposition. And though in the nineteenth century it may have tended to take the form of a 'dogma', especially when it was thought to be supported by the theory of evolution, for the eighteenth-century thinkers it had more the nature of a plastic hypothesis. Even when Turgot anticipated Comte's law of the three stages of human thought, he was propounding an hypothesis based on a study of the historical data rather than an *a priori* pattern to which the data were made to conform.

It is, indeed, obviously true that in the judgment of the thinkers of the Enlightenment the theory of progress was based on historical facts. They did not present it as a conclusion derived from metaphysical premises. But it is also true that it played the part of a presupposition, based on a value-judgment. That is to say, the Encyclopaedists and those who shared their outlook first formed their ideals of man and of society and then interpreted progress as a movement towards the realization of those ideals. There is, of course, nothing very strange in this procedure. But it meant, for instance, that they came to the study of human history with a presupposition which exercised an undue influence on their interpretation of history. For example, they were unable to appreciate the contribution of the Middle Ages to European culture: the Middle Ages inevitably appeared to them as the Dark Ages. For if progress meant advance towards the fulfilment of the ideals represented by *les philosophes* of the eighteenth century, it involved liberation from some of the leading features of mediaeval culture. Light was represented by the advanced thinkers of the eighteenth century, and the advance of 'reason' was incompatible with mediaeval religion or with a philosophy which was closely associated with theology. In this sense the men of the Enlightenment had a 'dogma' of their own.

Their point of view also meant, of course, that they were unable to do justice to important aspects of human nature and life. It is, indeed, an exaggeration to say that *les philosophes* had no understanding of any aspect of man other than the life of the analytic and emancipated reason. Hume, for instance, insisted on the great part played by feeling and asserted that reason is and ought to be the slave of the passions.[11] And Vauvenargues emphasized the importance of the affective side of human nature. Even if Rousseau's attacks on the Encyclopaedists were not without foundation, we cannot take his strictures as representing the whole truth. At the same time *les philosophes* showed little appreciation of, for example, man's religious life. It would be absurd to turn to Voltaire among the deists or to d'Holbach among the atheists for a profound understanding of religion. D'Holbach outlined a naturalistic philosophy of religion; but it will not bear comparison with the idealist philosophies of religion which we find in the next century. The rationalist freethinkers of the eighteenth century were too much preoccupied with the idea of man's emancipation from what they regarded as the deadening weight of the chains of superstition and priestcraft to have any profound understanding of the religious consciousness.

This element of superficiality shows itself, for instance, in the materialist current of thought in the philosophy of the Enlightenment. As we saw, the word 'materialist' cannot legitimately be used as a label to be applied indiscriminately to *les philosophes*. But there were materialists among them, and they present us with the somewhat comical spectacle of man as subject engaged in reducing himself, so to speak, to a purely material object. It is easy to understand the repugnance and disgust which d'Holbach's *System of Nature* aroused in the mind of Goethe as a student. And d'Holbach was not the crudest of the materialists.

But the superficiality of the philosophy of the French Enlightenment in some of its aspects should not blind one to the historical importance of the movement. Rousseau, indeed, stands in a class by himself. His ideas have an intrinsic interest and they exercised a considerable influence on subsequent thinkers such as Kant and Hegel. But though the Encyclopaedists and kindred philosophers, from whom Rousseau chose to dissociate himself, may not occupy a similar position in the development of philosophy, they nevertheless exercised an important influence which has to be estimated, I think, not so much in terms of definite 'results' to which we can point as in terms of their contribution to the formation of a mentality or outlook. Perhaps we can say that the typical philosophers of the French Enlightenment represent the idea that man's betterment, welfare and happiness rest in his own hands. Provided that he frees himself from the notion that his destiny depends on a supernatural power, whose will is expressed through ecclesiastical authority, and provided that he follows the path marked out by reason, he will be able to create the social environment in which true human morality can flourish and in which the greater good of the greatest possible number can be successfully promoted. The idea, which later became so widespread, that the growth of scientific knowledge and a more rational organization of society would inevitably bring with them an increase of human happiness and further the attainment of sound moral ideals was a development of the outlook of the Enlightenment. True, other factors, such as the advance of technical science, were required before the idea could assume its developed form. But the fundamental idea that human welfare depends on the exercise of reason emancipated from the trammels of authority, of religious dogmas and of dubious metaphysical doctrines came into prominence in the eighteenth century. It was not, as at the Reformation, a question of substituting Protestant for Catholic dogma but of substituting 'free thought', the autonomy of reason, for authority.

These remarks are not, of course, intended to express agreement with the point of view of men like Voltaire. Their idea of reason was limited and narrow. To exercise reason meant for them pretty well to think as *les philosophes* thought; whereas to anyone who believes that God has revealed Himself it is rational to accept this revelation and irrational to reject it. And in any case the men of the Enlightenment were not as free from presuppositions and prejudices as they fondly imagined. Further, their optimistic rationalism has obviously met with a powerful challenge in the twentieth century. But all this does not alter the fact that an outlook which has exercised a considerable influence in the modern world took clear shape in the eighteenth century. The ideals of freedom of thought and of toleration, which have played such a part in the civilization of western Europe and

of North America, found striking expression in the writings
of the eighteenth-century philosophers.[12] No doubt we can
add that the philosophers of the French Enlightenment gave
a powerful stimulus to the promotion of scientific studies,
in psychology, for example. And some of them, such as
d'Alembert, made real contributions in the advance of extra-philosophical pursuits. But their chief importance lies,
I think, in their contribution to the formation of a general
mentality or outlook.

To a certain extent the philosophy of the Enlightenment
expressed the development of the middle classes. From the
economic point of view the middle class had, of course, been
in process of development for a long time. But in the seventeenth and eighteenth centuries its rise was reflected in philosophical currents of thought which, in France, were hostile
to the *ancien régime* and which helped to prepare the way
for a different organization of society. Such remarks, it may
be said, have a Marxist flavour; but they are not for this reason necessarily erroneous.

In conclusion I wish to draw attention to one selected
problem which arises out of eighteenth-century philosophy.
We have seen that the typical representatives of the Enlightenment tended to insist on the separation of ethics from
theology and metaphysics. And I think that behind their
attitude there was a genuine philosophical question. But
some of the writers of the Enlightenment obscured rather
than clarified the nature of this question. I refer to those who
were concerned to argue that religion, especially dogmatic
Christianity, exercises a baneful influence on moral conduct,
with the implication that deism or atheism, as the case may
be, is more conducive to morality and virtue. This way of
talking obscures the nature of the philosophical question
about the relation between ethics on the one hand and metaphysics and theology on the other. For one thing, the question whether virtue is more prevalent among Christians or
non-Christians is not a philosophical question. For another
thing, if we say, for example, that deism is more conducive
to morality and virtue than are Catholicism and Protestant-
ism, we imply that there is a connection between metaphysical beliefs and morals. For deism is, of course, a form of
metaphysics. And we ought to make it clear precisely what
sort of connection we wish to affirm.

The philosophical question at issue is clearly not whether
talk about human conduct can be distinguished from talk

about the existence and attributes of God or about things considered simply as beings. For it obviously can be distinguished. In other words, it is clear enough that ethics or moral philosophy has its own subject-matter. This was recognized, for example, by Aristotle in the ancient world and by Aquinas in the Middle Ages.

The immediate question is rather whether fundamental moral principles can be derived from metaphysical or theological premisses. But this question can be reformulated in a broader way, without any specific reference to metaphysical or theological premisses. Let us suppose that someone says: 'We are creatures of God; therefore we ought to obey Him.' The first statement is a statement of fact. The second is a moral statement. And the speaker asserts that the first entails the second. We can ask, therefore, putting the question in a general form, whether a statement of what ought to be the case can be derived from a statement of what is the case, a moral statement from a statement of fact. This general formulation of the question would apply not only to the example which I have given but also, for instance, to the deduction of moral statements from statements of fact about the characteristics of human nature, when no reference is made to theological truths.

This question, we may note, was formulated explicitly by David Hume. 'In every system of morality which I have hitherto met with I have always remarked that the author proceeds for some time in the ordinary way of reasoning and establishes the being of a God or makes observations concerning human affairs, when of a sudden I am surprised to find that instead of the usual copulations of propositions, *is* and *is not*, I meet with no proposition that is not connected with an *ought* or an *ought not*. This change is imperceptible, but is, however, of the last consequence. For as this *ought* or *ought not* expresses some new relation or affirmation, it is necessary that it should be observed and explained, and at the same time that a reason should be given for what seems altogether inconceivable, how this new relation can be a deduction from others, which are entirely different from it'.[13] But though Hume explicitly raised this question, the utilitarians tended to pass it over; and it is only in modern ethical theory that it has been given prominence.

The question is obviously important. For it is relevant not only to authoritarian ethics but also to teleological ethics of the type which first asserts that human nature is of such a kind or that man seeks a certain end and then derives ought-statements from this statement of fact. And I have drawn attention to it because of its importance, not with a view to undertaking a discussion of the right answer. For such a discussion would involve, for instance, an analysis of ought-statements, and this is a task for the writer of a treatise on ethical theory rather than an historian of philosophy. However, to avoid any possible misunderstanding of my remarks it may be appropriate to state explicitly that I have no intention of suggesting that the idea of a teleological ethics must be abandoned. On the contrary I think that the concept of the good is paramount in morals, and that 'ought' must be interpreted in function of the idea of the good. At the same time any defender of a teleological ethical theory must take account of the question raised by Hume. And it is worth while having pointed out that behind the polemical utterances of French writers about the separation of ethics from metaphysics and theology there lies a genuine philosophical question. That it was Hume who gave a clear explicit formulation to this question is not, I think, surprising.

5. Mention has been made in the last section of the tendency shown by philosophers of the French Enlightenment to look on history as an advance towards the rationalism of the eighteenth century, an advance out of darkness into light, and to expect in the future further advance which would consist in the fuller implementation of the ideals of the Age of Reason. And in the present volume the fourth Part was devoted to the rise of the philosophy of history in the pre-Kantian modern period. It is appropriate, therefore, to make some general remarks in this Concluding Review about the philosophy of history. But the remarks must be brief. For the idea of philosophy of history is best discussed in connection with later thinkers who developed the theme on the grand scale. At present I wish to content myself with merely suggesting some lines of thought for the reader's reflection.

If by philosophy of history one means a critique of historical method, then philosophy of history is obviously a possible and legitimate undertaking. For just as it is possible to examine scientific method, so is it possible to examine the method or methods employed by historians. We can ask questions about the concept of historical fact, about the nature and role of interpretation of the data, about the part played by imaginative reconstruction, and so on. We can discuss the norms of selection which are observed by historians; and we can inquire what presuppositions, if any, are implicit in historical interpretation and reconstruction.

But when we speak of Bossuet or Vico or Montesquieu or Condorcet or Lessing or Herder as a philosopher of history, it is not of these meta-historical inquiries that we are thinking. For such inquiries are concerned with the nature and method of historiography rather than with the course of historical events. And when we speak of the philosophy of history we think of interpretations of the actual course of historical events rather than of an analysis of the historian's method, norms of selection, presuppositions, and so on. We think of the search for patterns or for a pattern in the course of history and of theories of universal laws which are supposed to be operative in history.

Talk about searching for patterns in history is somewhat ambiguous. We can perfectly well say that historians themselves are concerned with patterns. A man who writes a history of England, for instance, is obviously concerned to trace an intelligible pattern of events. He does not leave us with a series of unconnected historical statements such as the statement that William the Conqueror landed in England in 1066. He tries to show how this event came to pass and why the Conqueror acted as he did: he tries to illustrate the effects which the Norman invasion had on English life and culture. And in doing this he inevitably exhibits a pattern of events. But we do not for this reason call him a philosopher of history. Further, the mere fact that a given historian casts his net more widely and concerns himself with a great range of historical data does not of itself qualify him for the label 'philosopher of history'.

But searching for a pattern in history may mean something more than this. It may mean attempting to show that there is a necessary pattern in history, this pattern taking the form either of a movement towards a goal which will be attained whatever the motives of individuals may be or of a series of cycles the course and rhythm of which are determined by certain universal laws. In the case of such theories we should certainly speak of philosophy of history.

Here again, however, there is room for a distinction. On the one hand a man might believe that in his study of history he had discovered certain recurrent patterns, and he might then endeavour to explain this recurrence in terms of the operation of certain laws. Or he might think that the actual course of history manifests a movement towards a condition

of affairs which he regards as desirable and which has come
about in spite of obstacles. On the other hand a man might
come to the study of history with an already-formed belief,
derived from theology or from metaphysics, that human history moves inevitably towards the attainment of a certain
end or goal. With this belief in mind he then endeavours to
see how the actual course of historical events confirms this
belief. The distinction is thus between empirically-grounded
philosophy of history and one the main tenet of which is an
a priori theory, in the sense that the theory is brought ready-
made to the study of history.

The distinction, when expressed in this abstract way, seems
to be clear enough. But it does not follow, of course, that it
is always easy to assign a given philosopher of history to one
definite class. Perhaps we can assign Montesquieu to the first
class. For he seems to have thought that the laws which he
regarded as operative in history were derived from a study of
the actual course of events. Bossuet belongs definitely to the
second class. For his conviction that a providential divine
plan is worked out in history was obviously derived from
theology. And Hegel, in the nineteenth century, also belongs
to this class. For he explicitly asserts that in studying the
course of history the philosopher brings to it the truth (believed to have been demonstrated in what we would call
metaphysics) that Reason is the sovereign of history, that is,
that Absolute Reason manifests itself in the historical process. But it is not so easy to classify writers such as Condorcet.
At the very least, however, we can say that they made a
value-judgment about the spirit of the Enlightenment, and
that this judgment influenced their interpretation of history.
That is to say, they made an approving value-judgment about
the culture which they diagnosed as emerging out of the past
and as beginning to express itself in the spirit of the Enlightenment; and they then interpreted the past in the light
of this judgment. As has already been remarked, this affected,
for example, their interpretation of the Middle Ages, which
constituted in their eyes a retrogressive movement on the
upward path. In other words, their interpretation of history
and their tracing of a pattern were permeated and influenced
by judgments of value. The same sort of remark could be
made, of course, about some historians who are not generally
thought of as philosophers of history. Gibbon is a case in
point. But Condorcet seems to have assumed that a law of
progress operates in historical development (and his concept

of what constitutes progress obviously involved value-judgments). And for this reason he can be called a philosopher of history. True, he did not make this assumption very clear; and he laid stress on the need for human effort, particularly in the field of education, to perfect man and human society. But his confident optimistic belief in the advance of history from darkness into light involved an implicit assumption about a teleological movement in historical development.

It does not seem to me that one can justifiably dismiss all philosophy of history in a pure *a priori* manner. As far as those philosophies of history are concerned which purport to be generalizations derived from objective study of historical data, the main question is whether the empirical evidence is such as to render probable the truth of a given theory. We can, of course, raise the question whether the concept of historical laws, as found, for instance, in the philosophy of Vico, does not assume that there is repetition in history; and if we think that this assumption is in fact made, it is open to us to challenge it. But the challenge will have to be based on appeal to historical evidence. And if the reply is made that the concept of historical laws does not assume repetition in history but is based on similarities and analogies between different events or different periods, any discussion of these themes must be conducted in the light of the available evidence. We might, indeed, wish to say that the concept of historical laws can be ruled out *a priori* in virtue of an appeal to human freedom. But though human freedom and initiative would be incompatible with the operation of what one might call 'iron laws', it might be possible to elaborate a conception of historical law which would be compatible with human freedom. In other words, it might be possible to develop a theory of loose-texture cultural cycles which would not make nonsense of human choice. The question whether there was any sufficient ground for the development of such a theory would have to be decided in the light of historical data. At the same time, apart from the question whether the division of history into cultural cycles is legitimate and well-grounded, we should have to ask ourselves whether the so-called laws which are supposed to govern the rhythm of these cycles were anything better than truisms on the one hand or, on the other, propositions which the historian himself would be quite capable of enunciating, without the aid of any philosopher.

As for those philosophies of history in which the philosopher openly brings to the study of historical development a belief derived from theology or from metaphysics, there is at least this to be said in their favour, that they are honest, in the sense that the assumption is explicitly stated. In this respect they are preferable to those philosophies of history which do indeed assume that history moves inevitably towards a certain goal but in which this assumption is concealed. Further, the belief which is taken over from theology or from metaphysics may be quite true. It may be quite true, and in my opinion it is true, that divine providence operates in history and that the divine plan will be realized whether human beings like it or not. But it by no means follows that this belief can be of very much practical use for the study of history. Historical events have their phenomenal causes, and without revelation we cannot really tell how the actual course of events is related to divine providence. We can conjecture and speculate, it is true; we can see in the fall of a nation a symbol of divine judgment, or a symbol of the transitoriness of the things of this world. But neither conjecture nor a deciphering of symbols from the standpoint of faith permit prediction. If these activities are what we mean by philosophy of history, then philosophy of history is, of course, possible. But it is then a pursuit, perhaps profitable and in any case harmless, which the man of faith can undertake if he chooses; but it cannot be said to yield scientific knowledge. Moreover, if we rashly assume that we know the providential plan and that we can discern by philosophical reflection its operation in history, we shall probably find ourselves committed to justifying all that happens.

These remarks are not intended to indicate that the present writer entirely rejects the idea of a philosophy of history which goes beyond meta-historical inquiries such as analysis of the historian's method and presuppositions. But they are intended to express a serious doubt concerning the validity of the idea. I believe that a theology of history is possible; but its scope is extremely limited, being determined by the limits of revelation. And I very much doubt whether it is possible to go further than St. Augustine went. But when we turn from Bossuet to the philosophers of history in the eighteenth century, we find them substituting philosophy for theology in the belief that they are thereby giving to their theories of history the character of scientific knowledge. And I doubt whether philosophy of history is capable of assuming this character. No doubt, the philosophers make true statements;

but the question is whether these statements are not the sort of truths which can perfectly well be made by the historian himself. In other words, the question is whether the philosopher as such can achieve anything more in developing a synthetic interpretation of history than can be achieved by the historian. If not, there is no place for philosophy of history in the sense in which the term is being used. But it is, of course, difficult to draw any clear line of demarcation between history and philosophy of history. If by the latter term we mean broad generalizations, the historian himself can make them.

6. The three volumes of this *History* which are devoted to the philosophy of the seventeenth and eighteenth centuries end with a discussion of the Kantian system. And it will obviously be expected of any Concluding Review that it should contain some reflections on Kant's thought. I do not propose, of course, to give a summary of his philosophy. A preliminary summary was provided in the introduction to Volume 4, and after the extended treatment of Kant in the present volume a second summary would be superfluous. Nor do I propose to undertake a direct refutation of Kantianism. I propose instead to make some general reflections about its relations to preceding philosophy and to the German speculative idealism which followed it. And I also wish to draw attention to some of the questions which arise out of Kant's philosophy.

There is, I suppose, a natural temptation to represent the philosophy of Kant as the confluence of the two streams of continental rationalism and British empiricism. It is a natural temptation because there are some obvious grounds for representing his thought in this way. For instance, he was brought up, philosophically speaking, in the scholasticized version of Leibniz' philosophy as presented by Wolff and his successors, and he then underwent the shock, as it were, of Hume's empiricist criticism which awoke him from his dogmatic slumbers. Further, in the construction of Kant's own philosophy we can discern the influence of both movements. For example, his discovery of Leibniz himself, as distinct from Wolff and his successors, had a very considerable influence on Kant's mind; and we may recall that Leibniz had asserted the phenomenal character of space and time. Indeed, the Kantian theory of the *a priori* can be represented as in some sense a development of Leibniz' theory of virtually innate ideas, with the difference that the ideas became innate categorical functions. At the same time we can recall that Hume himself had maintained a subjective contribution to the formation of certain complex ideas, such as that of the causal relation. And thus we might represent Kant's theory of the *a priori* as being also influenced by Hume's position in the light of the former's conviction that Newtonian physics presents us with synthetic *a priori* propositions. In other words, Kant not only offered an answer to Hume's empiricism and phenomenalism but also, in formulating this answer, utilized suggestions made by the British philosopher himself, though the latter did not see their full significance and possibilities.

It would, however, be absurd, were one to represent the Kantian philosophy as a synthesis of continental rationalism and British empiricism in the sense of a conflation of elements borrowed from two mutually opposed currents of thought. Like any other philosopher, Kant was subject to influence by his contemporaries and by his predecessors. And though opinions may differ about the degree of influence which should be ascribed to Leibniz and Hume respectively, we cannot call in question the fact that each man exercised some influence on the development of Kant's thought. So, for the matter of that, did Wolff and his disciples. At the same time any elements which may have been derived from or suggested by other philosophies were taken up and welded together by Kant in a system which was very much more than a conflation. It was intended to supersede both rationalist metaphysics and empiricism, not to combine the incompatible.

The inappropriateness of describing Kant's system as a synthesis of rationalism and empiricism becomes clear if we recall his fundamental problem, the pervasive problem, so to speak, of his philosophy. As we saw, he was faced with the problem of effecting a harmonization between the world of Newtonian physics, the world of mechanistic causality and determinism, and the world of freedom. True, Descartes also had been faced with an analogous problem: it was not a problem peculiar to Kant but one which arose out of the historical situation when natural science had once begun its remarkable development. But the point is that in grappling with this problem Kant submitted to critical examination both rationalism and empiricism and worked out his own philosophy, not as a synthesis of these two movements, but as a triumph over them. Empiricism, he thought, is inadequate because it is unable to account for the possibility of synthetic *a priori* knowledge. If we take scientific knowledge seriously, we cannot embrace sheer empiricism, even if we agree that all knowledge begins with experience. We must have recourse to a theory of the *a priori* formal element in knowledge. That is to say, we cannot explain the possibility of scientific knowledge if we assume that experience is simply given: we have to allow for the subject's construction of experience if we are going to account for the possibility of *a priori* knowledge. But this does not mean that we should accept rationalist metaphysics. If anyone takes moral experience, freedom and religion seriously, it may seem to him that the dogmatic metaphysics of the rationalist philosophers, at least of those who allowed for freedom, offers a sure rational basis for the moral law and for belief in freedom, immortality and God. But this is not the case. Rationalist metaphysics cannot stand up to criticism; and the hollowness of its pretensions to knowledge is shown empirically by the conflict of systems and by the evident incapacity of metaphysics to reach assured results. And the theory of the *a priori*, the transcendental critique of knowledge, shows why this must be the case. But at the same time that this new science shows the hollowness of dogmatic metaphysics it also shows the limitations of scientific knowledge. And for anyone who takes seriously the moral consciousness and the beliefs and hopes which are intimately associated with it the way is left open for a rationally legitimate, though scientifically indemonstrable, belief in freedom, immortality and God. The great truths of metaphysics are then placed beyond the reach of destructive criticism by the very act of removing them from the position of conclusions to worthless metaphysical arguments and linking them with the moral consciousness which is as much a fundamental feature of man as his capacity of scientific knowledge.

In working out his philosophy Kant obviously made use of suggestions and ideas derived from other philosophers. And specialists can trace the origins and development of this or that idea. But this fact does not justify our saying that the Kantian system is a conflation of rationalism and empiricism. He agreed with empiricist criticism of rationalist metaphysics, and at the same time he agreed with the metaphysicians about the importance of the leading metaphysical problems and about the existence of a sphere of noumenal reality to which physical science has no access. But this does not mean that rationalism and empiricism can be combined. It is rather that Kant's measure of agreement, coupled with his measure of disagreement, with each movement drives him forward to the development of an original philosophy. The fact of scientific knowledge rules out sheer empiricism. And a critical analysis of the possibility and conditions of this knowledge rules out dogmatic metaphysics. But man is not simply 'understanding': he is also a moral agent. And his moral consciousness reveals to him his freedom and justifies a practical assurance of spiritual reality, while his aesthetic experience helps him to see the physical world as the manifestation of this reality. To a certain extent, of course, we can see in the Kantian philosophy the culmination of previous lines of thought. Thus it is not unreasonable to regard his theory of the subject's construction of experience as an original development which issued out of a combination of the rationalistic theory of virtually innate ideas with the empiricist tendency to speak as though the immediate objects of experience were phenomena or impressions or sense-data. I have no wish to deny continuity in the development of philosophy or the fact that Kant's philosophy took the form which it did largely because of the character of preceding philosophical thought. But at the same time it remains true that in a certain sense Kant turned his back on both rationalism and empiricism. In other words, if we wished to speak of the Kantian system as a 'synthesis' of rationalism and empiricism, we should have to understand the term in a sense approximating to that given it by Hegel, that is, in the sense that Kant subsumed the elements of positive value (estimated from his own point of view) in the preceding rival traditions or antitheses in an original system, incorporation in which at the same time transformed these elements.

Now, if Kant turned his back on rationalist metaphysics, which he called 'rotten dogmatism', it may appear difficult to explain how it came to pass not only that the critical philosophy was followed in Germany by a series of metaphysical systems but also that the authors of these systems looked on themselves as the true successors of Kant who had developed his thought in the right direction. But if one bears in mind the tension between Kant's theory of the subject's construction of experience and his doctrine of the thing-in-itself, it is an easy matter to understand how German speculative idealism grew out of the critical philosophy.

Kant's doctrine of the thing-in-itself was certainly not un-attended by difficulties. Apart from the fact that the nature of the thing-in-itself was declared to be unknowable, not even its existence as cause of the material of sensation could be positively asserted without misuse (on Kant's premisses) of the categories of causality and existence. To be sure, Kant was aware of this fact. And while it seemed to him that the concept of phenomenon demanded as its correlative the con-cept of thing-in-itself, the former not making any sense with-out the latter, he maintained that we must refrain from asserting dogmatically the existence of the thing-in-itself, though we cannot help thinking it. It is clear that Kant thought it absurd to reduce reality to a mere construction of the subject, and that he therefore looked on the retention of the concept of the thing-in-itself as a matter of common sense. At the same time he was aware of his difficult position and tried to find formulas which would save him from self-contradiction but which at the same time would enable him to retain a concept which he regarded as indispensable. One can understand Kant's attitude in this matter. But one can also understand Fichte's objections to the theory of the thing-in-itself, which he looked on as a superfluity, indeed as a monstrosity. In his view the thing-in-itself had to be elimi-nated in the interests of idealism. In his opinion Kant was a man who tried to have things both ways at once, and who therefore involved himself in hopeless inconsistencies. If one had once accepted the Kantian theory of the subject's part in the construction of experience, one was bound, thought Fichte, to go forward to a fully idealist philosophy.

This step involved inevitably a transition from theory of knowledge to metaphysics. If the thing-in-itself is eliminated, it follows that the subject creates the object in its entirety; it does not merely mould, so to speak, a given material. And the theory that the subject creates the object is obviously a metaphysical theory, even if the approach to it is by way of a critique of knowledge.

But what is this creative subject? When Kant spoke about the subject's construction of experience, he was talking about the individual subject. True, he introduced the concept of the transcendental ego as a logical condition of experi-ence; but here again it was of the individual ego that he was thinking, the 'I' which is always subject and never object. But if we transform this logical condition of experience into a metaphysical principle which creates the object, we can hardly identify it with the individual finite ego without being involved in solipsism. For John Smith all other human beings will be objects, and so they will be his own creation. For the matter of fact, John Smith as object, as a phenomenal ego, will be the creation of himself as transcendental ego. If, therefore, we eliminate the thing-in-itself and transform Kant's transcendental ego, a logical condition of experience, into the supreme metaphysical principle, we are driven in the end to interpret it as the universal infinite subject which is productive both of the finite subject and of the finite object. And at once we are involved in a full-blown metaphysical system.

I do not intend, of course, to discuss here the phases of the philosophy of Fichte or the history of German speculative idealism in general. These themes must be reserved for the next volume of this *History*. But I wished to point out that the seeds of speculative idealism were present in the Kantian philosophy itself. Of course, the speculative idealists were concerned to reduce all things to one supreme metaphysical principle from which, in one way or another, they could be philosophically deduced, whereas Kant did not share this concern. And there is an obvious difference in atmosphere and interest between the critical philosophy and the metaphysical systems which succeeded it. At the same time it is not merely a question of 'succeeding'; for the systems of speculative idealism have a more than temporal connection with the philosophy of Kant. And if one admits this and at the same time rejects what grew out of Kant's philosophy, one can hardly accept this philosophy in so far as it formed the point of departure for what one rejects. And this means in practice submitting the idealist and subjectivist aspects of Kant's thought to critical examination. For if one reaffirms these aspects and eliminates instead the thing-in-itself, it is difficult to avoid accompanying Kant's successors along the path which they trod.

It is, indeed, easy to understand that in the middle of the nineteenth century the cry was raised 'Back to Kant!', and that the Neo-Kantians set themselves to develop the critical, epistemological and ethical positions of Kant without falling into what they regarded as the fantastic extravaganzas of the speculative idealists. Kant was for them primarily the patient, methodical, meticulous, analytically-minded author of the first *Critique*; and they thought of the systems of the great idealist metaphysicians from Fichte to Hegel as representing a betrayal of the spirit of Kant. And this point of view is perfectly understandable. At the same time it is, I think, undeniable that the Kantian system lent itself to the very development (or exploitation, if preferred) which it received at the hands of the speculative idealists. In support of the attitude of the Neo-Kantians we can say, of course, that Kant deliberately substituted a new form of metaphysics, a metaphysics of knowledge or of experience, for the older metaphysics which he rejected, and that he regarded this new metaphysics as capable of giving real knowledge, whereas he would certainly not have looked on Hegel's metaphysics of the Absolute, for instance, as constituting knowledge. In other words, he would certainly have disowned those who claimed to be his children, just as he rejected Fichte's preliminary attempts to improve the critical philosophy by eliminating the thing-in-itself. But though one may feel assured that Kant would not have looked with much favour on the metaphysical flights of his successors, this does not alter the fact that he provided them with a promising foundation for their constructions.

It is possible, however, by stressing other aspects of Kant's philosophy than those stressed by his idealist successors, to regard it as pointing in quite a different direction. Kant's rejection of dogmatic metaphysics, it may be said, was more than a rejection of the systems of continental rationalism from Descartes to Leibniz and his disciples. For Kant exposed the fallacious character of all pretended demonstrations in metaphysics and showed that metaphysical knowledge is impossible. True, he offered a new metaphysics of his own; but this was to all intents and purposes analysis of the subjective conditions of experience. It did not pretend to give us a knowledge of so-called noumenal reality. Kant did, indeed, allow for belief in the existence of noumenal reality; but this was inconsistent with his account of the function of the categories. For the categories have content and meaning only in their application to phenomena. Hence it is meaningless, on Kant's premises, to talk of noumenal reality or of a 'supersensuous substrate' as existing. In fact, if reality is itself one of the categories, it is nonsense to talk about noumenal reality at all. We can, it is true, examine the nature of the scientific, moral and aesthetic judgments. But on Kant's premises we are really not entitled to use the moral judgment as the basis for any sort of metaphysics. He would not, of course, have admitted the validity of this interpretation of his thought. But in point of fact, it may be claimed, the valuable service performed by Kant was to show that whatever can be known belongs to the sphere of the sciences, and that metaphysics is not only not science but also meaningless. At best it can have only 'emotive' significance. And this is what Kant's theory of practical faith really amounts to, when it is given its cash-value.

In other words, it can be argued that though the Kantian system gave rise directly to the systems of speculative idealism it is really a half-way house on the road to positivism. And it is in this light, I suppose, that positivists would wish to regard it. They would not follow him, of course, in his theory of synthetic *a priori* propositions and of the conditions of their possibility. But they would regard his partial rejection of metaphysics as a step in the right direction; and they would wish, I think, to emphasize the aspects of his philosophy which seem to point the way to a more radical rejection, even if Kant himself did not understand the full implications of these aspects.

But the fact that both idealist metaphysicians and positivists can offer grounds for claiming that the Kantian system points in the direction of their types of philosophy obviously does not compel us to conclude that we must choose one of the two types. There is another possibility, namely that of rejecting the Kantian theories which lead to this choice. After all, Kant's Copernican revolution was an hypothesis designed to explain the possibility of synthetic *a priori* knowledge on the supposition that it could not be explained on a different hypothesis. And there is plenty of room for questioning here. We can ask whether there is in fact any synthetic *a priori* knowledge. And if we decide that there is, we can still ask whether its possibility cannot be better explained in a different way from that in which Kant explained it. Again, though it is widely taken for granted that Kant showed once and for all that speculative metaphysics cannot lead to knowledge, this assumption is open to question. But it is impossible to deal with these questions in a few words. A thorough discussion of Kant's Copernican revolution would involve discussion not only of Kant's own theories but also of the empiricism of Hume which was partly responsible for his thinking those theories necessary. And the only really satisfactory way of showing that there can be metaphysical knowledge is to produce examples and to show that they are examples. Such tasks cannot be attempted here.

But it can be remarked that in any genuine dialogue with Kant a philosopher must endeavour to ascertain his insights and to distinguish between them and what is weak or false. In other words, it would be absurd to suppose that in the case of a thinker of such stature his philosophy can simply be thrown on the rubbish-heap of rejected systems. To take but one example, Kant's insistence on the unity of apperception as a fundamental condition of human experience seems to me to represent a genuine and important insight. Even if he failed to see that the substantial subject affirms its own ontological reality in the judgment, he did not forget the subject.

7. In conclusion we might consider briefly the statement which has sometimes been made that whereas mediaeval philosophy was concerned with the problem of being, modern philosophy has been concerned with the problem of knowledge.[14]

This is a difficult statement to deal with. If it were understood in a sense similar to that of the statement that astronomy is concerned with the heavenly bodies and botany with plants, it would be obviously untrue. On the one hand mediaeval philosophers had a good deal to say about knowledge. On the other hand, if concern with the problem of being is taken to mean concern with problems of existence, with metaphysical explanation of empirical reality and with the problem of the One and the Many, we can hardly say that the problem of being was absent from the minds of men such as Descartes, Spinoza and Leibniz.

Further, statements which involve saying that 'mediaeval philosophy' and 'modern philosophy' are concerned respectively with this or that are obviously open to the criticism that they are, by their very nature, unjustifiable simplifications of complex situations. That is to say, such statements are open to the well-grounded objection that it is thoroughly misleading to speak about mediaeval and post-Renaissance philosophy as though each were a homogeneous unity. The former ranged, for example, from the systematic metaphysical syntheses of Aquinas or Duns Scotus to the critical reflections of Nicholas of Autrecourt, the mediaeval Hume. And the latter, namely post-Renaissance philosophy, was obviously not all of a piece. If we compare Aquinas with Kant, it is certainly true to say that the theory of knowledge occupies a much more prominent position in the latter's thought than it does in that of the former. But if we selected for comparison other mediaeval and modern thinkers, our judgment about the degree to which each was preoccupied with epistemological problems might be somewhat different.

Again, the attempt to give a general interpretation of the world and of human experience can be found both in mediaeval philosophy and in the philosophy of the seventeenth and eighteenth centuries. Even Kant was not concerned only with the question: What can I know? He was also concerned, as he put it, with the questions: What ought I to do? and, What may I hope for? Reflection on these questions leads us not only into moral philosophy proper but also to the postulates of the moral law. And though, for Kant, immortality and the existence of God are not demonstrable, a general world-view is opened up to us in which science, morals and religion are harmonized. A critique of the process of reason shows us the limitations of definite knowledge; but it does not destroy the reality or the importance of the chief metaphysical problems.[15] And though the solutions are a matter of practical or moral faith rather than of knowledge, it is both natural and legitimate for reason to attempt to form a general view of reality which goes beyond the field of mathematics and of science, the field, that is, of 'theoretical' knowledge.

True, the extent to which Hume could attempt any such general interpretation of reality was, on his own principles, extremely limited. The nature of reality in itself and the ultimate causes of phenomena were for him shrouded in impenetrable mystery. As far as metaphysical explanation was concerned, the world was for him an enigma. Agnosticism was the only sensible attitude to adopt. His philosophy, therefore, was primarily critical and analytic. But the same can be said of some of the thinkers of the fourteenth century. The difference is that they looked to revelation and theology to supply them with a general view of reality, whereas Hume did not.

But though exception can be taken on several grounds to the statement that mediaeval philosophy is concerned with the problem of being and modern philosophy with the problem of knowledge, the statement may serve to draw attention to certain differences between mediaeval and post-Renaissance thought. If we take mediaeval philosophy as a whole, we can say that the problem of the objectivity of knowledge is not prominent. And one reason for this is, I think, that a philosopher such as Aquinas believed that we perceive directly physical objects such as trees and tables. Our natural knowledge of purely spiritual beings is, indeed, indirect and analogical: there is no natural intuition of God. But we perceive trees and tables and men, not our own subjective modifications or our ideas of trees and tables and men. True, we can make erroneous judgments about the nature of what we perceive. I may judge, for example, that an object in the distance is a man when in point of fact it is a shrub. But the way to correct such error is to do what we are accustomed to do, namely to examine the object more closely. Problems of error arise against the background, so to speak, of a realist theory of perception, the common-sense theory that we enjoy immediate perception of the connatural objects of human cognition. Aquinas was not, of course, so naïve as to suppose that we necessarily know everything that we think that we know. But he believed that we enjoy direct access, as it were, to the world, that the mind is capable of apprehending things in their intelligible being, and that in the act of genuine knowledge it knows that it knows. While, therefore, he was prepared to discuss questions about the origins, conditions and limitations of knowledge and about the nature and causes of erroneous judgments, general questions about the objectivity of knowledge would not have had much meaning for him. For he did not think of ideas as a screen placed between our minds and things.

But if we follow Locke in describing ideas in such a way that they become the immediate objects of perception and thought, it is natural to ask whether our 'knowledge' of the world really is knowledge, that is, whether our representations correspond with reality existing independently of the mind. I do not mean to imply that all philosophers in the seventeenth and eighteenth centuries maintained a representative theory of perception and involved themselves in the problem of the correspondence between our representations and the things which they purport to represent. Locke himself did not maintain the representative theory consistently. And if, with Berkeley, we describe physical objects as clusters of 'ideas', the problem of correspondence between ideas and things simply does not arise. The problem arises only if ideas are said to have a representative function and to be the immediate objects of perception and knowledge. But if the problem does arise, the question whether our *prima facie* knowledge of the world is really objective knowledge pushes itself into the foreground. And it is then natural to treat this question before we embark on any metaphysical synthesis. Epistemology or theory of knowledge becomes basic in philosophy.

Again, while the mediaeval philosopher certainly did not think of the mind as a purely passive recipient of impressions, he regarded its activity as one of penetrating the objective intelligible structure of reality.[16] In other words, he thought of the mind as conforming itself to objects rather than of objects as having to conform themselves to the mind for knowledge to be possible.[17] He did not think of what we call the world as a mental construction. But, given the philosophies of Hume and Kant, it becomes natural to ask whether what we call the world is not a kind of logical construction which lies, as it were, between our minds and reality in itself or things in themselves. And if we think that this is a genuine problem, we shall naturally be inclined to give much more emphasis to the theory of knowledge than we should be if we were convinced that the subject does not construct empirical reality but grasps its intelligible nature.

My point is simply that if we bear in mind the development of post-Renaissance philosophy, especially in British empiricism and in the thought of Kant, it is easy to understand the prominence given in subsequent times to theory of knowledge or epistemology. Kant in particular exercised a most powerful influence in this respect. Of course, different attitudes are possible in regard to the emphasis which came to be laid in large areas of philosophical discussion on problems about the objectivity of knowledge. We may wish to say that it represents an advance from realist naïvety to a more sophisticated and profound understanding of the basic problems of philosophy. Or we may wish to say that the problem of the objectivity arises out of mistaken assumptions. Or we may wish to say that it is silly to talk, for example, about 'the critical problem'. We must try to formulate carefully-defined questions. And in the process of doing so we may find that some alleged problems which appear to be of great moment when they are expressed in vague terms turn out either to be pseudo-problems or to answer themselves. But whatever attitude we may wish to adopt in regard to the emphasis placed on the theory of knowledge, it is clear, I think, that it arose through the asking of questions which would not come naturally to the mind of the mediaeval philosopher but which were stimulated by developments in the philosophy of the seventeenth and eighteenth centuries.

These remarks are not meant to imply that the prominence given to epistemology or the theory of knowledge in modern philosophy was due exclusively to the British empiricists and to Kant. It is obvious that a theory of knowledge was prominent in the philosophy of Descartes. Indeed, we can describe the difference between rationalism and empiricism in terms of different beliefs about the origins of knowledge and about the ways of increasing knowledge. It is thus true to say that from the very beginning of modern philosophy epistemology occupied a prominent and important position. At the same time it is also true that Kant in particular exercised a powerful influence in pushing epistemology into the foreground of philosophical discussion, if only for the fact that his destructive criticism of metaphysics through a transcendental critique of knowledge seemed to imply that the proper subject-matter for the philosopher was precisely the theory of knowledge. And, of course, anyone who wished to refute his criticism of metaphysics had perforce to start with examining his epistemological doctrines.

The fact, discussed briefly in the last section, that the critical philosophy of Kant led, somewhat paradoxically, to a fresh outburst of metaphysical speculation may appear to count against the assertion that Kant exercised a powerful influence in concentrating attention on the theory of knowledge. In point of fact, however, the speculative idealism of the first half of the nineteenth century arose, not out of a revulsion against Kant's epistemology, but out of a development of what seemed to Kant's successors to be the proper implications of his point of view. Thus Fichte started with the theory of knowledge, and his idealist metaphysics grew out of it. The Neo-Kantians may have regarded speculative idealism as a betrayal of the true Kantian spirit; but this does not alter the fact that the approach to the new metaphysics was by way of the theory of knowledge. How this transition from the critical philosophy of Kant to idealist metaphysics took place will be recounted in the next volume of this *History*.

APPENDIX

A SHORT BIBLIOGRAPHY[1]

For general remarks and for General Works see the Bibliography at the end of Volume 4, *Descartes to Leibniz*.

For the benefit of the reader who desires some guidance in the selection of a few useful books in English about general movements of thought and the more prominent thinkers an asterisk has been added to some titles. But the absence of this sign must not be taken to indicate a negative judgment about the value of the book in question.

Chapters Eleven – Sixteen: Kant

Texts

Gesammelte Schriften. Critical edition sponsored by the Prussian Academy of Sciences. 22 vols. Berlin, 1902–42.

Immanuel Kants Werke. Edited by E. Cassirer. 11 vols. Berlin, 1912–18.

Kant's Cosmogony. Translated by W. Hastie. Glasgow, 1900. (Contains the *Essay on the Retardation of the Rotation of the Earth* and the *Natural History and Theory of the Heavens.*)

A *New Exposition of the First Principles of Metaphysical Knowledge* (contained as an Appendix in F. E. England's book, listed below).

An *Inquiry into the Distinctions of the Principles of Natural Theology and Morals* (contained in L. W. Beck's translation of Kant's moral writings, listed below).

Dreams of a Spirit-Seer Illustrated by the Dreams of Metaphysics. Translated by E. F. Goerwitz, edited by F. Sewall. New York, 1900.

Inaugural Dissertation and Early Writings on Space. Translated by J. Handyside. Chicago, 1929.

Critique of Pure Reason. Translated by N. K. Smith. London, 1933 (2nd edition).

[1] The abbreviation (*E.L.*) stands, as in previous volumes, for *Everyman's Library.*

Critique of Pure Reason. Translated by J. M. D. Meikle-john, with an introduction by A. D. Lindsay. London (E.L.).

Prolegomena to Any Future Metaphysic. Translated by J. P. Mahaffy and J. H. Bernard. London, 1889.

Prolegomena to Any Future Metaphysic. Translated by P. Carus, revised by L. W. Beck. New York, 1950.

Prolegomena to Any Future Metaphysics. Translated with introduction and notes by P. G. Lucas. Manchester, 1953.

Immanuel Kant: Critique of Practical Reason and Other Writings in Moral Philosophy. Translated and edited by L. W. Beck. Chicago, 1949. (Contains *An Inquiry*, as mentioned above, *Foundations of the Metaphysics of Morals, Critique of Practical Reason, What is Orientation in Thinking?, Perpetual Peace, On a Supposed Right to Lie from Altruistic Motives,* and selections from the *Metaphysics of Morals.*)

Kant's Critique of Practical Reason and Other Works on the Theory of Ethics. Translated by T. K. Abbott. London, 1909 (6th edition). (Contains a Memoir of Kant, *Fundamental Principles of the Metaphysics of Morals, Critique of Practical Reason,* the Introduction to the *Metaphysics of Morals,* the Preface to the *Metaphysical Elements of Ethics,* the first part of *Religion within the Limits of Reason Alone, On a Supposed Right to Lie from Altruistic Motives,* and *On the Saying 'Necessity has no Law'.*)

The Metaphysics of Ethics. Translated by J. W. Semple. Edinburgh, 1886 (3rd edition).

The Moral Law or Kant's Groundwork of the Metaphysics of Morals. Translated with an introduction by H. J. Paton. London, 1950.

Kant's Lectures on Ethics. Translated by L. Infield. London, 1930.

Critique of Judgment. Translated by J. H. Bernard. London, 1931 (2nd edition).

Religion within the Limits of Reason Alone. Translated by T. M. Greene and H. H. Hudson, with an introduction by T. M. Greene. Glasgow, 1934.

Perpetual Peace, A Philosophical Essay. Translated by M. Campbell Smith. London, 1915 (reprint).

Kant. Selections. Edited with an introduction by T. M. Greene. London and New York, 1929.

Studies

Adickes, E. *Kant als Naturforscher.* 2 vols. Berlin, 1924–5.
    Kant und das Ding an sich. Berlin, 1924.
    Kant und die Als-Ob-Philosophie. Stockholm, 1927.
    Kants Lehre von der doppelten Affektion unseres Ich als Schlüssel zu seine Erkenntnistheorie. Tübingen, 1929.

Aebi, M. *Kants Begründung der 'deutschen Philosophie'.* Basel, 1947.

Aliotta, A. *L'estetica di Kant e degli idealisti romantici.* Rome, 1950.

Ardley, G. *Aquinas and Kant.* New York and London, 1950.

Ballauf, T. *Ueber den Vorstellungsbegriff bei Kant.* Eleda, 1938.

Banfi, A. *La filosofia critica di Kant.* Milan, 1955.

Basch, V. *Essai critique sur l'esthétique de Kant.* Paris, 1927 (enlarged edition).

Bauch, B. *Kant.* Leipzig, 1923 (3rd edition).

Bayer, K. *Kants Vorlesungen über Religionslehre.* Halle, 1937.

Bohatec, J. *Die Religionsphilosophie Kants in der 'Religion innerhalb der Granzen der blossen Vernunft'.* Hamburg, 1938.

Borries, K. *Kant als Politiker.* Leipzig, 1928.

Boutroux, E. *La philosophie de Kant.* Paris, 1926.

Caird, E. **The Critical Philosophy of Immanuel Kant.* 2 vols. London, 1909 (2nd edition).

Campo, M. *La genesi del criticismo Kantiano.* 2 vols. Varese, 1953.

Carabellese, P. *La filosofia di Kant.* Florence, 1927.
    Il problema della filosofia da Kant a Fichte. Palermo, 1929.
    Il problema dell'esistenza in Kant. Rome, 1943.

Cassirer, A. W. **A Commentary on Kant's Critique of Judgment.* London, 1938.
    *Kant's First Critique: an Appraisal of the Permanent Significance of Kant's Critique of Pure Reason. London, 1955.

Cohen, H. *Kommentar zu Kants Kritik der reinen Vernunft.* Leipzig, 1917 (2nd edition).
    Kants Theorie der reinen Erfahrung. Berlin, 1918 (3rd edition).
    Kants Begründung der Ethik. Berlin, 1910 (2nd edition).

Vom Kants Einfluss auf die deutsche Kultur. Berlin, 1883.

Kants Begründung der Aesthetik. Berlin, 1889.

Coninck, A. de. *L'analytique de Kant (Part I: La critique kantienne).* Louvain, 1955.

Cornelius, H. *Kommentar zur Kritik der reinen Vernunft.* Erlangen, 1926.

Cousin, V. *Leçons sur la philosophie de Kant.* Paris, 1842.

Cresson, A. *Kant, sa vie, son œuvre. Avec un exposé de sa philosophie.* Paris, 1955 (2nd edition).

Daval, R. *La métaphysique de Kant. Perspectives sur la métaphysique de Kant d'après la théorie du schématisme.* Paris, 1951.

Delbos, V. *La philosophie practique de Kant.* Paris, 1905.

Denckmann, G. *Kants Philosophie des Aesthetischen.* Heidelberg, 1949.

Döring, W. O. *Das Lebenswerk Immanuel Kants.* Hamburg, 1947.

Duncan, A. R. C. **Practical Rule and Morality. A Study of Immanuel Kant's Foundations for the Metaphysics of Ethics.* London and Edinburgh, 1957.

England, F. E. *Kant's Conception of God.* London, 1929.

Ewing, A. C. **Kant's Treatment of Causality.* London, 1924.

*A Short Commentary on Kant's Critique of Pure Reason. London, 1938.

Farinelli, A. *Traumwelt und Jenseitsglaube bei Kant.* Königsberg, 1940.

Fischer, K. *Kants Leben und die Grundlage seiner Lehre.* 2 vols. Heidelberg, 1909 (5th edition).

Friedrich, C. J. *Inevitable Peace.* New Haven, 1948. (Contains *Perpetual Peace* as Appendix.)

Garnett, C. B. Jr. *The Kantian Philosophy of Space.* New York, 1939.

Goldmann, L. *Mensch, Gemeinschaft und Welt in der Philosophie Kants.* Zürich, 1945.

Gottfried, M. *Immanuel Kant.* Cologne, 1951.

Grayeff, P. *Deutung und Darstellung der theoretischen Philosophie Kants.* Hamburg, 1951.

Guzzo, A. *Primi scritti di Kant.* Naples, 1920.

Kant precritico. Turin, 1924.

Heidegger, M. *Kant und das Problem der Metaphysik.* Bonn, 1929.

Heimsoeth, H. *Studien zur Philosophie I. Kants. Metaphysische Ursprünge und ontologische Grundlagen*. Cologne, 1955.

Herring, H. *Das Problem der Affektation bei Kant*. Cologne, 1953.

Heyse, H. *Der Begriff der Ganzheit und die kantische Philosophie*. Munich, 1927.

Jansen, B., S.J. *Die Religionsphilosophie Kants*. Berlin and Bonn, 1929.

Jones, W. T. **Morality and Freedom in the Philosophy of Immanuel Kant*. Oxford, 1940.

Kayser, R. *Kant*. Vienna, 1935.

Klausen, S. *Die Freiheitsidee in ihrem Verhältnis zum Naturrecht und positivem Recht bei Kant*. Oslo, 1950.

Körner, S. **Kant*. Penguin Books, 1955.

Kronenberg, M. *Kant. Sein Leben und seine Werke*. Munich, 1918 (5th edition).

Kroner, R. *Von Kant bis Hegel*. 2 vols. Tübingen, 1921–4. **Kant's Weltanschauung*. Translated by J. E. Smith. Chicago, 1956.

Krüger, G. *Philosophie und Moral in der kantischen Kritik*. Tübingen, 1931.

Kühnemann, E. *Kant*. 2 vols. Munich, 1923–4.

Külpe, O. *Immanuel Kant*. Leipzig, 1921 (5th edition).

Lachièze-Rey, P. *L'idéalisme kantien*. Paris, 1950 (2nd edition).

Lehmann, G. *Kants Nachlasswerk und die Kritik der Urteilskraft*. Berlin, 1939.

Lindsay, A. D. **Kant*. London, 1934.

Litt, T. *Kant und Herder als Deuter der geistigen Welt*. Leipzig, 1930.

Lombardi, F. *La filosofia critica: I, La formazione del problema kantiano*. Rome, 1943.

Lotz, B., S.J. (editor). *Kant und die Scholastik heute*. Munich, 1955.

Lugarini, C. *La logica trascendentale di Kant*. Milan, 1950.

Marc-Wogau, K. *Untersuchungen zur Raumlehre Kants*. Lund, 1932.
Vier Studien zu Kants Kritik der Urteilskraft. Uppsala, 1938.

Maréchal, J., S.J. *Le point de départ de la métaphysique*. 5 vols. Bruges, 1923–46. (Cahiers 3 and 5.)

Martin, G. *Arithmetik und Kombinatorik bei Kant*. Itze-
hoe, 1938.
   *Kant's Metaphysics and Theory of Science. Translated
by P. G. Lucas. Manchester, 1955.
Massolo, A. *Introduzione all'analitica kantiana*. Florence,
1946.
Menzer, P. *Kants Aesthetik in ihrer Entwicklung*. Ber-
lin, 1952.
Messer, A. *Kommentar zu Kants ethischen und religions-
philosophischen Hauptschriften*. Leipzig, 1929.
Miller, O. W. *The Kantian Thing-in-itself or Creative
Mind*. New York, 1956.
Natorp, P. *Kant über Krieg und Frieden*. Erlangen, 1924.
Nink, C., S.J. *Kommentar zu Kants Kritik der reinen
Vernunft*. Frankfurt, 1930.
Noll, B. *Das Gestaltproblem in der Erkenntnistheorie
Kants*. Bonn, 1946.
Oggiani, E. *Kant empirista*. Milan, 1948.
Pareyson, L. *L'estetica dell'idealismo tedesco: I, Kant*.
Turin, 1950.
Paton, H. J. **Kant's Metaphysic of Experience: A Com-
mentary on the First Half of the Kritik der reinen
Vernunft*. 2 vols. London, 1952 (2nd edition).
   **The Categorical Imperative: A Study in Kant's Moral
Philosophy*. London, 1948.
Paulsen, F. *Immanuel Kant: His Life and Doctrine*. Trans-
lated by J. E. Creighton and A. Lefèvre. New York,
1902.
Pfleiderer, E. *Kantischer Kritizimus und englische Phi-
losophie*. Tübingen, 1881.
Reich, C. *Die Vollständigkeit der kantischen Urteilstafel*.
Berlin, 1932.
   *Kants Einzigmöglicher Beweisgrund zu einer Demon-
stration des Daseins Gottes*. Berlin, 1932.
Reinhard, W. *Ueber das Verhältnis von Sittlichkeit und
Religion bei Kant*. Berne, 1927.
Reininger, R. *Kant, seine Anhänger und Gegner*. Munich,
1923.
Rickert, H. *Kant als Philosoph der modernen Kultur*.
Tübingen, 1924.
Riehl, J. *Kant und seine Philosophie*. Berlin, 1907.
Ross, Sir D. *Kant's Ethical Theory. A Commentary on the
'Grundlagen zur Metaphysik der Sitten'*. Oxford, 1954.
Rotta, P. *Kant*. Brescia, 1953.

Ruyssen, T. *Kant*. Paris, 1909.

Scaravelli, L. *Saggio sulla categoria kantiana della realtà*. Florence, 1947.

Scheenberger, G. *Kants Konzept des Moralbegriffs*. Basel, 1952.

Schilling, K. *Kant*. Munich, 1942 (2nd edition).

Schilpp, P. A. *Kant's Pre-Critical Ethics*. Evanston and Chicago, 1938.

Sentroul, C. *La philosophie religieuse de Kant*. Brussels, 1912.
Kant et Aristote. Paris, 1913.

Simmel, G. *Kant*. Munich, 1921 (5th edition).

Smith, A. H. *Kantian Studies*. Oxford, 1947.

Smith, N. K. *A Commentary to Kant's 'Critique of Pure Reason'*. London, 1930 (2nd edition).

Souriau, M. *Le jugement réfléchissant dans la philosophie critique de Kant*. Paris, 1926.

Specht, E. K. *Der Analogiebegriff bei Kant und Hegel*. Cologne, 1952.

Stuckenberg, J. H. W. *The Life of Immanuel Kant*. London, 1882.

Teale, E. *Kantian Ethics*. Oxford, 1951.

Tönnies, I. *Kants Dialektik des Scheins* (dissert.). Würzburg, 1933.

Troilo, E. *Kant*. Milan, 1939.

Vaihinger, H. *Kommentar zur Kritik der reinen Vernunft*. 2 vols. Stuttgart, 1922 (2nd edition).

Vanni-Rovighi, S. *Introduzione allo studio di Kant*. Milan, 1945.

Vleeschauwer, H. J. de. *La déduction transcendentale dans l'œuvre de Kant*. 3 vols. Antwerp, 1934–7.
L'évolution de la pensée kantienne. Histoire d'une doctrine. Paris, 1939.

Vorländer, K. *Immanuel Kant. Der Mann und das Werk*. Leipzig, 1924.

Vuillemin, J. *L'héritage kantien, et la révolution copernicienne*. Paris, 1954.
Physique et métaphysique kantiennes. Paris, 1955.

Wallace, W. *Kant*. Oxford, Edinburgh and London, 1882.

Webb, C. C. J. *Kant's Philosophy of Religion*. Oxford, 1926.

Weldon, T. D. *Introduction to Kant's Critique of Pure Reason*. Oxford, 1945.

Whitney, G. T., and Bowers, D. F. (editors). *The Heritage of Kant* (essays). Princeton, 1939.

Wundt, M. *Kant als Metaphysiker*. Stuttgart, 1924.

Notes

1. R. Eisler's *Kantlezion* (Berlin, 1930) is a useful aid to the study of Kant.
2. *Kantstudien*, the periodical founded in 1896 by H. Vaihinger, contains many important articles on Kant.
3. There are various collections of articles on Kant.
   For example:
   Revue internationale de philosophie, n. 30; Brussels, 1954.
   A *Symposium on Kant*, by E. G. Ballard and others. Tulane Studies in Philosophy, vol. III. New Orleans, 1954.
4. The more metaphysical aspects of Kant's philosophy are emphasized in the works, listed above, by Daval, Heimsoeth, Martin (second work mentioned) and Wundt. For a discussion of the relations between Kant's thought and Thomism see the works by Audley and Maréchal (Cahier V). Besides the works of Professors Paton and N. K. Smith those of de Vleeschauwer are highly recommended.

NOTES

CHAPTER ELEVEN

[1] References to Kant's writings in Chapters XI–XIII are to be interpreted as follows. A denotes the first edition and B the second edition of the *Critique of Pure Reason*. These will be found respectively in Volumes IV and III of the critical edition of Kant's works edited by the Prussian Academy of Sciences (see Bibliography). The numbers placed after A and B refer to sections as given in this edition (the sections corresponding to pagination in the original German editions). For the translation of passages I am responsible. But as the great majority of passages quoted in translation are taken from B, the references are generally valid for Professor N. Kemp Smith's translation of B (see Bibliography), as this translation embodies the division into sections referred to above. (Professor Kemp Smith's translation also contains the preface to A, as well as the Deduction of the Categories as given in A.)

Prol. denotes *Prolegomena to Any Future Metaphysics*, which is contained in Volume IV of the critical German edition. Numbers following *Prol.* refer to sections in the German edition. This division into sections is reproduced in, for example, the translation by J. P. Mahaffy and J. H. Bernard (see Bibliography).

[2] A, viii.

[3] *Prol.*, 4.

[4] B, xv.

[5] A, x.

[6] B, xxxv.

[7] A, xii.

[8] The distinction between understanding and reason can be passed over for the moment. It will be explained later.

[9] A, xvii.

[10] B, xxxvi.

[11] See, for example, B, 869–70.

[12] B, 1.

[13] Universality which is based on induction is not, for Kant, strict but 'assumed and comparative' and admits of exceptions. If, on the basis of my personal experience, I say that human beings do not live more than a hundred years, the universality of the judgment is 'assumed'. Strict universality admits of no possible exception.

[14] B, 4.

[15] B, 4–5.

[16] *Prol.*, Foreword.

[17] B, 5.

[18] *Prol.*, Foreword.

[19] B, 11; A, 7.

[20] *Ibid.*

[21] The judgment could, of course, be turned into an analytic judgment by so defining membership of the tribe that it

includes the idea of shortness. But then we should be moving in the realm of verbal definitions and their implications; we should not be dealing with empirical reality, with the tribe as it actually exists.

22 B, 13; A, 9.

23 B, 14.

24 B, 16.

25 Ibid.

26 B, 17.

27 B, 18.

28 Ibid.

29 B, xvi.

30 For purposes of this analogy I must be allowed to use ordinary everyday language. It is obviously an analogy or illustration, not a considered statement about the ontological status of colours.

31 Obviously, Kant does not envisage the physicist as simply reading preconceived theories into Nature. He is thinking of the process of hypothesis, deduction and controlled experiment, in which the physicist is clearly no mere passive recipient of impressions from Nature.

32 In the Foreword to the Prolegomena Kant rightly notes that Hume never questioned the fact that the concept of cause is indispensable for life.

33 B, 29; A, 19.

34 'Unconditioned' as transcending the subjective conditions of sensibility and understanding.

35 'I call all knowledge transcendental which is occupied not so much with objects as with our mode of cognition of objects, so far as this is possible a priori' (B, 25; A, 11–12).

36 B, 735–6.

37 B, 28; A, 13.

38 B, xxx.

CHAPTER TWELVE

1 The word 'intuition' (Anschauung) can refer either to the act of intuiting or to what is intuited. In the present context the word is used in the first sense. But Kant frequently uses it in the second sense.

2 B, 33; A, 19.

3 B, 34; A, 19.

4 Ibid.; A, 20.

5 Ibid. In A, 20 the wording is somewhat different.

6 A, 248.

7 A, 50; B, 74; Prol., 11.

8 Cf. A, 20–2; B, 35–6.

9 Strictly speaking, the form of appearance is, as we have seen, that which enables the manifold of appearances (sensations or that which corresponds to sensations) to be ordered in certain relations. But we can speak of the relations as the formal element in appearance.

10 Kant would agree with Hume that in introspection we perceive psychical states but not a permanent ego or soul. More will be said on this subject later.

11 B, 42; A, 26.

12 Kant is referring to the empirical ego, not to the spiritual soul.

13 B, 49; A, 33.

14 We may recall that Hume remarked that we cannot properly speak of one internal state as being to the left or right of another.

15 Das Gemüt is customarily translated 'mind'. The word is used by Kant in a very wide sense, and it must not, of course, be taken as equivalent to 'understanding' (Verstand).

16 See p. 239, note 1.

17 'Object' must here be taken, of course, in the sense of object of human knowledge or object for us.

18 We must remember that to appear means being subjected to the *a priori* forms of sensibility.

19 Whether or not he could do so consistently is a question which need not concern us for the moment.

20 B, 40.

21 That is, if we take the section entitled 'transcendental exposition of the conception of space' together with the relevant parts of the 'general remarks on the Transcendental Aesthetic'.

22 B, 40.

23 *Prol.*, 13, remark 1.

24 Leibniz had also understood by space Euclidean space.

25 B, 268; A, 220–1.

26 In a sense Leibniz also maintained the transcendental ideality of space and time, but with reference to God's thinking, not, as with Kant, to ours. And for Kant the difference is all-important.

27 B, 75; A, 51.

28 For example, in systematically mapping out, so to speak, the forms of deductive thinking we are concerned simply with these forms themselves. And the whole matter can be expressed symbolically, without reference to objects.

29 B, 94; A, 69.

30 According to Kant, judgment is *mediate* knowledge of an object, a representation of a representation of an object. No representation, except an intuition, relates immediately to an object. A concept relates immediately only to some other representation, either to an intuition or to another concept.

31 B, 94; A, 69.

32 B, 95 and 106; A, 70 and 80.

33 Thus the concept of a necessary being would be the concept of a being whose possibility involves existence, that is, which cannot be merely possible. But *this* concept is not, for Kant, objectively applicable.

34 B, 137.

35 B, 129–30.

36 B, 130.

37 B, 132.

38 B, 143.

39 B, 144.

40 B, 176; A, 137–8.

41 B, 179–80; A, 140.

42 B, 184; A, 145.

43 B, 178; A, 139.

44 Reality, as we learn in the section on the categories of quality, is that whose concept indicates a being in time.

45 B, 183; A, 144.

46 *Ibid.*

47 B, 183–4; A, 144.

48 P. 340: see Bibliography.

49 B, 187; A, 147.

50 B, 186; A, 147.

51 B, 200; A, 161.

52 B, 202; A, 162.

53 B, 207; A, 166.

54 B, 218; this differs from the version in A, 176–7.

55 B, 224; A, 182.

56 B, 232; A, 189.

57 B, 256; A, 211.

58 B, 265–6; A, 218.

59 15.

60 *Ibid.*

61 *Ibid.*

62 *Prol.*, 23.

63 For Kant physics very naturally meant the Newtonian physics: given the historical context,

it could hardly mean anything else. And it is evident that there is a connection between Kant's principles, as listed in the *Analytic of Principles*, with the Newtonian conception of the physical world. For instance, a principle asserting that all changes take place according to necessary causal relations, would not fit in with a physics which admitted the concept of indeterminacy.

64 B, 147.
65 B, 294.
66 Cf. *Prol.*, 32; B, 309.
67 A, 248–9.
68 A, 253.
69 B, 307.
70 *Ibid.*
71 *Ibid.*
72 B, 311.
73 B, 312.
74 A, 19; B, 34.
75 *Prol.*, 13, remark 2.
76 Kant is speaking, of course, of the empirical ego, which I perceive introspectively only in its successive states. The transcendental ego is not determined in time, but it is not given as an object of self-consciousness. It is thought as the condition of the transcendental unity of apperception.
77 B, 276.
78 B, 278.
79 *Ibid.*

CHAPTER THIRTEEN

1 Objective experience, that is to say, in the sense of experience or knowledge of objects. The analysis of moral experience has not yet been considered. And moral experience is not an experience of objects in the sense in which we have been using the term.
2 B, 349; A, 293.
3 B, 88; A, 63–4.
4 B, 697.
5 This deduction of the Ideas of pure reason corresponds to the metaphysical deduction of the categories of the understanding, that is, to the systematic derivation of the categories from the forms of judgment. In the *Dialectic* there cannot be anything exactly corresponding to the transcendental deduction or justification of the application of the categories to objects. For the Ideas cannot be applied to objects. However, as the Ideas have a 'regulative' function, the exhibition of this fact is in some way remotely analogous to the transcendental deduction of the categories.
6 Mediate inference because the conclusion in a syllogism is derived from the major premiss only by means of the minor premiss, which is a condition of the deduction.
7 Kant admits that the theory according to which the mere form of the disjunctive syllogism necessarily involves the supreme Idea of pure reason, namely the Idea of a Being of all beings (*Wesen aller Wesen*), 'seems at first sight to be extremely paradoxical' (B, 393). But he promises a further treatment later (cf. the sections on the Transcendental Ideal; B, 599 ff.). We cannot, however, discuss the matter further here.
8 B, 391–2; A, 334–5.
9 B, 401; A, 343.
10 *Tractatus logico-philosophicus*, 5.632.

11 *B*, 410–11; cf. A, 348.

12 *B*, 454–5.

13 My references here to me-diaeval philosophy must not be understood as involving the suggestion that Kant had the mediaevals in mind. As far as I know, there is no evidence that he knew enough about them for this to have been even possible. But the references are, I think, of general interest.

14 For a statement of Aquinas's position, see Vol. 2, Part II of this *History*, pp. 85, 86.

15 See Vol. 2, Part I of this *History*, pp. 292–4.

16 It does not follow, of course, that we have to follow Kant in saying that they are valid. We might wish to say that neither is valid, or that while one is invalid, the other is valid. For a discussion of Kant's proofs of the theses and antitheses in the four antinomies the reader can consult, for instance, Professor N. Kemp Smith's *Commentary to Kant's Critique of Pure Reason*, pp. 483–506.

17 *B*, 462–3.

18 It is arguable that there is in fact no antinomy, on the ground that the thesis must be interpreted as referring to Leibnizian monads, whereas the antithesis refers to extended bodies in space.

19 *B*, 472–3.

20 *B*, 480–1.

21 Kant's approach was suggested by the Wolffian philosophy. Baumgarten, for example, approached the idea of God through the idea of the *Ens perfectissimum*, which is then identified with the *Ens realissimum*.

22 For the ontological argument as given by St. Anselm, see Vol. 2, Part I of this *History*, pp. 183–5. For the variants given by Descartes and Leibniz, see Vol. 4, pp. 119–24 and 324–7.

23 *B*, 623.

24 *B*, 630.

25 *B*, 632–3.

26 *B*, 649–50.

27 Kant did not, of course, have in mind Paley's *Evidences*; for this work was not published until 1802.

28 *B*, 655.

29 *B*, 660.

30 *B*, 664.

31 The term does not, of course, refer to moral theology in the sense of a study of the practical application of Christian moral principles. It refers to a philosophical theology, or doctrine of God, based on the demands or postulates of the moral law.

32 *B*, 662.

33 *B*, 667–8.

34 *B*, 665.

35 *B*, 670; cf. A, 297–8.

36 *B*, 670.

37 *B*, 671.

38 *B*, 692; cf. A, 302.

39 Kant believed, of course, that there are noumenal realities which we call the soul and God, though he would say that he did not and could not know that this is the case. The arguments to show that there are a soul and God are fallacious; but the ideas, by themselves, do not produce antinomies. The cosmological Idea, however, does produce antinomies. And to this extent it stands in a class by itself.

40 *B*, 707.

41 *B*, 710.

CHAPTER FOURTEEN

1 In references in this chapter G. denotes the *Groundwork of the Metaphysics of Morals*, *Pr.R.* the *Critique of Practical Reason*, and *Rel.* the *Religion within the bounds of Reason Alone*. These three works are contained respectively in Volumes IV, V and VI of the critical edition. Numbers after the abbreviated titles indicate sections or (if preceded by p.) pages in this edition. In the case of G. and *Pr.R.* corresponding references (by page) will be given to the translations contained in T. K. Abbott's *Kant's Theory of Ethics* (see Bibliography) which will be referred to as *Abb.* In the case of *Rel.* corresponding references will be given to the translation by T. M. Greene and H. H. Hudson, abbreviated as *G.-H.* References to volume and page, preceded by the letter *W.*, are to the edition of Kant's Works by the Prussian Academy of Sciences. See Bibliography.

2 The word 'reason' must be understood here in the wide sense indicated by the titles of the first two *Critiques*, not in the narrow sense of the power of mediate inference.

3 G., p. 391; *Abb.*, p. 7.

4 *Critique of Pure Reason*, B, x.

5 *Pr.R.*, 29–30; *Abb.*, p. 101.

6 The difference in meaning between these two words will be mentioned later.

7 W., VI, p. 217; *Abb.*, p. 272.

8 G., Preface, p. 389; *Abb.*, pp. 3–4.

9 It is conceivable that Kant had at the back of his mind the picture of Satan deceiving men. The precept would apply also to 'the father of lies'.

10 G., Preface, p. 389; *Abb.*, p. 4.

11 *Ibid.*

12 *Pr.R.*, 70; *Abb.*, p. 129.

13 G., Preface, pp. 389–90; *Abb.*, p. 4.

14 G., Preface, p. 392; *Abb.*, p. 7.

15 G., p. 393; *Abb.*, p. 9.

16 G., p. 397; *Abb.*, p. 13.

17 G., p. 398; *Abb.*, p. 14.

18 G., p. 400; *Abb.*, p. 16.

19 G., p. 402; *Abb.*, p. 18.

20 There is obviously no question here of *deducing* concrete rules of conduct from the concept of universal law as such. The concept is used as a test of the admissibility or inadmissibility of maxims, but not as a premiss from which they can be deduced.

21 G., p. 403; *Abb.*, p. 20.

22 He does not make much use of it, however. So there is no real need to bother about it.

23 G., p. 413; *Abb.*, p. 30.

24 For an outline of Aristotle's ethical theory, see Vol. 1 of this *History*, *Chapter Thirty-One*.

25 G., p. 415; *Abb.*, p. 32.

26 G., p. 421; *Abb.*, p. 38.

27 *Ibid.*; *Abb.*, p. 39.

28 G., p. 424; *Abb.*, p. 41.

29 *Ibid.*; *Abb.*, p. 42.

30 G., p. 436; *Abb.*, p. 54.

31 *Pr.R.*, 122; *Abb.*, p. 161.

32 This formula is clearly presupposed by Kant's first example of the application of the categorical imperative, namely of the man who is reduced to hopeless

misery and who asks himself whether he may commit suicide (G., pp. 421–2; Abb., pp. 39–40).

33 G., p. 425; Abb., p. 43.
34 G., p. 428; Abb., p. 46.
35 G., pp. 428–9; Abb., p. 47.
36 G., p. 429; Abb., p. 47.
37 G., p. 431; Abb., p. 50.
38 G., p. 434; Abb., p. 52.
39 Pr.R., 54; Abb., p. 119.
40 G., p. 440; Abb., p. 59.
41 Pr.R., 58; Abb., p. 122.
42 G., p. 441; Abb., p. 59.
43 Pr.R., 58; Abb., p. 122.
44 Pr.R., 69; Abb., p. 129.
45 G., p. 433; Abb., p. 51.
46 G., p. 434; Abb., p. 52.
47 G., p. 433; Abb., p. 52.
48 G., p. 438; Abb., p. 57.
49 G., p. 448; Abb., p. 67.
50 G., p. 454; Abb., pp. 73–4.
51 G., p. 461; Abb., p. 81.
52 Pr.R., 167–8; Abb., p. 187.
53 Pr.R., 170; Abb., p. 189.
54 Pr.R., 171; Abb., p. 189.
55 Pr.R., 175; Abb., p. 191.
56 Pr.R., 199; Abb., pp. 206–7.
57 Pr.R., 220; Abb., p. 218.
58 Ibid.
59 Pr.R., 224; Abb., p. 221.
60 Pr.R., 225; Abb., p. 221.
61 Pr.R., 238; Abb., p. 229.
62 Pr.R., 240; Abb., p. 231.
63 Pr.R., 243; Abb., p. 233.
64 Pr.R., 244; Abb., p. 233.
65 Pr.R., 246; Abb., p. 234.
66 Pr.R., 255; Abb., p. 239.
67 This way of speaking can, of course, be misleading. For ultimately, as we saw earlier, there is only one reason, though it has distinguishable functions or modes of employment.
68 Pr.R., 216–17; Abb., p. 216.
69 Ibid.

70 Pr.R., 233; Abb., p. 226.
71 Pr.R., 235; Abb., p. 227.
72 Rel., p. 3; G.-H., p. 3.
73 Rel., p. 6; G.-H., p. 5.
74 Rel., p. 103; G.-H., p. 95.
75 Rel., p. 170; G.-H., p. 158.
76 The reader can consult, for example, Kant's Philosophy of Religion by C. C. J. Webb (see Bibliography).
77 I do not mean to imply that the defenders of the emotive theory of ethics in its various developed forms do not allow for this feature of the moral judgment.

CHAPTER FIFTEEN

1 The Critique of Judgment (Kritik der Urteilskraft), contained in Volume V of the critical edition of Kant's works, will be referred to in footnotes as J.; and references will be given according to sections. Corresponding references will also be given, by page, to the translation by J. H. Bernard (see Bibliography), which will be referred to as Bd.
2 J., xx; Bd., p. 13.
3 Ibid.
4 J., LVIII; Bd., p. 41.
5 The term used for mind in general is das Gemüt. As already noted, Kant uses this term in a very wide sense to cover all psychical powers and activities.
6 J., v; Bd., p. 2.
7 J., xxv; Bd., p. 16.
8 J., xxvi; Bd., pp. 16–17.
9 J., xxvii; Bd., p. 18.
10 J., xxviii; Bd., pp. 18–19.
11 J., xxxi; Bd., p. 20.
12 J., xxxix; Bd., p. 27.
13 J., xlviii–xlix; Bd., p. 34.
14 J., lii; Bd., p. 37.
15 Ibid.

[16] Cf. *J.*, LVI; *Bd.*, p. 40.

[17] *J.*, LVI; *Bd.*, p. 40.

[18] *J.*, 16; *Bd.*, p. 55.

[19] *J.*, 32; *Bd.*, p. 67.

[20] In introducing the idea of the moral imperative, I do not mean to imply, of course, that it is a private condition, as inclination is. I introduce it simply to complete the notion of being 'free' as Kant uses this term in connection with the aesthetic judgment.

[21] *J.*, 25; *Bd.*, p. 62.

[22] *J.*, 43; *Bd.*, p. 76.

[23] *J.*, 61; *Bd.*, p. 90.

[24] *J.*, 47; *Bd.*, p. 79.

[25] *Ibid.*; *Bd.*, p. 80.

[26] *J.*, 60–1; *Bd.*, p. 90.

[27] *J.*, 68; *Bd.*, p. 96.

[28] *J.*, 62–3; *Bd.*, p. 91.

[29] *J.*, 64–5; *Bd.*, p. 93.

[30] I do not intend to imply by this remark that Burke was the first to make this distinction.

[31] *J.*, 128; *Bd.*, p. 147.

[32] *J.*, 77; *Bd.*, p. 103.

[33] *J.*, 80; *Bd.*, p. 106.

[34] *J.*, 84; *Bd.*, p. 109.

[35] Kant's remark that the spectacle of, say, the might of the storm-tossed ocean or of a volcano in eruption becomes pleasing when beheld from a safe vantage-point incited Schopenhauer to some sarcastic remarks.

[36] For the details of the deduction the reader is referred to the *Critique of Judgment* itself (*J.*, 131 ff.; *Bd.*, pp. 150 ff.).

[37] To judge by the way in which Kant cites the tulip as an example, he appears to have had a predilection for this flower.

[38] *J.*, 173; *Bd.*, p. 183.

[39] *J.*, 179; *Bd.*, p. 187.

[40] *J.*, 180; *Bd.*, p. 187.

[41] *J.*, 181; *Bd.*, p. 188.

[42] *J.*, 192; *Bd.*, p. 197.

[43] *J.*, 183; *Bd.*, p. 190.

[44] He also adds to the first part of the *Critique of Judgment* an appendix on the 'Doctrine of Method of Taste'. But this is extremely brief.

[45] *J.*, 234; *Bd.*, p. 231.

[46] *J.*, 258; *Bd.*, p. 250.

[47] *J.*, 263; *Bd.*, p. 255.

[48] *Nach inneren Volksgesetzen* (*J.*, 256; *Bd.*, p. 249) is Kant's phrase. Perhaps he has at the back of his mind Rousseau's idea of law as the expression of the general will.

[49] *J.*, 264; *Bd.*, p. 255.

[50] *J.*, 272; *Bd.*, pp. 262–3.

[51] *J.*, 279, note; *Bd.*, p. 268, note.

[52] *J.*, 286; *Bd.*, pp. 273–4.

[53] *J.*, 291; *Bd.*, p. 277.

[54] *J.*, 295–6; *Bd.*, pp. 280–1.

[55] *J.*, 296; *Bd.*, p. 281.

[56] *J.*, 304; *Bd.*, p. 287.

[57] *J.*, 307–8; *Bd.*, pp. 289–90.

[58] *J.*, 314; *Bd.*, p. 294.

[59] *J.*, 314–15; *Bd.*, pp. 294–5.

[60] *J.*, 325; *Bd.*, p. 302.

[61] *J.*, 327; *Bd.*, pp. 304–5.

[62] *J.*, 335–6; *Bd.*, p. 311.

[63] *J.*, 408; *Bd.*, p. 368.

[64] *Ibid.*

[65] *J.*, 410; *Bd.*, p. 370.

[66] *J.*, 413; *Bd.*, p. 372.

[67] *J.*, 410; *Bd.*, p. 369.

[68] *J.*, 424, note; *Bd.*, p. 381, note.

[69] *J.*, 462; *Bd.*, p. 409.

CHAPTER SIXTEEN

[1] The *Opus Postumum* is contained in Vols. XXI–XXII of the Berlin critical edition, and references will be given according to volume and page.

2 XXI, p. 526.

3 XXII, p. 497.

4 Experience is described as the 'absolute unity of the knowledge of the objects of the senses'; XXII, p. 497.

5 XXI, pp. 525–6.

6 XXII, p. 323.

7 XXI, p. 291.

8 *Ibid.*

9 *Ibid.*

10 XXI, p. 81.

11 XXI, p. 104.

12 XXI, p. 77.

13 XXI, p. 81.

14 XXI, p. 82.

15 XXI, p. 150.

16 XXI, p. 6.

17 XXI, p. 35.

18 XXI, p. 20.

19 XXI, p. 22.

20 XXII, p. 62.

21 XXI, p. 34.

22 XXI, pp. 36–7.

23 XXI, p. 93.

24 XXI, p. 105.

25 XXI, p. 82.

26 XXI, p. 20.

27 XXI, p. 21.

28 XXI, p. 85.

29 XXII, p. 36.

30 XXII, p. 37.

31 XXII, p. 24.

32 XXII, p. 34.

33 XXII, p. 33.

34 'Subjective' in the sense that the ultimate principle of being and knowledge is the subject; 'transcendental' in the sense that the subject is the pure or transcendental subject, not the empirical ego; 'idealism' in the sense that there is no factor which is not ultimately reducible to the self-positing of the transcendental subject or ego.

35 XXII, p. 23.

36 XXI, p. 440.

37 XXI, p. 19.

38 XXI, p. 17.

39 *Ein Gedankending.*

40 XXI, pp. 32–3.

41 XXI, p. 27.

42 XXI, p. 33.

43 Some passages of the *Opus Postumum* seem at first sight to contradict this statement. They will be referred to presently.

44 XXI, p. 12.

45 XXI, p. 15.

46 *Ibid.*

47 Cf. XXII, p. 64.

48 XXII, p. 104.

49 XXII, p. 62.

50 XXII, p. 109.

51 XXII, p. 113.

52 XXII, p. 111.

53 XXI, p. 42.

54 *Ibid.*

55 XXI, p. 18.

56 XXI, p. 61.

57 XXI, p. 42.

58 XXI, p. 24.

59 XXI, p. 25.

60 XXI, p. 50.

CHAPTER SEVENTEEN

1 As was pointed out in the Introduction to Vol. 4 rationalism in the present context does not signify simply an attempt to base philosophy on reason rather than on mystical insights. Nor must the term be understood in the sense which has been given it in later times, namely as involving a denial of revealed religion, and perhaps of all religion. There were, indeed, rationalists in this sense in the seventeenth and eighteenth centuries; but the term is not used in this way when we speak of Descartes, for example, as a rationalist.

2 I use the term 'reality' in preference to 'the world', because

the knowledge in question might concern a Being, God, which transcends the world.

[3] The statement can, of course, be expressed in more 'linguistic' fashion, without the use of the word 'idea'. One might say, for instance, that we learn the meanings of the terms through experience, or through ostensive definition.

[4] I have used the Kantian term 'synthetic *a priori* proposition'. And the use of this particular term can be misleading: for though I agree with Kant that there are propositions which are neither tautologies nor merely probable empirical generalizations, I do not accept Kant's interpretation of their status. In my opinion they express insight into the objective intelligible structure of being. But the term is a convenient one; and it is frequently used today without its use involving, or being thought to involve, the interpretation peculiar to Kant.

[5] What Hume called 'experimental philosophy', namely physics, is now, of course, no longer accounted part of philosophy. And one may be tempted to comment that part at any rate of what he regarded as pertaining to the science of man has also tended to separate itself from philosophy, especially if one bears in mind the methodological limitations which he imposed. I am thinking principally of empirical psychology.

[6] As we saw in Volume 5, Hume admits the possibility of exceptions to this rule. When presented with a graded series of shades of blue in which one shade was missing, we might be able to supply the missing member in the sense of producing the 'idea' though there has been no preceding impression. But, apart from such possible exceptions, Hume presses his general rule throughout.

[7] The principle, be it noted, says nothing about the mode of operation of the cause. That is to say, its application is not confined to mechanical or determined causality.

[8] Obviously, we should have to avoid defining 'understanding the meanings of the terms' as 'seeing a necessary connection between the meanings of the terms'. For in this case the statement that whoever understands the meanings of the terms sees the necessary connection would be equivalent to the tautological statement that whoever sees the necessary connection sees it.

[9] This idea of 'emotive' significance also has a basis in Hume's philosophy. For though he complicated his ethical theory by introducing utilitarian elements, his root-idea of the moral judgment was that it expressed 'feeling', specific feelings, that is to say, of approbation or disapprobation. Moral predicates are 'emotive' rather than descriptive terms.

[10] For example, though professedly concerned with the limits of our knowledge rather than with the nature of reality in itself, he now and again makes incursions into ontology. And his tendency to speak as though the objects of perception are subjective modifications is an unfortunate legacy from his predecessors.

11 For the meaning of this statement see Vol. 5, Part II, p. 123 and pp. 130–1.

12 I do not mean to imply that toleration and a belief in revealed religion are necessarily incompatible. I am speaking of an historical rather than of a logical connection, unless, of course, one interprets 'freedom of thought' in such a way that it becomes tautological to say that the ideals of 'freedom of thought' and toleration are inseparable.

13 *Treatise*, 1, 3, 1 (Selby-Bigge, p. 469).

14 Some Thomist writers maintain that Aquinas was concerned with the act of existing whereas post-Renaissance rationalist metaphysicians were primarily concerned with the deduction of essences. And there is, I think, some truth in this contention. At the same time we cannot justifiably say that Descartes, for example, bypassed problems of existence. In any case I am concerned in this section with the position occupied by the theory of knowledge in mediaeval and modern philosophy respectively, not with the Thomist contention which I have just mentioned.

15 As was remarked in the last section, it is arguable that Kant's doctrine of the categories leads to the conclusion that properly metaphysical problems must be excluded from the rank of meaningful problems. But Kant himself did not think so, of course. On the contrary, he emphasized the importance of what he regarded as the leading problems of metaphysics.

16 This is true of the metaphysicians at least.

17 In a certain sense we can say that for Aquinas things must conform themselves to the subject for knowledge to be possible. For though in his view all being is intelligible in itself, the human subject is of such a kind and possesses such a cognitional structure, so to speak, that the natural scope of its knowledge is limited. For human knowledge as such to be possible conditions are required on the part both of subject and object. But this point of view is different from that represented by Kant's Copernican revolution.

INDEX

OTHER IMAGE BOOKS

These prices subject to change without notice

OTHER IMAGE BOOKS

These prices subject to change without notice

OTHER IMAGE BOOKS

These prices subject to change without notice